"GUNS DON'T KILL PEOPLE, PEOPLE KILL PEOPLE"

"GUNS DON'T KILL PEOPLE, PEOPLE KILL PEOPLE"

And Other
Myths About
Guns and
Gun Control

Dennis A. Henigan

Beacon Press
Boston

Beacon Press
Boston, Massachusetts
www.beacon.org

Beacon Press books
are published under the auspices of
the Unitarian Universalist Association of Congregations.

© 2016 by Dennis A. Henigan
All rights reserved
Printed in the United States of America

19 18 17 16   8 7 6 5 4 3 2 1

This book is printed on acid-free paper that meets the uncoated paper
ANSI/NISO specifications for permanence as revised in 1992.

Text design and composition by Kim Arney

This is an entirely revised and completely updated edition of *Lethal Logic:
Exploding the Myths That Paralyze American Gun Policy* (Washington, DC: Potomac
Books, 2009). Published by arrangement with the University of Nebraska Press.

Library of Congress Cataloging-in-Publication Data

Names: Henigan, Dennis A., author.
Title: "Guns don't kill people, people kill people" : and other myths about
    guns and gun control / Dennis A. Henigan.
Other titles: Lethal logic
Description: Boston : Beacon Press, [2016] | Originally published in 2009 as:
    Lethal logic : exploding the myths that paralyze American gun policy. |
    Includes bibliographical references.
Identifiers: LCCN 2016014812| ISBN 9780807088845 (paperback) |
    ISBN 9780807088852 (ebook)
Subjects: LCSH: Gun control—United States. | BISAC: SOCIAL SCIENCE /
    Violence in Society. | POLITICAL SCIENCE / Public Policy / General. |
    LAW / Constitutional.
Classification: LCC HV7436 .H46 2016 | DDC 363.330973—dc23
LC record available at https://lccn.loc.gov/2016014812

To the memory of Jim and Sarah Brady

Contents

A Tortured Mythology

The issue of guns in America causes people in other parts of the developed world to look at our country and shake their heads. They just don't get it. They don't understand why so many Americans have such passion for their guns. They don't understand why gun control is such a contentious issue. Most of all, they don't understand how America can tolerate its chronic carnage of deaths and injuries from gunfire, particularly among our children and particularly after the horror of the mass shooting at Sandy Hook Elementary School in Newtown, Connecticut, in December 2012 in which twenty first graders and six adults lost their lives. American children ages five to fourteen are eighteen times more likely to die of a gun homicide and eleven times more likely to die of a gun suicide than children in twenty-two other high-income countries.[1] Across all those high-income nations, the United States accounts for more than 90 percent of the gun deaths of children under fifteen years of age.[2] President George W. Bush, of all people, once noted that an American teenager is more likely to die from a gunshot than from all natural causes of death combined.[3] God bless America.[4] Particularly her children.

This uniquely American tragedy is often viewed from a political perspective. At every level of government, a powerful lobby, the National Rifle Association, disproportionately influences gun policy. The *Washington Post* has called the NRA "arguably the most powerful lobbying organization in the nation's capital and certainly one of the most feared."[5] A 2005 poll of congressional "insiders" by the *National Journal* found that Democrats rated the NRA the "most effective" interest group on Capitol Hill; Republicans ranked it number two. One "insider" hastened to add: "Effective does not necessarily mean ethical."[6] In fact, a 2006 Harris Poll found the NRA one of the most recognizable, and least trusted, public policy organizations in the nation.[7]

What is truly astounding is that the NRA is able to block the enactment of legislation that is spectacularly popular with the American people. Reinstating the ten-year ban on AK-47s, UZIs, and other military-style assault weapons, enacted in 1994, enjoyed the support of 78 percent of the American people, with only 16 percent opposed,[8] when Congress, under NRA pressure, allowed it to lapse. Despite surveys taken after the Newtown shooting, showing almost 90 percent public support for requiring background checks for all gun sales,[9] legislation to extend the Brady Bill background checks to private sales failed to muster the necessary sixty Senate votes to cut off debate; the legislation never even reached the floor of the House of Representatives. Even mandatory registration of handguns has the support of 75 percent of Americans,[10] yet it has no serious support in Congress. Gun owners and non-owners alike favor proposals to strengthen gun laws. A poll conducted by Republican messaging guru Frank Luntz showed that 74 percent of current and former NRA members, as well as 87 percent of other gun owners, support universal background checks.[11] A majority of self-identified NRA members supports handgun registration and mandatory safety training before purchasing a firearm.[12] These are positions vehemently opposed by the NRA's leadership.

The NRA's power, of course, can be overcome. The Brady Bill was enacted into law in 1993 and is still stopping criminals from buying guns from gun dealers. Yet even the successful struggle to enact the Brady Bill can be seen as an illustration of the NRA's clout. Though the bill had public support consistently in the 85–90 percent range,[13] it took *seven years* to become law.

THE CURRENT STALEMATE

After the 2000 election, the NRA did a masterful job of deceiving the political punditry, and many in the Democratic Party, into believing that Al Gore's support for gun control cost him the election. (The gun lobby successfully distracted commentators from the highly material fact that Gore won more popular votes than his NRA-supported opponent.) President Bill Clinton has asserted that the party's support for the Brady Bill and the assault weapons ban cost it a decisive number of congressional seats in the 1994 elections. "The NRA could rightly claim to have made [Newt] Gingrich the House Speaker," the former president wrote in his autobiography.[14]

The conventional wisdom formed around the idea that the gun issue is too politically risky for Democrats, particularly in swing rural and outer suburban areas. When in 2005 the party chose Howard Dean, who had received the NRA's support in Vermont, as chair of the Democratic National Committee, an insider Capitol Hill publication called it "the last nail in gun control" and "a crippling blow to the gun-control movement."[15]

The conventional wisdom did not account for President Clinton's success in campaigning on the gun issue in 1996 (two years after the issue supposedly cost the Democrats control of the Congress) or for the stunning defeats of NRA-supported candidates in key 2000 Senate races (the names John Ashcroft of Missouri, Spencer Abraham of Michigan, Bill McCollum of Florida, and Slade Gorton of Washington State come to mind). Nor did the "run from gun control" Democrats explain why both John Kerry and George W. Bush endorsed renewal of the assault weapon ban during the 2004 presidential campaign. If gun control had become such political poison, how could this be?

The case of President Bush is particularly striking. When asked about the assault weapon ban in the third presidential debate, Bush not only endorsed its renewal; he went further to support closing the "gun show loophole" through requiring Brady Bill background checks for all gun-show sales, *even though he was not even asked about gun shows.* Karl Rove obviously thought there was a political price to be paid for Bush to be associated with the NRA's opposition to sensible gun laws.

Of course, President Bush wasn't sincere about his support for gun control. The NRA knew this and also knew that it would be politically damaging for Bush to publicly support the NRA's agenda.

The gun lobby worked to elect a candidate who claimed to support two of the major priorities of the gun control movement, but who could nonetheless be counted on to do the NRA's bidding once elected. Their confidence was well placed, as President Bush later signed into law sweeping legal immunity for the gun industry.

The conventional wisdom would have an even more difficult time explaining the 2008 elections, particularly Barack Obama's decisive victory. After solidly pro-gun candidates like Fred Thompson, Mike Huckabee, Ron Paul, and Bill Richardson failed in the primaries, the NRA had little choice but to endorse a candidate—John McCain—whom the gun lobby had long vilified for his support of legislation to mandate background checks at gun shows. In 2001, the NRA had called McCain "one of the premier flag carriers for the enemies of the Second Amendment."[16] To the gun lobby, however, he was by far a "lesser evil" than Barack Obama.

To put it mildly, the NRA went "all in" to defeat Obama. It said Obama and his vice presidential nominee, Joe Biden, constituted "the most anti-gun ticket ever to run for the White House" and "a clear and present danger" to Second Amendment rights. It launched a website, www.gunbanobama.com, dedicated solely to defeating Obama, and claimed to have spent at least $10 million on the presidential race (and millions more in the election generally). Top NRA officials personally campaigned for McCain in states including Pennsylvania, Colorado, Nevada, and Minnesota—all won by Obama. The group ran TV and radio ads against Obama in Colorado, New Mexico, Ohio, Virginia, Florida, Michigan, Minnesota, Wisconsin, North Carolina, and Pennsylvania—all also won by Obama. It advertised nationally in *USA Today*.

Although the NRA consistently lied about Obama's gun control record—outrageously accusing him of favoring a ban on the "use of firearms for home self-defense,"[17] for example—it is certainly true that no presidential ticket in history had a stronger record supporting gun control than Obama-Biden. Nor did candidate Obama run away from the gun issue during the campaign or retreat from any of the pro-control policy positions he had taken in the past.

Indeed, in his convention acceptance speech—arguably the single most important speech of his campaign—Obama directly addressed the issue with the words "don't tell me we can't uphold the Second Amendment while keeping AK-47s out of the hands of criminals." The NRA did everything in its power to defeat Obama, yet he won a commanding victory.

In politics, however, perception is power. Despite the evidence that the NRA's capacity to affect elections is vastly overstated, during its first term, the Obama administration, as well as the Democratic leadership in Congress, governed according to the continuing perception that the Democratic Party still had everything to fear from the gun lobby. During his first year in office, Obama did nothing to stop amendments to credit-card reform legislation and transportation legislation (added by a Democratic Congress) that permitted loaded guns in national parks and unloaded guns in luggage areas on Amtrak trains, ultimately signing those bills without a word of protest about their gun provisions. In its "report card," the Brady Campaign to Prevent Gun Violence gave the president straight F's for his first-year gun control record.

The president's moving remarks following the January 2011 Tucson mass shooting, in which six were killed and fourteen wounded, including Congresswoman Gabby Giffords, did not mention the word "gun." In 2012, mass shootings in an Aurora, Colorado, theatre and a Sikh temple in Oak Creek, Wisconsin, prompted eloquent, consoling remarks from the White House, but no presidential statements calling for stronger gun laws. The gun issue played virtually no role in the 2012 presidential campaign. Indeed, in his second debate against Republican nominee Mitt Romney, when asked, about his 2008 campaign pledge to keep assault weapons out of the hands of criminals, the president responded by downplaying the role of assault weapons in crime and emphasizing the need to enforce current laws, a standard NRA talking point.[18]

At least for the Democratic Party, the politics of guns seemed to shift when the Newtown massacre horrified the nation on December 14, 2012, the day President Obama later said was the worst day of his presidency. A few days later, in a tearful memorial service, the president asked, "Can we truly say, as a nation, that we're meeting our obligations?" and pledged to use the full scope of his powers to prevent more gun tragedies. In addition to taking a host of executive actions, he proposed an ambitious legislative agenda, including a new assault-weapons ban and universal background checks. Neither was enacted. The universal-background-check bill failed even though its bipartisan sponsors, Democratic senator Joe Manchin (West Virginia) and Republican senator Pat Toomey (Pennsylvania), as previously steadfast NRA allies, should have been able to provide political cover to others with largely pro-gun voting records. Even in the wake of Newtown, the gun lobby prevailed. It prevailed again in December 2015 when, the day after a terrorist gun attack on a holiday office party in San Bernardino, California, the Republican-controlled Senate voted down legislation to bar persons on the terror watch list from buying guns, as well as legislation, identical to that blocked after Newtown, to extend Brady background checks to all gun sales. The NRA's chokehold on the Republican Party in Congress has reached the point where Republican leaders are unabashed about admitting that they would do nothing without the approval of the gun lobby. When the NRA announced its opposition to Merrick Garland, President Obama's nominee to replace Justice Scalia on the Supreme Court, Senate Majority Leader Mitch McConnell (R-Kentucky) commented that he "can't imagine that a Republican majority in the United States Senate would want to confirm, in a lame-duck session, a nominee opposed by the National Rifle Association."[19] It also is hard to imagine another special interest group so influential that a congressional leader would recognize it by name as having veto power over a Supreme Court nominee.

The gun control issue also has been the subject of fierce battles in the states, and both sides can claim their share of victories. At the state level, the NRA's top priority has long been to make it easier to carry concealed handguns in public places, and it has been impressively successful in doing so. From 1981 to 2013, thirty-five states passed so-called "shall issue" concealed-weapons laws.[20] These laws require police to issue permits allowing the carrying of concealed weapons in public places to anyone who does not have a criminal record. Four other states have no permit requirement at all for concealed carry. In contrast, in the few states that still have "may issue" concealed-weapons laws, the police have discretion to deny a permit to someone whom they believe to present a risk of violence, even though he may not have a criminal record. The gun lobby also has been successful in enacting state laws that preempt local gun regulation, provide legal protection to the gun industry, and, in a few states, even in removing restrictions on guns in bars and on college campuses.[21]

Still, gun control forces also have an impressive list of victories in the states. Since 1989, they have succeeded in passing Child Access Prevention (CAP) laws in eighteen states.[22] These laws hold gun owners criminally responsible for leaving guns accessible to children. During that same period, the NRA also suffered key legislative defeats in New Jersey (legislation requiring that guns be "child-proofed"), Maryland (legislation requiring internal locks on guns and limiting handgun sales to one per month), and Illinois (legislation requiring background checks for private sales at gun shows), while Colorado and Oregon (two states traditionally unfriendly to gun control) extended background checks to private sales at gun shows, both by voter referendum. Since the Newtown shooting, Connecticut, Colorado, Delaware, New York, and Washington State have extended background checks to all gun sales; Washington State did so by a referendum that won with 60 percent of the vote. Maryland enacted licensing and fingerprint identification for handgun sales.

The gun control movement has found its most fertile ground in California, where the NRA and its allies have suffered repeated setbacks. Since 1989, in addition to enacting a CAP law, California passed legislation to ban semiautomatic assault weapons, require background checks for all gun sales from all sources, restrict handgun sales to one per month to curb gun trafficking, require gun dealers to sell child-safety locks with guns, require handgun buyers to pass a safety test and be fingerprinted, mandate certain safety features on handguns, and ban .50 caliber sniper rifles. After most states had acceded to NRA demands to immunize gun sellers from lawsuits brought by municipalities, in 2002, California went in the other direction and repealed a twenty-year-old law protecting the industry from certain lawsuits. Considering that one of every eight Americans resides in California, and that it is the largest gun market in the United States, this record is deeply embarrassing for the NRA.

Despite these state victories for gun control, it is fair to say that the nation is at a stalemate on the gun issue. To explain our inability to move decisively toward sensible gun regulation entirely in terms of raw political power, or the perception of that power, somewhat begs the question. Surely the NRA could not command such strength if there weren't something in its message that resonates with large numbers of people. Is there something about the gun control debate itself that contributes to the policy paralysis on the gun violence issue? Speaking as a longtime participant in that debate, I believe the answer is yes.

THE TRIUMPH OF BUMPER-STICKER LOGIC

Shortly after I began my tenure as a lawyer and advocate for the Brady gun control group, I started to notice a peculiar repetitiveness in my opponents' arguments. Whether it was on radio or TV talk shows, panel discussions, or speeches with audience Q&A, there was a striking similarity in the substance of the arguments, and even the language, used by my opponents. Over and over again, I would hear "Guns don't kill people. People kill people." I would hear "When guns are outlawed, only outlaws will have guns." I would hear "An armed society is a polite society." I had seen these sayings on bumper stickers for years, but I discovered that my opponents actually argued in these terms. Even when these exact phrases weren't used, the thoughts they express were conveyed in other words. In more scholarly settings, critics of gun regulation would dress up their arguments in the arcane language of academia and in mountains of statistics, but their basic claims could, to a remarkable degree, be boiled down to the same themes I had heard on countless talk shows.

For gun control advocates, the sad fact is that the bumper-sticker arguments of the National Rifle Association and its allies have an impact on the gun debate that needs to be acknowledged. I am not suggesting that these arguments cause most people to oppose specific gun control proposals; as already noted, a wide range of proposed restrictions on guns has broad public support. However, because the arguments sound like they have more than a kernel of truth, they have had an important long-term effect on the intensity with which the public favors gun control, particularly as it is reflected in its level of activism on the issue and its voting behavior.

Years of public-opinion polls on guns suggest that support for gun control is a mile wide and an inch deep. People will tell a pollster that they favor a host of gun restrictions, but surveys show a far smaller percentage will act on their support or will make it a major factor in determining their support or opposition to a particular candidate for office. Surveys show that opponents of gun control are far more likely than gun control supporters to give money, contact a public official, express an opinion on a social networking site, or sign a petition on the gun issue.[23] Although there is little doubt that the level of gun control activism increased after Newtown, surveys still indicate that gun-rights supporters are more likely to say they are "single-issue" voters than are gun control supporters. According to a 2015 Gallup poll, 40 percent of voters who want gun laws to be "less strict" say they would only vote for a candidate who shares their views on gun control, whereas only 21 percent of voters who want gun laws to be "more strict" say they would make their election choices solely on the gun issue.[24] A 2014 Yale University survey showed an even more dramatic gap: among voters who thought gun laws should be less strict, 71 percent said they would never vote for a political candidate who did not share their position on gun control, compared with just 34 percent of those who support stricter gun laws.[25] This gap is ameliorated to some extent by the fact that far more Americans favor making our gun laws more strict than favor weakening them, by a margin of 55 percent to 11 percent, with 33 percent wanting them kept as they are, according to a 2015 Gallup poll.[26] Nevertheless, this intensity gap strikes fear in the hearts of politicians who perceive that, particularly in swing districts or states, where a relatively small number of committed single-issue voters can make the difference in a close election.

As veteran Democratic pollster Peter Hart explained, "You can win the vast majority of the public, but it becomes a nonvoting issue for them. And the people opposed to gun control make it their single most important issue. That's the challenge."[27] President Obama, expressing frustration that Congress would not act to strengthen gun laws during his administration, recognized the "single-issue" problem. Indeed, he declared that he would no longer support candidates who do not support "common-sense gun reform" and challenged other gun-law supporters to join him in that pledge.[28]

This continuing intensity gap may well be related to the resonance of at least some of the NRA's oft-used bumper-sticker arguments. Let's take, for example, the declaration "Guns don't kill people, People kill people." The suggestion that the violence that has long plagued our society is rooted in the evil that lurks in our souls is effectively used to marginalize, as relatively insignificant, issues related to the specific instrumentalities of violence. As discussed in chapter 1, the slogan has been remarkably effective in diverting attention from the issue of gun regulation to the endless, and often fruitless, search for more "fundamental" causes of criminal violence.

To take another example, discussed at greater length in chapter 2, a great paradox of opinion polling on gun issues is that the public consistently supports enactment of gun legislation, even though it does not think it will be effective. In 1994, the year following the enactment of the broadly popular Brady Bill and the year the assault weapon ban passed with overwhelming public support, one poll showed that only 34 percent of the American people believed that gun control laws would reduce violent crime, while 62 percent said they would not.[29] Thirteen years later, an ABC News poll revealed similar attitudes; although 61 percent of those surveyed supported stricter gun laws, only 27 percent thought they would do "a lot" to reduce gun violence."[30] A CNN poll in 2015 found that 58 percent thought it unlikely that expanded background checks would keep guns out of the hands of convicted criminals.[31] In other words, at some basic level, the public is convinced that "When guns are outlawed, only outlaws will have guns." This belief cannot help but diminish the intensity of public support for further gun restrictions and the likelihood that such support will be translated into activism and voting behavior. It is difficult to motivate people to work and vote for gun control if they are not convinced it will make a difference.

The gun advocates' bumper-sticker messages, when examined critically, reveal themselves as mythology compounded by convoluted reasoning. Yet they continue to exert an outsized influence on public attitudes toward guns and gun control. Unless these messages are challenged and discredited, our national paralysis in addressing gun violence is likely to persist.

ARE LOGIC AND EVIDENCE IRRELEVANT?

Some may think this discussion reflects an embarrassing level of naiveté about the politics of gun control. If the barrier to progress is the continued fear of the NRA's raw political power, they will say, it will never be enough to show that the NRA's arguments make no sense. As one columnist said about the gun control debate, "This dispute isn't about logic any more than the stem-cell dispute is about science. It's about the power of an interest group to impede what looks to most of us like genuine public progress."[32] Let me be clear: I am not arguing that destroying the NRA's mythology will be sufficient to overcome the NRA's political influence. I believe, however, that the gun lobby's political power will never be overcome until these myths are destroyed. Political power is not unconnected to ideas. The source of the NRA's disproportionate political power is not simply its money and the intensity of its supporters' beliefs; it is also its effective communication of several simple themes that resonate with ordinary Americans and function to convince them that gun control has little to do with improving the quality of their lives.

The connection between politics and ideas on the gun issue is nicely demonstrated in the 2006 book *Take It Back* by Democratic

Party strategists James Carville and Paul Begala. Carville and Begala were solidly in the camp of Democrats who believe their party has been damaged by its identification with the gun control issue. They argued that Democrats should "defuse" the gun issue, essentially by agreeing with the NRA that we should simply enforce existing gun laws, but not pass any new ones.[33]

Those who believe that exposing the gun lobby's bumper-sticker fallacies would have no effect on the politics of gun control should consider this passage from the Carville-Begala book on the issue of whether the Democrats should push to require background checks on gun sales at gun shows:

> Sponsored by Senators Joe Lieberman (D-CT) and John McCain (R-AZ), the bill would require that people who buy guns at gun shows pass the same background check required for purchases made in stores. Okay. Sounds reasonable. But what is the political cost-benefit analysis? A study by the Clinton Justice Department showed that just 1.7 percent of criminals who used guns in the commission of a crime obtained their gun from a gun show. By extending the Brady Bill to catch such a small percentage of transactions, Democrats risk inflaming and alienating millions of voters who might otherwise be open to voting Democratic. But once guns are in the mix, once someone believes his gun rights are threatened, he shuts down.[34]

Notice the question: *What is the political cost-benefit analysis?* What Carville and Begala are saying is that gun control simply doesn't do enough good, as a policy matter, to be worth the political cost of advocating it. Presumably, the "political cost-benefit analysis" would be different if they were convinced that stricter gun laws would really save thousands of innocent lives and prevent untold suffering.

Dig beneath the surface of this passage and it is easy to uncover two of the NRA's favorite myths. The cavalier dismissal of the need for gun-show background checks is a variation on the theme of "When guns are outlawed, only outlaws will have guns." It turns out that, on the issue of gun shows, the Carville-Begala analysis is highly misleading. They cite a Justice Department survey of federal firearms offenders showing that only 1.7 percent of the offenders said they got their guns at gun shows.[35] This ignores the well-established fact that many gun criminals buy their guns from gun traffickers who, in turn, bought their inventory at gun shows. Many criminals simply don't know that their guns originated at gun shows. Carville and Begala overlook the joint Justice-ATF (the Bureau of Alcohol, Tobacco, and Firearms)[36] study of federal trafficking investigations showing "a disturbing picture of gun shows as a venue for criminal activity and a source of firearms used in crimes."[37]

The reference by Carville and Begala to gun owners feeling that their "gun rights are threatened" by background checks implicitly invokes the classic "slippery slope" argument treated in chapter 3. Carville and Begala obviously see some validity to the idea that gun-show background checks will lead to serious invasions of the right to bear arms. Chapter 3 will address the slippery slope argument from several angles, including the impact of the Supreme Court's rulings in *District of Columbia v. Heller*[38] and *McDonald v. City of Chicago*,[39] which struck down handgun prohibitions in those two cities, recognizing a Second Amendment right to possess handguns in the home enforceable against the federal government and the states. The political conclusion reached by Carville and Begala follows directly from their policy conclusion about the impact of gun control.

It seems clear that the persuasive power of the Carville-Begala political argument to fellow Democrats likely was enhanced because the NRA's bumper-sticker logic has managed to sink in to our collective consciousness about the relationship between guns and violence. Conversely, exposing the NRA's mythology as transparently empty and dangerous would have made it more difficult for Democrats to "defuse" the gun issue by embracing the NRA's view. On the gun issue, as with other issues, politics and policy *are* connected.

In December of 2003, former President Clinton, speaking at the Brady Bill's ten-year anniversary celebration in Washington, DC, cogently addressed the way the gun debate is conducted in this country and how it impacts our nation's ability to make greater progress in preventing injury and death from gunfire. He said he was always struck by the disconnect between the gun lobby's arguments and what is happening in real life. "This is all about getting people to stop thinking," he said, "ignoring the human consequences of a practical problem." He went on: "But the consequences here are quite severe, because the landscape of our recent history is littered with the bodies of people that couldn't be protected, under sensible gun laws that wouldn't have had a lick of impact on the hunters and sportsmen of this country."

I was in the audience that day and I was struck with his observation that "this is all about getting people to stop thinking." This is, in fact, the impact of the pro-gun slogans. They do not stimulate thoughtful, rational discussion of the "human consequences of a practical problem." They end thoughtful, rational discussion and replace it with clever catchphrases in service to an immovable ideology. I think President Clinton was getting at the disturbing truth about the gun debate in America. Our nation does a bad job of thinking about guns. Until we get the reasoning right, we will do little to address the "human consequences" of gun violence. It is no exaggeration to say that our nation's gun policy is paralyzed by a series of fallacies—arguments that appear sound on first hearing, but crumble when subject to careful thought and analysis.

Although exposing these fallacies is necessarily an exercise in reason, it should not be coldly intellectual. It is my hope that the task will awaken the same emotions in the reader that it did in me: Sadness. Then anger. When President Obama unveiled a series of executive actions on guns three years after the Newtown massacre, he reminded the nation that it was a mass killing of first graders. "Every time I think about those kids, it gets me mad," said the president, wiping away tears. It should, in fact, make all of us angry. It should lead us to realize that too many of our fellow citizens have perished or been severely injured because the pro-gun fallacies have held sway for far too long. They have excused inaction and justified misguided policies. Because gun violence is, literally, a life-or-death issue, the NRA's tortured mythology has cost innocent lives. Too many have died for us to tolerate it any longer.

CHAPTER ONE

GUNS DON'T KILL PEOPLE, PEOPLE KILL PEOPLE

This is, no doubt, one of the greatest advocacy slogans ever conceived. Its first sentence seems plainly false on its face; that is, until one reads the second sentence, which is plainly true and, at the same time, appears to confer truth on the first sentence. The first sentence captures our attention; the second persuades us with a proposition we cannot deny.

The slogan is, of course, intended to convey the idea that guns are simply inanimate objects that are not dangerous unless and until they come into contact with human beings. As pro-gun partisans have been known to say, "I've never seen a gun get up off a table and fire itself." The slogan makes the point that guns are morally neutral. They are not dangerous in and of themselves. They become dangerous only in the hands of evil, or disturbed, or careless people. As one Idaho gun dealer put it, "Firearms are not guilty of crime; the individuals who possess the firearm are guilty of doing something with it."[1] Countless gun owners have observed that they have owned guns for years and none of their guns has ever been involved in a crime or other violent act. Best-selling author Tom Clancy has pointed out that "no firearm has ever killed anyone unless directed by a person who acted either from malice, madness or idiocy."[2] There is no gun problem. There is only a people problem. For the gun partisan, this means that the only laws that make sense are those directed at how people use guns, not at guns themselves. When Charlton Heston was the NRA's president, he was asked by then Senator John Ashcroft during a congressional hearing, "What can be done, and specifically what can Congress do, to stem the tide of violent crime?" Heston's answer: "Punish criminals, Senator."[3]

How does this thinking fit with how we treat other "inanimate objects" that tend to become dangerous only when they come into contact with human beings? Are we content simply to punish the person who misuses the product? Or are we interested also in placing barriers between the product and those most likely to misuse it?

CARS DON'T KILL PEOPLE, PEOPLE KILL PEOPLE

Cars do not often exceed the speed limit without a driver behind the wheel. Sitting in a driveway, a car seems pretty innocuous indeed. Does this mean that the sum total of our public policy response to reckless driving should be severe punishment of drivers who violate the law? Few would think so.

For example, most of us are quite comfortable with the idea that before anyone is permitted to operate an automobile, she must be licensed by the government to do so. Although the requirements vary from state to state, this generally means prospective drivers must be of a legal age to drive, have undergone driver training, have passed a written test, and have shown they can safely operate a car. When I was a teenager in the Commonwealth of Virginia, I had to endure a "behind-the-wheel" test (which included the dreaded parallel-parking requirement) with a very large and intimidating state trooper in the passenger seat. No one seriously argues that since cars are not dangerous unless driven by dangerous people, we don't need to license drivers, only to punish dangerous driving. It makes sense to have a system in place to prevent potentially high-risk people from driving in the first place.

If you find this logic compelling, you will be mystified that for decades in this country convicted felons were legally prohibited from buying guns from gun dealers, yet there was no uniform system of background checks to ensure against such sales. Before the Brady Bill was signed into law by President Clinton in 1993, in thirty-two states it was possible for a convicted felon to walk into a gun store, fill out a federal form falsely claiming to have no criminal record, and walk out with a gun. The NRA vehemently opposed the Brady Bill, arguing that background checks at gun stores make no sense because criminals don't buy guns at gun stores; they either steal them or get them "on the street." An NRA lawyer wrote that the Brady Bill was "simply not workable" because "[c]riminals do not, to any appreciable degree, buy handguns from federally licensed firearms dealers."[4] This, of course, was always an example of muddled thinking: even if some criminals acquire guns through theft or "on the street," it is hard to believe that other criminals don't simply go into gun stores and lie on the federal form. After all, as we will explore in more detail later, gun stores *are where the guns are.* There is a nice selection, there is a store clerk to offer help, and you even get a warranty against defects. A Justice Department survey of adult prison inmates, taken before the Brady Bill was enacted, asked those who had used a handgun in a crime where the gun had been acquired. The guns were as likely to have come from a gun store as from the "black market" and three times more likely to have come from a gun store as from theft.[5]

One additional reason we know the NRA was wrong in saying criminals don't buy from gun stores is that they are still trying to do it *after* the enactment of the Brady Bill. According to the Department of Justice, since Brady became law and through 2012, over two million legally prohibited gun buyers have been blocked from completing their purchases at licensed gun dealers, or denied gun permits, with felony conviction being the most common reason.[6] Not only do the Brady background checks block these prohibited gun purchases; they also establish that the prospective buyer violated federal law by lying on the federal form. If thousands of criminals still try to buy guns from stores in the face of a background-check system that provides evidence of their criminal culpability, can you imagine how many bought them from stores before such a system existed?

That guns are inanimate objects that require the intervention of people to inflict injury is, therefore, not a sound argument against public policies designed to screen those who seek to own and use guns. Thanks to the Brady Act, we at least have a system to screen gun buyers at gun stores. In all but a handful of states, however, gun buyers do not face the equivalent of a parallel-parking test; that is, there is no licensing requirement for gun ownership that would require training and testing to establish that those who want to handle guns know what they are doing. If we are to treat guns like cars, such licensing, with its training and testing mandates, should be part of a sound gun policy. Nothing in the notion that "guns don't kill people, people kill people" should counsel otherwise.

The NRA has a creative response to the guns/cars licensing analogy. "[A] license and registration," it points out, "is not required to merely own a vehicle or operate it on private property, only to do so on public roads."[7] If all you do with your car is drive it on your own property, as opposed to a public thoroughfare, you need no license. (I presume they have in mind a rancher driving his pickup around the North Forty, not a suburbanite driving the family Volvo up and down the driveway.) Therefore, the argument goes, you should not need a license merely to own a gun but only to carry it, concealed, in a public place. (As explained above, the NRA position is, however, that the police should be required to give concealed-carry licenses to anyone who does not have a criminal record and can legally buy a gun.)[8]

The problem with this argument is that the risk posed by the gun owner's use of a gun on her property is far greater than the risk posed by the car owner's use of a car on her property. How many auto accidents occur on the property of the owner of the automobile? It is surely true that a virtually undetectable percentage of driver miles occurs within the confines of the owner's real estate. On the other hand, a substantial part of the risk posed by guns is created by the use of guns in or around the home of the gun owner. Large numbers of unintentional shootings occur in the home. Indeed, one study, examining only shootings in which the gun involved was known to be kept in the home, showed that guns in the home were four times more likely to be involved in accidents than to be used to injure or kill in self-defense.[9] Suicide, a significant but often underemphasized part of the gun violence problem, also occurs largely in the home. A landmark study by Arthur Kellermann and his colleagues, published in the *New England Journal of Medicine*, showed that a gun in the home increases the risk of suicide by nearly five times.[10] Many of those suicides are committed by depressed adolescents with guns left accessible by adults. Indeed, firearms are the most common method of suicide in adolescents, accounting for 60 percent of suicide deaths among youth under the age of nineteen.[11] The risk of unintentional shootings and adolescent suicide could be substantially reduced by safety training emphasizing the increased risk posed by guns in the home and the elements of safe handling and storage practices. Thus, the analogy between cars and guns strongly supports licensing gun owners. With respect to both products, persons should be licensed before they engage in the risk-producing activity with the product. With cars, that activity is driving on public streets. With guns, the activity is possession of the gun, whether in the home or on the person in a public place.

Not only is there broad consensus favoring government intervention to screen drivers of cars, that consensus extends to regulation directed to the cars themselves. The fact that an automobile is innocuous sitting in the owner's driveway does not persuade us against government regulation to make the car safer when a driver is at the wheel. The National Highway Traffic and Safety Administration (NHTSA) has long had the power to issue minimum safety standards for cars, to test cars for their crashworthiness, and to recall defective cars. Only the most extreme libertarians would argue that government has no proper role in the design of cars, even though traffic injuries and fatalities often are caused by some form of driver negligence, recklessness, or illegal behavior. Does any reasonable person argue that the government should not mandate seat belts, air bags, shatterproof windshields, and crash-resistant bumpers because "cars don't kill people, people kill people"? No, because it is more likely that people will kill people with unsafe cars than with safe ones.

REGULATE TOY GUNS, NOT REAL ONES

The authority of NHTSA regarding cars is loosely replicated by the Consumer Product Safety Commission regarding consumer products generally. For lawn mowers, playpens, cigarette lighters, and a myriad of other consumer products, there are federal regulations designed to reduce the risk of harm to consumers and others. Most Americans are quite surprised to learn that no federal agency has the power to set safety standards for guns, test guns for safety, or recall defective guns. As is typical of statutory provisions that bestow inexplicable benefits to a special interest, the consumer-safety exemption for guns is buried in the morass of parts and subparts in the law that gave birth to the Consumer Product Safety Commission (CPSC). The pertinent language is the exemption for "any article which, if sold by the manufacturer, producer or importer, would be subject to the tax imposed by section 4181 of the Internal Revenue Code of 1954." Those "articles" are guns. Of course, Congress could simply have written that the law "does not apply to guns," but then the irrationality of the exemption would leap screaming from the face of the statute.

The father of this clever indirection was Democratic representative John Dingell, the famously combative former congressman from Michigan who had been a proponent of strong consumer-protection laws as long as he had been an opponent of strong gun control laws. He quietly inserted the exempting language in the bill. Later, Representative Dingell led the effort to use the power of the CPSC against lawn darts, which were banned in 1988 because their use in outdoor games had killed three children.[12] Nevertheless, he opposed legislation to extend safety standards to guns, even though, in a typical four-year period, 1996–2000, an average of 270 children and teens lost their lives in unintentional shootings alone[13] and four times as many were injured.[14] For Representative Dingell, three dead children were enough to ban lawn darts, but hundreds of dead children every year and thousands injured were not enough to justify imposing minimum safety standards on guns.

Due to Representative Dingell's handiwork and the power of the gun lobby, we have a federal consumer-protection agency with power to regulate toy guns, but not real guns. The CPSC's regulatory authority over toy guns has resulted, for example, in a recall of a toy cork-shooting shotgun because of a single incident involving an eye injury to a small boy,[15] as well as a recall of caps for toy cap guns that resulted in burns to at least five children.[16] The cruel irony of it all was obvious to Ann Brown, when she was chair of the CPSC in 1994. In October of that year, Brown issued a statement challenging the toy industry to stop producing toy guns that look like real guns. "Fatal accidents with guns involving kids are tragic," she said. "Real-looking toy guns may be a small part of the problem of violence in our society, *but it is the part of the problem we can solve* [emphasis added]."[17] There is something truly plaintive in those words. Brown was faced with the absurd reality that she could address the risk that a child might be shot because he was holding a toy gun that *looked* real, but was powerless to address the far greater risk that he (or someone else) would be shot because he was holding a gun that *was* real.

It ought to be clear, at the very least, that the "morally neutral" status of guns is hardly a good reason to resist the regulation of guns both to screen those who would use them and ensure that the weapons meet minimum safety standards. However, "guns don't kill people, people kill people" also conveys the idea that if dangerous people are denied access to guns, they will simply use some other dangerous product to inflict harm. The homicidal have lots of alternatives: knives, baseball bats, fists. The suicidal have alternatives as well. Therefore, the argument goes, policies directed at guns themselves, rather than their users, are destined to fail.

The "guns don't kill people, people kill people" argument requires us to more seriously consider what it is about guns that may distinguish them from other products that can inflict serious injury or death. Automobiles are subject to far more regulation than knives and baseball bats. Are guns more like cars or more like knives and baseball bats? For purposes of deciding appropriate public policy toward guns, what characteristics of guns are relevant? How are they relevant?

Let's start by stepping back and asking the question: What, exactly, is a gun, anyway?

GUNS AS WEAPONS

Listen to any of the endless series of talk-radio shows on gun control and you will eventually hear the following point made, in virtually the same words: "Guns are merely devices to expel a projectile at a high rate of speed. A gun is simply a tool. It can be a tool for good, or for evil, depending on the user."

Well, yes, but the question is: Why does the user want a device to expel a projectile at a high rate of speed? The answer is undeniable. Such a device is an effective and efficient weapon. Unlike other dangerous products we allow to be widely available, guns are desired by their users primarily because they can be used to inflict serious injury or death on living beings, whether human or animal. This proposition is implicit in the survey results when gun owners explain why they own guns. Although pro-gun interests like to emphasize the use of guns to shoot holes in paper targets or blast clay pigeons out of the sky, relatively few gun owners report target or sport shooting as their primary reason for owning guns. According to a survey done for the Police Foundation, three-quarters of handgun owners cited "self-defense" as their primary reason for gun ownership, while only 11 percent cited "target and sport shooting" and less than 1 percent said "gun collection." For long-gun (rifle and shotgun) owners, 70 percent named hunting as the reason and 15 percent named self-defense, while only 6 percent named target and sport shooting and less than 1 percent named gun collecting.[18]

There is, of course, another major reason for owning a gun that will never be measured by a survey of gun owners: its use as a weapon in crime. No gun owner will admit in a survey that he owns a gun to engage in illegal activity. Yet we know that, for example, in 2011, a total of 478,400 violent crimes were committed with a firearm.[19] More crimes are committed with firearms than with knives, baseball bats, or any other products.[20]

Whether they are owned for lawful or criminal purposes, therefore, it is undeniable that guns are owned primarily for their use as weapons. This distinguishes guns from other potentially dangerous products. Autos, of course, can be used as weapons, as is proven from time to time by disgruntled spouses who have been known to run down their mates in the family Mercedes. They are, however, not generally purchased for their killing capacity. Baseball bats are another example. They can also, of course, be used as weapons. Just ask former Los Angeles Dodger catcher John Roseboro, who was attacked by a bat-wielding Juan Marichal of the San Francisco Giants in perhaps the most famous baseball brawl in major league history.[21] Despite Roseboro's painful injuries, it is nevertheless true that baseball bats are not designed to be weapons nor desired by consumers primarily for use as weapons.

The gun industry is fond of claiming that it is the "most regulated" industry in America because the sale of guns is regulated in ways that transactions in other products are not. A car dealer can sell me a car without contacting the authorities for a criminal background check. There is no minimum legal age to buy a baseball bat, as there is for the purchase of guns. (Under federal law, you must be twenty-one to buy a handgun, eighteen to buy a rifle or shotgun.)[22] That's true, but so what? Of course guns are, and should be, subject to such regulations *because guns are designed and sold as weapons.* Because few purchasers of cars and baseball bats buy these products to use as weapons, there is little reason to subject their purchasers to the same screening for past criminal conduct that is justified for gun purchasers.

The point is that the kind and extent of regulation should follow from the nature of the risk from the transaction. The purchase of a product sold as a weapon presents a different kind of risk than the purchase of a product sold for another purpose. As compared to other potentially dangerous products, the weapon will, by its nature, attract a far higher percentage of consumers who desire it to inflict injury on others (or themselves). The issue is not whether the gun industry is "more regulated" than other industries. The issue is whether the regulations we have are appropriate to the nature and extent of the risk.

It would be overstating matters to say that guns are the only widely available products desired primarily as weapons. For example, certain kinds of knives are designed and marketed as weapons to be used against human beings and animals. As weapons, however, even the most lethal knives are inferior substitutes for guns. It turns out that being able to "expel a projectile at a high rate of speed" is a most valuable attribute for a weapon.

For one thing, such a feature makes it unnecessary for the user to be in close physical proximity to the victim, thus reducing the attacker's risk of detection and making successful resistance by the victim more difficult. As Gary Kleck of Florida State University, one of the NRA's favorite researchers, has recognized, "Guns provide a more impersonal, emotionally remote, and even antiseptic way of attacking others, and could allow some attackers to bypass their inhibitions against close contact with their victims."[23] In October of 2002, this advantage was on horrifying display in the Washington, DC, area, as snipers used a Bushmaster XM-15 E2S .223 caliber military-style assault rifle in a series of long-range shootings that killed ten innocent people and wounded four more, while paralyzing an entire metropolitan area in fear for weeks. Sniper Lee Boyd Malvo told authorities he could "hit you with metal sights from 300 yards away."[24] Although not all the shootings were from that range (Malvo accurately estimated that his shooting of a Home Depot shopper was from about 160 yards away),[25] they were far enough that witnesses could not locate where the shots had come from. No knife has yet been invented that can afford such anonymous killing power.

The sniper scenario is only an extreme illustration of the obvious advantage of a gun over other potential weapons in most scenarios. Although handguns (pistols and revolvers) lack the range of rifles, they can do far more damage at longer distances than knives or other weapons. A cheap handgun in the hands of a dangerous racist terrorized two Midwestern states on Independence Day weekend in 1999. Benjamin Nathaniel Smith, a white supremacist with a shaved head and the words "Sabbath Breaker" tattooed on his chest, rampaged through Illinois and Indiana, targeting ethnic and religious minorities by firing his Bryco .380 pistol from his car and driving away. He drove to a predominately Jewish neighborhood in Chicago and shot six people in front of a synagogue. In a quiet, residential neighborhood in Skokie, Smith killed Ricky Byrdsong, an African American and the former Northwestern University basketball coach, as he walked along the street with his children. The next day, he shot and wounded an African American minister and an Asian American student at the University of Illinois. On July 4, Smith fired into a crowd of people entering a Korean Methodist Church in Indiana and mortally wounded Won-Joon Yoon, a doctoral student in economics.

Smith's choice of a gun, over other weapons, was no accident. To put the general point another way: seldom do criminals undertake to commit drive-by knifings.

A second advantage of the gun as a weapon is that it affords the opportunity to inflict multiple wounds, quickly and efficiently, on the same target. Even a six-shot revolver can inflict horrendous damage on the human body in a matter of seconds; fully automatic or semiautomatic guns with high-capacity ammunition magazines can inflict scores of wounds, again in seconds, with little physical effort by the attacker. As high-capacity semiautomatics replaced revolvers as street guns in the 1980s, urban trauma centers reported a substantial increase in the average number of gunshot wounds suffered by victims.[26]

A third advantage of the gun is that it can inflict wounds, quickly and efficiently, on multiple targets. This capacity has been tragically demonstrated time and again in recent American history, from Charles Whitman's sniper attacks from the University of Texas tower in 1966 (fourteen dead and at least thirty-one wounded), to Patrick Purdy's on a schoolyard in Stockton, California, in 1989 (five killed, all children; thirty wounded, all but one a child), to Eric Harris and Dylan Klebold's at Columbine High School in Littleton, Colorado, in 1999 (twelve students and one teacher dead, twenty-three students wounded), to Seung-Hui Cho's at Virginia Tech in 2007 (thirty-two students and faculty killed, seventeen wounded), to James Holmes's at a movie theatre in Aurora, Colorado, in 2012 (twelve killed and fifty-eight wounded), to Adam Lanza's at

Newtown (twenty-six killed, twenty of them first graders, and two wounded). If only these killers had been armed with knives or baseball bats—so many lives would have been saved. Researchers generally classify as "mass murders" any murder of three or more people. More than 75 percent of mass murderers kill with guns.[27]

It is remarkable how often the obvious lethal advantages guns have over other weapons are forgotten by the opponents of gun regulation. For example, after the September 11 attacks, the NRA repeatedly pointed out that the terrorists' weapon of choice was not the gun but the box cutter. According to NRA lawyer Stephen Halbrook, "The hijackers of September 11, armed with box cutters and then with airliners, proved terrorists don't need firearms."[28] Is this observation meant to suggest that the hijackers would not have preferred to carry semiautomatic pistols on those planes rather than box cutters? For all the failings of our airport security system, at least it deterred the terrorists from using guns. Indeed, the terrorists were forced to use a product not even designed to be a weapon at all. If they had been able to use guns, perhaps the heroic passengers of United Flight 93 would not have been able to bring their plane down in a field in western Pennsylvania, thus preventing the destruction of the Capitol building or the White House.

The NRA's box-cutter argument illustrates a recurring fallacy in the gun debate: simply because other weapons (or products used as weapons) can be used to do great harm, does not mean that guns should be subject to no greater regulation than other weapons or dangerous products. To make the point another way, the case for stringently regulating guns does not require a showing that guns are the only product that can be used to cause harm. Yes, Juan Marichal did great damage to John Roseboro with a baseball bat. What would have happened if the Giants' right-hander had had a revolver strapped to his waist?

THE INSTRUMENTALITY EFFECT

Every fan of rock music knows that two members of the Beatles were victims of criminal attacks during their lifetimes. John Lennon was shot. George Harrison was stabbed. John died. George survived. Of course, we can't necessarily say that if John had been stabbed and George shot, their fates would have been different. We can say that, as a statistical matter, John's death and George's survival were the most likely outcomes.

On the same day Adam Lanza used a gun to attack the Sandy Hook elementary school, an assailant used a knife to attack the Chenpeng Village Primary School near Xinyang, China. Of the twenty-eight children and adults shot at Sandy Hook, twenty-six died. Twenty-two children were injured in the Chenpeng knife attack. None died.

Simply put, *guns are more lethal than other weapons.*

The pioneering work on this "instrumentality effect" of guns has been done by Franklin Zimring, whose landmark 1968 study compared fatal and nonfatal gun and knife assaults in Chicago over a three-year period. The study found that gun attacks were about five times as likely to kill as knife attacks, a ratio that held true even when the comparison was controlled for the number of wounds inflicted and the specific location of the most serious wound.[29] In other words, a gunshot wound is more likely to be lethal than a comparable knife wound. Almost a quarter-century later, Zimring's instrumentality effect was confirmed by a study in the *Journal of the American Medical Association* of fatal and nonfatal assaults involving family members or other intimates. Domestic assaults with firearms were three times more likely to result in death than assaults with knives or other cutting instruments; firearm assaults were more than twenty-three times as likely to be deadly than assaults with other weapons or bodily force.[30]

It is hardly coincidental that, although guns are not used in most crimes, they are the weapon of choice for homicide. Guns are used in only 4 percent of all felonies, which, of course, include many nonviolent offenses. As to felonies involving threatened or actual bodily injury—homicide, rape, robbery, and aggravated assault—the involvement of guns increases five-fold, to 20 percent. For homicides alone, gun involvement jumps to 70 percent.[31] It is true that guns do not kill without people to use them. It is also true that people kill people more often with guns. Guns don't kill people. They *enable* people to kill people.

The data suggesting that firearms are more lethal than other weapons used in criminal assault is consistent with the data on the use of firearms versus other methods of suicide. Suicide attempts with firearms are more likely to be successful than attempts by other means. One study of more than 1,000 suicides and more than 1,600 attempted suicides in Allegheny County, Pennsylvania, found that attempted suicides by gun were successful 92 percent of the time.[32] The next most-lethal means were carbon monoxide (78 percent), hanging (77 percent), and drowning (66 percent). The differences in lethality, however, were far greater when gun suicide attempts are compared to attempts with other instruments that can be considered weapons. The 92 percent lethality of guns far exceeded the lethality of poison (23 percent), drugs (11 percent), or, most relevantly, cutting with a knife or other sharp object (4 percent). Thus, for persons trying to kill themselves, guns were over twenty-two times more deadly than knives. Again, as weapons go, whether used against others or against oneself, guns are more deadly.

Pro-gun critics respond to these lethality figures by suggesting that those who use guns in crimes against others or to hurt themselves may simply be more determined to kill than those who choose other weapons. According to this argument, if guns weren't available, these highly motivated killers would simply try harder with other weapons and would succeed just as often. Note the premise of this argument: persons more serious about killing will choose guns over other weapons. This implies, of course, that the truly motivated killers at least *believe* that guns are more lethal. They could, of course, be wrong. Zimring's research suggests that they are not. Zimring analyzed the location and number of wounds inflicted in assaults for a one-month period in Chicago in 1967 as a basis for judging the seriousness and intent of the assailants.[33] During this period, there were 366 serious knife attacks, of which eight (or 2 percent) were fatal, and 247 serious gun attacks, of which thirty-four (13.8 percent) were fatal. The implication is that if a higher percentage of the serious knife attackers had used guns, more victims would have died.

For suicides, it turns out that the choice of a gun as the instrument of self-destruction does not necessarily indicate a greater determination to complete the task. The Allegheny County suicide study found that those who unsuccessfully attempt suicide with guns are actually less likely to later commit suicide (by any means) than those who unsuccessfully employ other means. Although gunshot was the most lethal suicide method, it ranked only sixth as a predictor of future suicide, behind smothering oneself with a plastic bag, carbon monoxide, drowning, gas, and poison. Unsuccessful suicide attempters using guns were only slightly more likely to eventually kill themselves as unsuccessful attempters who cut themselves. Whereas 6.25 percent of the gun attempters eventually committed suicide by some means, 4.83 percent of the cutting attempters did so. Even if this reflects a somewhat greater determination among the gun users, it does not come close to explaining the overwhelming difference in lethal results described earlier (92 percent versus 4 percent).

Of course, any suicide is a devastating tragedy. But suicides of young people, who have everything to live for but often don't realize it, are particularly tragic. The *Omaha World-Herald* did a series on guns and teen suicide, finding that the unique deadliness of guns and their ready availability to teens in Nebraska were taking far too many innocent young lives. In 2003, Nebraska hospitals treated 553 children for self-inflicted injuries or suicide attempts. The hospitals discharged 386 of those children who had swallowed pills or poisons, but only three who had used guns.[34] The gun users generally went from the hospital to the morgue. "If we can get them to take pills instead of a gun," said Seattle pediatrician and researcher David Grossman, "it is more likely to turn a suicide into a suicide attempt."[35]

But the "guns don't kill people" myth has a powerful hold on people, even parents whose children have become victims. The *World-Herald* interviewed Darrell Schramm, whose fifteen-year-old son Ryan had killed himself with a hunting rifle after finding out he had to attend summer school and his mother had discovered he was abusing amphetamines. Four years after the tragedy, Mr. Schramm was still ambivalent about guns. "I suppose if I wouldn't have ever owned a gun, he might be alive today. But the gun didn't kill the boy. The boy killed the boy."[36]

The question, therefore, is not whether people can kill other people (or themselves) with weapons other than guns. Of course they can. The question, rather, is whether guns are more effective and efficient in achieving lethal results than other weapons. Of course they are.

THE INSTRUMENTALITY EFFECT ACROSS NATIONS

If guns are more lethal than other weapons, we would expect that nations with a greater use of guns in crime would have more lethal crime. On the other hand, if the lethality of a nation's criminal activity were relatively low despite its relatively high involvement of guns in crime, we might begin to doubt the instrumentality effect. In their landmark 1997 book, *Crime Is Not the Problem: Lethal Violence in America*, Zimring and his collaborator, Gordon Hawkins, focused on comparative analyses of US crime with other Western industrialized nations. The Zimring-Hawkins findings will be surprising to most Americans, although they are entirely consistent with the instrumentality effect.

We generally think of our country as comparatively crime ridden when stacked up against other Western democracies. Indeed, there has been endless speculation about the causes of peculiarly high American crime rates, with possible answers found in everything from the unique individualism of American social thought, to the violent conquests that made possible our western expansion, to various demographic explanations. Zimring and Hawkins found, however, that the basic premise is wrong. America actually does not have dramatically more crime than other Western democracies. America's crime is simply more deadly.

Zimring and Hawkins's analysis of crime-victimization rates for eighteen industrialized nations showed, for example, that high rates of property crime are not unique to the United States. They found that the United States had a rate of property crime slightly lower than Poland's and only slightly higher than that of New Zealand, the Netherlands, Australia, and Czechoslovakia. Even as to violent offenses, the rate in Australia actually exceeded that of the United States, and three other countries—New Zealand, Poland, and Canada—had rates within 10 percent of those prevailing in the United States. Perhaps most surprising, rates for assault in the United States were actually lower than those in Canada, New Zealand, and Australia, and were nearly identical to those in Finland, the Netherlands, and Poland. However, the rate of assaults leading to death was four times higher in the United States than in Canada, New Zealand, and Australia. Homicide rates in Finland, the Netherlands, and Poland were a tiny fraction of the American homicide rate.[37] A more recent review of the data by researchers at the Harvard School of Public Health confirmed the conclusion:

> The United States is not a more violent country than other high-income nations. Our rates of car theft, burglary, robbery, sexual assault, and aggravated assault are similar to those of other high-income countries; [citation omitted] our adolescent fighting rates are also similar [citation omitted]. . . . However, when Americans are violent, the injuries that result are more likely to prove fatal.[38]

Other Western countries have our crime problem. No country has our lethal-crime problem.

No country, moreover, has our gun-crime problem. The United States is the only large industrial democracy that reports firearms as involved in a majority of its homicides.[39] To take one dramatic example, Zimring and Hawkins reported a comparison of the United States with England and Wales. Killings by all means other than guns occurred in the United States at a rate per million population that is 3.7 times the non-gun killings in England and Wales. However, the gun homicide rate in the United States was *sixty-three times* that of England's and Wales', yielding an overall homicide rate that was 8.5 times greater in the United States.[40] More recent data shows the United States with an overall homicide rate almost four times that of England and Wales (2013 data), driven by a gun homicide rate *forty-two* times that of the United Kingdom (2007 data). (See appendices 3 and 4.) The United States is a far more homicidal nation not because of its people, but because of its guns. In 2010, the gun homicide rate for the United States was over twenty-five times that of the combined rates of twenty-two other high-income countries, while its homicide rate for all means other than guns was less than three times that of other high-income countries.[41] As noted above, the US gun-homicide rate for children ages five to fourteen is thirteen times the rate in twenty-five other high-income countries; in contrast, the US non-gun homicide rate for that age group is less than two times that for other high-income countries.[42]

Because these international comparisons show that greater gun involvement in crime yields more deadly crime, they are entirely consistent with the basic proposition that guns are more lethal than other widely available weapons. As might be expected, it turns out that, across twenty-six developed nations of the world, there is a significant correlation between gun-ownership levels, gun homicides, and total homicides.[43]

THE LETHALITY OF GUN ACCIDENTS

The instrumentality effect, as discussed above, has to do with the deadliness of guns when used intentionally, either in crimes or suicide attempts. However, unintentional uses are also instructive on the relative dangerousness of guns. Unlike other weapons, guns often kill or inflict serious injury even when the user does not intend to inflict injury at all.

My earliest recollection of ever thinking about guns concerned an incident in my neighborhood when I was about twelve years old. I was a child of the 1950s American suburbs; my family lived in the solidly middle-class community of Springfield, Virginia. One day our neighbor, Mrs. A., was rushed to the hospital with a bullet wound. She had been accidentally shot by her husband while he was cleaning his handgun at the kitchen table. The bullet shattered her leg, and Mrs. A walked with a pronounced limp from that day on. Even the idea that a family three doors away would own a gun was jarring to my Leave-It-to-Beaver childhood. That the family's own gun would end up changing Mrs. A's life forever was absolutely chilling to me. That the bullet might have taken a different, and deadly, path was unthinkable.

The Mrs. A. incident also provides a different kind of response to the "guns don't kill, people do" argument. If Mr. A. had owned a knife for self-defense, or a baseball bat, he likely would not have seriously injured his wife unless he intended to do so. He could not have come close to killing her accidentally. In the words of the late columnist and humorist Molly Ivins, "People are seldom killed while cleaning their knives."[44] Guns are meant to shoot projectiles, potentially lethal projectiles. This feature means that they have a certain complexity that other weapons, like knives, do not have. For example, many gun accidents occur because the user did not know the gun was loaded. Others occur when the gun is dropped. Hunting accidents often occur because the long range of hunting rifles and shotguns makes it sometimes difficult to know whether one is shooting at an animal or human target. (Just ask Dick Cheney.) Of course, there is much that can be done to train gun users to avoid accidents through myriad gun safety and safe-hunting courses. But even those who teach gun-safety classes have been known to accidentally discharge their guns. Just consider the NRA gun instructor who accidentally shot one of his students in the foot during a class to certify applicants for a concealed-carry license, or the Drug Enforcement Administration agent who shot himself in the thigh with a .40 caliber Glock pistol while talking to schoolchildren about gun safety.[45] There is no denying that the relative complexity of guns makes their users more susceptible to accidents than users of knives.

Instead of comparing accidents with guns to accidents with other weapons, defenders of firearms would rather compare guns to other potential causes of accidental deaths. For example, criminologist Gary Kleck points out that the accidental death rate for motor vehicles is thirty-three times that for guns, when based on the total number of cars and guns in existence.[46] Kleck offers this comparison as "a meaningful point of reference,"[47] but it is meaningful only in the absence of serious reflection. As pointed out earlier, guns are owned primarily as weapons; cars are not. This means, of course, that the uses of guns and cars will be dramatically different. The average American car owner uses her car virtually every day, sometimes for lengthy periods of time. Moreover, auto owners use their cars in a way that involves constant interaction with other car owners using their cars, that is, on crowded roadways. Gun owners, on the other hand, do not typically use their guns every day, nor for long periods of time during the day, nor in a manner involving interaction with other gun owners using their guns. This is true even if we define the "use" of guns to mean contact with them (i.e., carrying them) that does not involve shooting. Indeed, many gun owners go for months, if not years, without ever touching their guns. It is difficult to even imagine a general usage of guns that could be meaningfully comparable to our use of cars. (Such a comparison would be only fanciful; for example, suppose virtually all gun owners went hunting virtually every day of the year.) The point is a simple one: if gun owners actually used their guns as frequently as car owners use their cars, there is every reason to expect that the accidental death rate from guns would be far *greater* than the accidental death rate from cars. Since there is no way to actually control for differences in usage between guns and cars, Kleck's comparison is the classic "apples and oranges" fallacy. It makes no sense to conclude from such a comparison of accidental death rates that guns are somehow "less dangerous" than cars or should be less regulated than cars.

Kleck also cannot resist another common comparison of accidental death rates that frequents gun debates: that between drownings of young children in swimming pools and shootings of young children. Of all categories of gun deaths, shootings of young children are the most shocking and senseless. For this reason, gun advocates are particularly determined to minimize their significance. Kleck points out that each year about five hundred children under the age of five accidentally drown in residential swimming pools, compared to about forty killed in gun accidents. Considering that far more households have guns than swimming pools, Kleck estimates the risk of a fatal accident among young children is over one hundred times higher for swimming pools than for guns.[48]

Again, if this comparison is meant to suggest that swimming pools are one hundred times more dangerous for young children than guns, it doesn't hold water. The comparison is illegitimate because it fails to control for exposure to the risk. To make the accidental-death-rate comparison meaningful, we would have to imagine a world in which young children are as exposed to the risks posed by guns as they are exposed to the risks posed by residential swimming pools. Of course, we can't imagine such a world, because most adults are not crazy enough to expose young children to guns in any way similar to their exposure to swimming pools. Parents typically allow five-year-olds to use residential swimming pools, with active adult supervision. Indeed, the benefits of teaching young kids to swim are widely acknowledged. What would the accidental death rate for gunshots among five-year-olds be if gun owners frequently allowed five-year-olds to use loaded guns under active adult supervision? Of course it would be astronomical, to say nothing of the likely fatal casualties inflicted on the adults supervising their young shooters. This is why no rational gun owner would think of allowing a five-year-old to handle a loaded gun under any circumstances. (Tragically, though, rationality is sometimes in short supply. Witness the 2014 incident in which a nine-year-old girl at a shooting range outside Las Vegas accidentally killed her instructor when she lost control of an Uzi[49] or the 2008 incident in which an eight-year-old boy killed himself when he lost control of a machine gun at the Machine Gun Shoot and Firearms Expo in Westfield, Massachusetts.)[50]

Guns are weapons. They are purchased as weapons. They are used as weapons. When assessing relative risks, they must be compared with other weapons. When such a comparison is made, it is striking that guns are far more likely to kill, even when their users have no intention of killing. This is a measure of the lethality of guns that should not be obscured by phony comparisons of guns with other potentially dangerous products.

IT'S THE GUNS, STUPID

What, then, is the core fallacy of the argument "guns don't kill people, people kill people"?

If the argument is meant to convey the idea that guns cannot inflict injury without human involvement, it is both true and irrelevant. As to policy issues involving regulation of cars and other dangerous products, it is hardly sufficient to oppose regulation simply because injuries from those products occur only when they are used by human beings. Why should such reasoning have any more validity when the issue is regulation of guns?

If the argument is meant to convey the idea that gun regulation cannot be effective because criminals will simply substitute other weapons for guns, it ignores the central reality that guns are more lethal than other weapons. Thus, reducing gun involvement in violent crimes (as well as in suicide attempts) can be expected to save lives.

In other words, "guns don't kill people, people kill people" is a fallacy because, although guns *alone* do not kill people, they *enable* people to kill people more effectively than other weapons. They more effectively enable those with criminal intent to inflict mortal injury on others; they more effectively enable the suicidal to inflict mortal injury on themselves. They enable mortal injury even when such injury is intended by no one. This lethal *enabling* potential is a key justification for regulation designed to reduce access to guns by those likely to use them in violent acts and to make guns themselves less susceptible to unintentional discharge.

"Guns don't kill people, people kill people" is, however, a fallacy with a powerful hold on how the problem of gun violence is addressed in America. Consider, for example, the public response to the Columbine school shooting of 1999.

On April 20 of that year, two seniors at Columbine High School in Littleton, Colorado, Eric Harris and Dylan Klebold, entered the school with two sawed-off shotguns, a Hi-Point semiautomatic rifle, and an Intratec TEC-DC9 assault pistol. In sixteen minutes, they killed twelve fellow students and one teacher, and wounded twenty-one others, before taking their own lives.[51] Until Newtown,

Columbine was the most deadly of the horrifying series of school shootings in suburbs and small towns that is now a recurring American nightmare. In the wake of the Columbine attack, a stunned nation struggled to answer the question "Why?" Because Klebold and Harris had planned their assault for months without detection from their parents, many said lack of parental involvement was to blame. Since the killers were fans of *Doom*, others said violent video games were responsible. The Family Research Council cited the "alleged bisexuality" of the shooters.[52] In his first speech after leaving Congress, Newt Gingrich blamed the shootings on a combination of the elimination of school prayer, violent movies and video games, and high taxes that force parents to spend more time working and away from their children, as well as the decline in "core values" among youth, "so that young people may not know who George Washington is . . . but they know what MTV is."[53] The NRA's Charlton Heston blamed the absence of an armed security guard in the school, even though there actually *was* an armed security guard in the school.[54] Heston also said the school should not have allowed Klebold and Harris to wear black trench coats to school.[55]

A national discussion of how teenagers like Klebold and Harris could be so alienated and infected by hatred as to massacre their classmates was well worth having. With hindsight, however, it is now clear that the "Why?" debate served to obfuscate the most obvious and simple lesson of the tragedy. Columbine was a national tragedy not because two teenagers were morally bankrupt and filled with hatred, but because two morally bankrupt and hate-filled teenagers *were able to kill thirteen innocent people and seriously injure twenty-one others.* They were *enabled* to be mass killers because of guns. Knives or baseball bats would have been woefully inadequate to the task. Yes, the killers also were armed with homemade bombs, but most of them did not detonate.[56] If explosives were regulated as loosely as are guns, Klebold and Harris would not have had to resort to the less dependable homemade variety. The killing and wounding was done with guns. Without the guns, the problem was two deeply troubled kids. With the guns, the problem was fourteen dead kids, including Klebold and Harris. A bumper sticker emerged after Columbine with the message "It's the guns, stupid."

Nevertheless, the aftermath of Columbine was a triumph for the "guns don't kill people, people kill people" fallacy. No new federal laws to curb access to guns by dangerous kids were enacted, even though Klebold and Harris obtained their guns by exploiting the weaknesses in America's gun laws. At the federal level, and in most states, gun sales by licensed dealers are regulated, but sales by private citizens are not. The Brady Act's background-check system, for instance, applies only to sales of guns by licensed gun dealers, not to sales by private citizens who claim they are merely selling guns from their personal collections. This leaves a huge, unregulated "secondary market" of gun sales between private citizens at gun shows, through the Internet, and by other means. About 40 percent of gun sales occur in these private transactions.[57]

Klebold and Harris turned to this secondary market to acquire their arsenal. Indeed, Eric Harris was chillingly well informed about the loophole allowing purchases from private sellers at gun shows. In his personal journal, amid the nauseating profanity, racism, and promises to "burn the world" and "kill everyone," he wrote: "If we can save up about 200$ [sic] real quick and find someone who is 21+ we can go the next gun show and find a private dealer and buy ourselves some bad-ass AB-10 machine pistols." Because, at age seventeen, the boys were under the minimum age of eighteen to buy guns from a dealer, they recruited Klebold's eighteen-year-old prom date, Robyn Anderson, to act as a "straw purchaser" for them. (She was not old enough to be an effective straw purchaser for the "machine pistol" referred to by Harris, for which the minimum age was twenty-one, but she was old enough to buy rifles and shotguns.) Anderson first went to a licensed dealer but did not complete the purchase because she would have had to fill out a federal form to trigger the Brady background check. Even though she presumably would have passed the check, she later said: "The dealer asked me if I would fill out some paperwork and I said, 'No, I didn't feel comfortable with that.' I didn't want to put my name on something that

I wasn't going to have control of." She and the two boys instead went to the Tanner Gun Show in Adams County, Colorado, where she paid a private seller cash for the two shotguns and the Hi-Point semiautomatic. Anderson said it was clear to the seller that the guns were for the boys. "They were the only ones asking all the questions and handling the guns." There were no questions asked and no paperwork to fill out. She said, "I would not have bought a gun for Eric and Dylan if I had had to give any personal information or submit to any kind of check at all."[58] The fourth gun—a machine pistol—was purchased directly by Klebold and Harris from a private seller who, in turn, had purchased it from an unlicensed vendor at the Tanner Gun Show.[59]

Paradoxically, however, this tragic illustration of the weakness of America's gun laws failed to result in a new surge of public support for stronger laws. An analysis of public opinion before and after the Columbine shootings by the National Opinion Research Center concluded that "there is little indication that Littleton generally increased support for gun control in the short term and no sign that it did so after about six months."[60]

In July of 2003, more than four years after Columbine, a survey conducted by the Marttila Communications Group showed that the school shootings had hardly shaken the power of the "people, not guns" fallacy. The survey asked the following question:

> Recently, there have been a series of school shootings in the news, perpetrated by high school and elementary school students. Which of the following statements is closest to your own view?
>
> A. Weak gun laws deserve a large part of the blame for these tragedies. It is much too easy for children to get access to guns.
> B. People kill people, not guns. Stronger gun laws would make little difference in stopping school shootings. It is not fair to blame guns or gun owners when children take guns to school.

Fifty-one percent of those responding said "People kill people, not guns" was closest to their view, while only 43 percent attributed blame to weak gun laws.[61]

In May of 1999, a month after the Columbine shootings, legislation to extend the Brady background checks to private sales at gun shows passed the US Senate, but only by Vice President Al Gore's tie-breaking vote. A month later, however, the House of Representatives defeated a similar proposal by a comfortable margin of 235–193.[62]

The echo of "guns don't kill people, people kill people" could be heard throughout the floor debate in the House. Listen to Representative Lamar Smith of Texas: "The violence and crimes committed with guns are not the root problem, just the manifestation of it. The root problem is the destruction of American values. Our efforts should be directed towards strengthening those values, and not passing restrictive amendments which are going to be considered later tonight and which do not solve the problem."[63] Or Representative Terry Everett of Alabama: "The erosion of America's morality has desensitized our children's ability to discern right from wrong, and even to value human life. This debate should not be about more laws on guns, or adding even more laws at any point. It should be about our culture and values that have gone really, really wrong."[64] Or Representative John Peterson of Pennsylvania: "Something has changed in this country. The people do not value life. That is what we need to deal with. It is not guns."[65]

If it is true that Dylan Klebold and Eric Harris were typical of large numbers of young people who truly do not know the value of human life, that would seem to be a compelling reason to limit their access to the instruments of killing. Shouldn't Columbine have made keeping guns out of the hands of violent kids our most urgent national priority, while we also figure out how to deal with the far tougher challenge of the hardness of so many young hearts? No one can deny the importance of addressing the "root causes" of youth violence, but the need to do so is simply not a good reason to oppose laws to make it more difficult for kids to get guns. Representative

Steven Rothman of New Jersey responded to the "root causes" argument during the House debate: "There were many factors that contributed to the recent school killings: lack of parental involvement, the prevalence of violent, cruel and sadistic video games, television shows, and movies. But when all is said and done, the main culprit was the easy accessibility of guns to the children."[66]

Congress, however, was not persuaded. As the House debate drew to a close in the wee hours of the morning on June 18, Representative Carolyn McCarthy of New York, the primary sponsor of the gun-show legislation, took the podium knowing that defeat was inevitable. She had been elected to Congress three years before as a strong gun control advocate after her husband was killed and her adult son was badly wounded in the Long Island Railroad shooting of 1993. The futility of the debate had brought her to tears. "I am sorry that this is very hard for me. I am Irish, and I am not supposed to cry in front of anyone. But I made a promise a long time ago. I made a promise to my son and to my husband. If there was anything that I could do to prevent one family from going through what I have gone through . . . then I have done my job." Carolyn McCarthy thought what she was trying to do seemed so simple and sensible. "I am trying to stop the criminals from being able to get guns. That is all I am trying to do." She concluded, "If we do not do it, shame on us."[67]

Today, it is still possible, in all but a few states, for another Dylan Klebold or Eric Harris to buy high-firepower guns at gun shows. The search for the "root causes" of youth violence continues.

CHAPTER TWO

When Guns Are Outlawed, Only Outlaws Will Have Guns

In her first network interview as a candidate for vice president, Sarah Palin was asked by ABC's Charlie Gibson whether she supported a ban on semiautomatic assault weapons, as did 70 percent of the American people at the time. She responded by proudly proclaiming her lifetime membership in the NRA and then explaining that she opposes an assault-weapons ban because if "you start banning guns . . . you start taking away guns from people who will use them responsibly" and then it's "the bad guys who have the guns, not those who are law-abiding citizens."[1] In other words, "When guns are outlawed, only outlaws will have guns."

This clever slogan embodies several ideas, each of which has some surface plausibility. First, it invokes the "futility argument"; that is, the belief that criminals are so determined to arm themselves, no gun control laws can possibly disarm them. Second, it implies the corollary argument that, because gun control laws will be obeyed only by law-abiding citizens, the law-abiding will be defenseless against the well-armed criminal.

Although those two propositions are embodied in the slogan, they are not directly expressed by it. Instead, the slogan, by its literal terms, addresses the imagined consequences of the most extreme of gun control proposals, that is, the legal prohibition of gun ownership. It is worth noting that the proposal to "outlaw" all guns, or even just handguns, has little to do with the contemporary gun-policy debate. A legal ban on the manufacture, sale, and possession of handguns has had virtually no support in the US Congress. Some localities have enacted broad handgun bans, but no state has done so. Public-opinion surveys show large majorities supporting virtually every conceivable proposal for stricter gun laws, with the conspicuous exception of a handgun ban, which polls currently in the 25–30 percent range.[2]

This is not to say that the proposal to ban handguns, or even all guns, is not worthy of public debate. Indeed, entire books have been written in support of a handgun ban, and there are organizations that have actively worked toward that end.[3] It is merely to note that the argument "when guns are outlawed, only outlaws will have guns" does not address most proposals for strengthening our gun laws, including the ones that have dominated the gun debate for at least the past two decades. Instead, the argument often functions as a classic red herring.[4]

For example, the proposal to require background checks for all gun sales, including private gun sales at gun shows and through the Internet, obviously is not equivalent to a proposal to "outlaw guns." Indeed, the evidence indicates that requiring background checks at gun shows does not even have an adverse effect on the number of gun shows, as shown by the experience of various states that have closed the "gun-show loophole." One study found that of the five states that hosted the most gun shows, three—Pennsylvania, Illinois, and California—already require background checks or licenses for private purchases.[5] Nor would the extension of background checks to gun shows have the effect of depriving gun buyers with no criminal background or other disqualifying record of their access to arms. Whatever the arguments against outlawing guns, they appear quite irrelevant to this and other policy ideas that have been animating the gun debate in recent years.

This does not, however, stop opponents of gun control from invoking the specter of banning guns in response to far more modest policy proposals. Indeed, this is one reason gun control debates often have a "ships passing in the night" quality. The gun control advocate will argue for additional regulation on some aspect of gun manufacture, sale, or possession (e.g., required safety devices on guns, limits on the numbers of guns sold to specific buyers, or requirements that guns be stored safely). The gun control opponent will respond, at least in part, by talking about how important gun possession is for self-defense and to preserve our basic liberties, as if the issue were whether the government should allow people to own guns at all. This is an understandable, if objectionable, effort to "change the subject," that is, to shift the debate from proposals that enjoy broad popular support to a more radical idea that does not. "What the opposition *really* wants," said one NRA official, "is a total ban on the private ownership of all firearms. I have no doubt whatsoever."[6] This "change the subject" tactic also enables the NRA to make the gun control issue salient to hunters and sportsmen, convincing them that even modest controls are merely a "first step" on the slippery slope to the eventual elimination of recreational shooting.[7] We will explore the "slippery slope" argument more fully in chapter 3.

One of the challenges for gun control advocates is that their opponents have had great success in causing many people to equate the words "gun control" with the concept of banning gun possession. This was not always the case. After all, when I was a teenager, Congress enacted the Gun Control Act of 1968, which did not ban a single gun and is still the foundation for federal gun control. However, a poll taken thirty-five years later by the Marttila Communications Group showed a large minority of likely voters—45 percent—agreed with the statement "The hidden agenda of most gun control advocates is to ban all guns."[8] The equating of "gun control" with "banning guns" is aided and abetted by the media, which frequently uses the shorthand label "anti-gun" in reference to any person advocating stronger gun laws. The use of this label assumes that the advocate is motivated by an animus towards guns per se and that his agenda really is to ban gun ownership. The use of the "anti-gun" label more likely reflects the tendency of the media (particularly television) to oversimplify issues and to portray most every issue (whether it be guns, abortion, immigration, or others) in the starkest possible terms as a clash between polar-opposite positions. The intention, obviously, is to make the coverage as dramatic and interesting as possible, but in the case of guns, it plays directly into the NRA's hands.

To the extent that the NRA and others have been able to frame the debate as about "outlawing guns," their success, surprisingly, may be threatened by the greatest "gun rights" victory in American legal history, in *District of Columbia v. Heller*. In a 5–4 decision issued in June 2008, the Supreme Court found that the Second Amendment's "right of the people to keep and bear Arms" was violated by DC's handgun ban, as well as its highly restrictive requirements for storage of guns, which the Court read to make impossible the use of those guns for self-defense. *Heller* marked a radical departure from the long-standing view, endorsed by the Court almost seventy years before, that the right to be armed relates exclusively to service in a "well regulated Militia." Justice Antonin Scalia's majority opinion in *Heller* found that the amendment "elevates above all other interests the right of law-abiding, responsible citizens to use arms in defense of hearth and home."[9] In Justice Scalia's words, "The enshrinement of constitutional rights necessarily takes certain policy choices off the table," including, in this case, "the absolute prohibition of handguns held and used for self-defense in the home." There is, as we will see, considerable mythology surrounding the use of handguns, and other guns, for self-defense in the home.

If a handgun ban is "off the table," this may make it more difficult for the pro-gun partisans to change the subject when the issue is reasonable gun laws, such as universal background checks, that fall far short of a handgun ban. How can the gun lobby argue as if the issue is whether to allow guns for self-defense if the issue now *cannot* be whether to allow guns for self-defense? If the argument is "When guns are outlawed, only outlaws will have guns," now a new response is possible: "Not only are we not talking about outlawing guns, but guns *cannot* be outlawed. So let's talk about ways of strengthening our laws to keep guns out of the wrong hands, while abiding by the new constitutional right created in *Heller*."

In succeeding chapters, I will explore the implications of *Heller* for the gun lobby's slippery-slope argument, as well as the decision's legal significance. For now, it is sufficient to at least recognize the possibility that, in achieving a great legal victory, gun-rights advocates may well have made it easier for their opponents to focus the debate on a set of policy proposals that have broad public support, free from the distracting charge that the debate is really about whether law-abiding citizens should be allowed to have guns.

WHAT CRIMINAL WOULD OBEY GUN LAWS?

Putting aside, for the time being, the problem of "hidden agendas" and "slippery slopes," the core of the "when guns are outlawed . . ." argument is that because gun control laws, by their very nature, are obeyed only by the law-abiding, they cannot possibly be effective in curbing violent behavior by criminals. "Criminals will always break the law and obtain firearms illegally," says NRA president Sandra Froman.[10] Here is how two academic critics of gun control laws put it:

> Attempts to reduce drive-by shootings by restricting access to firearms are doomed to failure. It must be borne in mind that in all cases of drive-by shooting, the weapons themselves and the use to which they are put are already illegal and carry heavy penalties. . . . The prospect of all these penalties appears not to deter drive-by shooters, and why should it? They are, after all, on their way to commit first-degree murder, punishable by no less than a death penalty. Further gun control laws could hardly be expected to offer more deterrence than that.[11]

If, in fact, the effectiveness of gun control laws depended on the willingness of determined killers to obey them, their success would be unlikely indeed. In fact, however, the premise of the argument is wrong. The success of gun control laws in curbing access to guns by dangerous people is not at all dependent on the willingness of hardened criminals to obey them.

First, let's take the drive-by shooter himself. If he is a minor, already has a felony record, or has a domestic-violence record, his mere possession of a gun is illegal. This creates the possibility that he may be arrested and charged with a gun crime before he is able to shoot anyone. Were it not for gun control laws barring gun possession by certain categories of high-risk people, the police would not have this enforcement tool at their disposal.

Gun-possession offenses also can be valuable even if the offender is successful in committing a crime with the illegal gun. They can be useful to prosecutors in obtaining longer sentences in plea bargains, particularly since they may be easier to prove than the more serious, violent offense. Even the NRA says it supports laws barring possession of guns by convicted felons,[12] although it goes without saying that many convicted felons will not obey those laws.

The problem is that, under federal law, the categories of prohibited possessors are insufficiently broad. For example, although a misdemeanor involving domestic violence—such as violence committed by the victim's current or former spouse, parent, or guardian—bars the offender from gun possession, other violent misdemeanors do not. One study showed that violent misdemeanors are predictors of future, more serious violent behavior.[13] Persons with at least two violent misdemeanors are fifteen times more likely to be charged with murder, rape, robbery, or aggravated assault. The "prohibited person" gun control laws would be an even greater law-enforcement tool if they were broadened to include more high-risk people. Their value, even in dealing with hardened criminals, in no way depends on whether such criminals will obey them.

Moreover, there is an obvious circularity in arguing that gun laws must be futile because criminals disobey them. Of course, as to the criminals who are willing to disobey them, the laws are futile by definition. But what about the possibility that there are potentially violent individuals who are deterred from carrying guns by the illegality of doing so? It should be clear that compliance with a law cannot be determined merely by looking at the instances of when the law is violated. If it could, we would regard all our criminal laws as ultimately futile because all of them are frequently violated. Should we repeal our laws against murder because murderers don't obey them?

It turns out that there is substantial evidence that many criminals may refrain from gun carrying because of gun control laws. In one survey, incarcerated felons who had not carried weapons during the commission of their crimes were asked why they decided against being armed. Seventy-nine percent chose the response "Get a stiffer sentence" and 59 percent chose "Against the law."[14] It seems clear that, although some criminals will ignore gun laws, others will be deterred by them.

Returning again to the drive-by shooter (who obviously is not worried about a possible illegal-gun-possession charge), what about laws designed to prevent him from getting his hands on guns in the first place? Does the effectiveness of these laws depend on the willingness of hardened criminals to obey the law? To answer this question, we must think about the sources of guns for the criminal market.

WHERE DO CRIME GUNS COME FROM?

Guns do not fall from the sky into the hands of criminals. Few "black market" guns started their lives as "black market" guns. Virtually every gun illegally possessed or used in a criminal act was first made by a government-licensed gun manufacturer and sold by a government-licensed gun dealer. This establishes a critical connection between the legal and the illegal market in firearms. As the director of ATF put it some years ago,

> Virtually every crime gun in the United States starts off as a legal firearm. Unlike narcotics or other contraband, the criminals' supply of guns does not begin in clandestine factories or with illegal smuggling. Crime guns, at least initially, start out in the legal market, identified by a serial number and required documentation.[15]

This does not mean that every crime gun was sold directly by a licensed dealer to a criminal, although this was a more frequent kind of transaction before the Brady Act was passed. It does mean that the gun used by our drive-by shooter is very unlikely to have been smuggled across the border or manufactured in a garage gun factory. It also means that regulation directed at the legal sources of guns—those who are in the business of legally making and selling them—may well have an impact on their availability to illegal users. Take the Brady Act, for example. The effectiveness of the Brady Act does not depend on criminals' willingness to obey the law. The act's requirements are not directed at the gun user but at the licensed dealer who is selling the gun. The act requires gun dealers to submit the purchaser's name for a background check and to refuse the sale if the check reveals a disqualifying record. If the dealer is willing to obey the law, the criminal's preferred source of guns will be denied him. Of course, there are scofflaw dealers who will sell guns "under the table" without doing the necessary background checks. Increasing enforcement resources and criminal penalties directed at those dealers may well reduce the incidence of illegal-dealer sales. The point, however, is that the effectiveness of the Brady Act in curbing retail sales to criminals does not depend on the willingness of prospective murderers to obey gun laws.

Of course it may be argued that those who are blocked from buying guns from retailers will simply get them elsewhere. Some, of course, will succeed in doing so. It is perfectly plausible to believe, however, that some prohibited gun buyers will either lack the determination or the knowledge or the money to find guns from other sources. We have already seen that prohibited gun buyers have continued, even with the Brady Act, to try to buy guns from gun stores. If alternative sources are so readily available, why aren't they using them instead of running the risk of criminal prosecution by lying on a federal form about their criminal history and being nabbed by a Brady background check? As gun salesman Ed Riddle told the *Pittsburgh Tribune-Review*, "So-called 'bad guys' often are so eager to get their hands on a weapon that they'll submit to a background check—only to be arrested on the spot for outstanding warrants."[16]

To look at it another way, if criminals are so dumb as to continue to subject themselves to Brady background checks, why are we so sure they are smart enough to find alternative sources of guns?[17] One study showed that individuals who were denied purchases of handguns because of prior felony convictions were less likely to commit subsequent crimes than those who had been arrested but not convicted and thus were able to legally obtain handguns.[18] The study found that denial of a handgun purchase is associated with a reduction in risk for later criminal activity of approximately 20–30 percent.

Of course some criminals will obtain guns despite being closed off from retail gun dealers. This does not mean that there is no benefit to preventing criminal access to guns from that source. As prominent gun control critic Gary Kleck has acknowledged, even though some highly motivated criminals may evade the Brady background checks by resorting to unlicensed sellers or other alternatives, "there are some persons who will commit serious acts of violence in the future but who would not be sufficiently motivated and able to make use of these evasion strategies."[19]

Kleck's conclusion is supported by the statistics. Although, as the NRA often points out, violent-crime rates began declining shortly before Brady went into effect; the use of firearms in violent crime did not begin its sharp decline until after Brady's inaugural year of 1994. In the five years preceding Brady, the percentage of violent crimes committed with firearms increased every year.[20] Beginning in 1995, the first full year the Brady Act was in effect, a stunning reversal occurred. The proportion of nonlethal violent crimes committed with firearms declined by 33 percent from its high point in 1994 to 2003. Even more remarkable was the decline in the absolute number of violent gun victimizations, from 1,529,700 in 1994 to 467,300 in 2003, *a drop of 70 percent*.[21] (See appendix 1.) During the same period, the number of gun murders dropped 31 percent.[22] During those same years, over one million criminals and other prohibited purchases were blocked by Brady background checks from buying guns from licensed gun dealers or denied gun permits.[23]

The causes of this steep drop in crime have been widely debated, and no doubt there were multiple factors at work. Although violent-crime rates have remained relatively stable since 2004,[24] is it plausible to believe that the Brady Act, by repeatedly interfering with the preferred method of gun acquisition by dangerous individuals, was not one of the factors contributing to our nation's historic decline in gun crime in the decade following its enactment? The impact of the Brady Act in no way depends on criminals being willing to obey gun laws. And, as we will see later, the existence of alternative sources of guns for criminals is a reason to shut off those sources, not to despair of the futility of gun laws.

A particularly strong indication of the close relationship of the legal to the illegal gun market is the impact of so-called "one gun a month" laws. Here the surprising pioneer was my home state of Virginia, also now home to the National Rifle Association, whose impressive headquarters building sits astride Route 66 in Fairfax. Although the NRA's move some years ago from the District of Columbia to Virginia took it to a far more gun-friendly environment, in July of 1993, the Old Dominion had a moment of gun control sanity that made the NRA cringe. It enacted a statute limiting handgun purchases by individuals to one gun a month, with an exception for gun collectors. The law was in effect until 2012, when Republican governor Bob McDonnell signed a bill repealing it, despite personal pleas from families of the Virginia Tech shooting victims not to sign it and polls showing that 66 percent of Virginians opposed repeal. While it was in effect, however, its impact exposed the fallacy in the argument that gun laws are doomed to fail because criminals don't obey them.

To many observers, the Virginia law was an odd gun control law indeed, because it seemed unlikely that a law allowing individuals to purchase twelve guns a year would have much of a beneficial impact on the availability of guns. The law, however, was a direct response to Virginia's burgeoning reputation as a primary "source state" for crime guns in the cities of the northeast. Since 1989, the Bureau of Alcohol, Tobacco, and Firearms has used the unique serial numbers on guns to trace many thousands of "crime guns"—guns confiscated in connection with criminal investigations—to their last retail seller. When ATF traces a gun, it begins with the manufacturer, who reveals its distributor, who then reveals its retailer. Based on its database of these crime gun traces, ATF had determined that 41 percent of a sample of guns seized in New York City in 1991 had originated with Virginia gun dealers. Virginia similarly was a primary source state for crime guns traced in Washington, DC, and in Boston.[25] Indeed, Interstate 95, from the Southeast to the Northeast, became known to ATF as the "Iron Pipeline." Interstate gun-trafficking investigations revealed that traffickers could make impressive profits by recruiting Virginia residents as "straw buyers" to purchase guns in bulk in Virginia gun stores for shipment in the trunks of cars going up Route 95 to the illegal gun markets of the large cities of the Northeast.[26] Virginia wasn't the only source state; Florida and Georgia also accounted for large shares of northeastern crime guns.

The Iron Pipeline, however, ran in only one direction: from the states of the Southeast, with their weak gun control laws, to the states of the Northeast, with their strong laws. Because New York, Massachusetts, and the District of Columbia had strong gun laws that made it difficult for criminals to get guns at gun stores, the "street value" in those cities of Virginia crime guns greatly exceeded their legal retail price. As one ATF agent observed, "On the streets of New York, an illegal handgun often can be sold for more than $1,000 in cash or drugs—a markup of five times or more over the price in Virginia."[27] The trafficker could maximize profits and keep costs down by buying large numbers of guns from Virginia dealers during each gun-store visit. In fact, the purchase of multiple hand-guns by a single buyer has long been regarded by law-enforcement authorities as an "indicator" that the buyer intends to traffic the guns to the illegal market. If someone buys two or more hand-guns in a five-day period, the purchases are regarded as so suspect that the seller is required by federal law to file a special "multiple sale" report with ATF.[28] Federal law does not, however, prohibit multiple sales. By restricting handgun purchases to one per month, Virginia sought to disrupt these trafficking operations by under-mining their profitability.

A landmark study by Douglas Weil and Rebecca Knox in the *Journal of the American Medical Association* showed a dramatic de-cline in Virginia's relative contribution to the Northeast crime-gun problem following the statute's enactment. Prior to the law, 35 percent of all guns originating in the Southeast and traced in the Northeast came from Virginia gun shops. Shortly after the law took effect, Virginia accounted for only 16 percent of the Southeastern guns traced to crime in the Northeast.[29] For Southeastern-sold guns traced in New York State alone, Virginia's share dropped from 38 percent to 15 percent.[30] The law's statistical impact was confirmed by the experience of federal law enforcers. The *Washington Post* cited an ATF spokesperson as saying that the law's impact has been dramatic in stopping criminals from literally filling their car trunks with guns in Virginia and taking them north. "We do not see the trafficking the way we used to," he said.[31]

Of course, it is possible that gun traffickers could simply avoid Virginia and use gun shops in other states. To some extent, this may have happened. In one particularly high-profile case, in July 2000, a West Virginia pawnshop, Will's Jewelry and Loan, sold twelve handguns in a single all-cash transaction to a New Jersey cocaine dealer named James Gray and his recently recruited West Virginia straw buyer and drug user, Tammi Lea Songer. Despite her history with drugs, Songer had a clean record. She would buy Gray his guns. She would get drugs and cash in return. Songer stood next to the cash register while Gray told the clerk which guns Songer would buy. Songer filled out the ATF purchase forms and paid the clerk thousands of dollars in cash. Gray carried the guns out of the store, destined for the streets of northern New Jersey. Songer said she "kind of" suspected she was getting involved in a criminal enterprise, but "I was so strung out I didn't care."[32]

On a frigid night six months later, one of those guns, a Ruger 9mm semiautomatic, serial number 313–07198, was in the hands of three-time felon Shuntez Everett, as he approached a gas station in Orange, New Jersey, that repeatedly had been victimized by armed robbers. Everett matched the description of someone who was suspected in several gas-station robberies in the area. When approached by Detective David Lemongello, who was staking out the gas station, Everett drew a gun out of his pocket and started firing.

Lemongello was hit in the chest, stomach, and left arm. Unable to return fire, he radioed for help. Officer Ken McGuire responded and chased Everett into the backyard of a nearby house. Everett again started firing, hitting McGuire in the stomach and leg. Knocked to the ground, McGuire returned fire and killed Everett at the scene. Both officers survived, but their police careers were over.[33] Incredibly, some months before the shooting, McGuire had taken a handgun from a suspect that was traced back to the same batch of twelve guns. What happened in that West Virginia pawnshop turned out to be a clear and present danger to a community and two of its bravest police officers, several states and hundreds of miles away.

If Virginia's law drove traffickers to West Virginia and other states, it proves two propositions. First, the Virginia law worked to curb trafficking from Virginia gun shops. Its effectiveness, moreover, did not depend on traffickers like James Gray obeying Virginia law. If the licensed gun dealers obey the law, the traffickers find it far more difficult to conduct their deadly business in Virginia. Second, if the Iron Pipeline was being detoured to West Virginia or other states, it means we should adopt a strong *federal* one-gun-a-month law. To the extent that the weak laws of other states undercut the effectiveness of Virginia's law, the solution is a federal law that bans multiple sales in *all* states. Like the Virginia law, a federal statute would reduce gun trafficking because the new legal mandates would be directed at legal gun dealers, not the criminal element. The law's success would depend not on the willingness of criminals to obey the law, but on the willingness of gun dealers to adhere to new legal requirements that curb a primary avenue by which criminals get their guns.

Another indication that the illegal market is largely the result of guns trafficked from gun stores is how quickly the guns are traced to crime after they leave the store. According to ATF, "experienced trafficking investigators" have found that recovery of crime guns within three years of their last retail sale is a "significant indicator" that the gun was trafficked out of a gun shop.[34] This "time to crime" is merely a rough measure of how long it took a gun to move from the retail shelf to the illegal market; indeed, a gun could have been possessed by a criminal, or used in a crime, long before it was recovered and traced by police. In twenty-seven communities in which tracing of all guns recovered in crime was being done, ATF found that between 32 percent and 49 percent of the guns recovered from persons aged eighteen to twenty-four had been sold by a retail dealer or pawnshop less than three years before. The range for adult purchasers was 27 percent to 40 percent.[35] This suggests a flood of guns moving quickly from retail gun outlets into the illegal market.

Opponents of gun regulation are anxious for the public to think about the "black market" in guns as mysterious in its origins and somehow self-generating. If the public believes that criminals get their guns "on the street," without asking how those guns got to the street in the first place, it is more likely to support the NRA's idea that the only productive response to gun crime is merely to punish the criminal. If the "black market" is generated by the criminal element itself, with no relationship to the legal market, then it is easier to make gun control seem ultimately futile. The fast-flowing stream of guns from dealers to the illegal market tells a different story. So does the successful operation of the Brady Act and the Virginia one-gun-a-month law.

WAR BETWEEN THE STATES

Virginia's long-held position as the prime supplier of guns to crime markets in northeastern states is but one example of a broader pattern of the movement of guns across state lines. For many cities, crime guns are largely homegrown; that is, they originate with gun dealers in their home states. For example, over 80 percent of the crime guns in Houston, Atlanta, and New Orleans originate from gun dealers in Texas, Georgia, and Louisiana, respectively.[36] For other cities, the vast majority of crime guns originate in other states. For New York City and Newark, New Jersey, for instance, about 85 percent of the crime guns originate with gun shops outside New York State and New Jersey.[37] For Boston, about 60 percent originate outside Massachusetts. What explains the difference between these groups of cities? It is almost universally true that cities in states with relatively strong gun laws "import" their crime guns from other states. Cities in states with relatively weak gun laws get their crime guns right at home.

What does this pattern tell us? There obviously is no reason for a criminal in New Jersey to prefer out-of-state sources for his weaponry. If it were easy to get guns from New Jersey gun dealers, he would do so. If the opponents of gun regulation were right that gun laws can have no effect on the arming of criminals because criminals don't obey laws, Newark's crime guns would come from New Jersey gun shops just as often as Houston crime guns come from Texas gun shops. The fact is that the strict gun laws in states like New Jersey, New York, and Massachusetts have the effect of forcing gun traffickers in those states to use sources in other states for their guns. Strict gun laws have a direct impact on the arming of criminals in those states, not because criminals obey gun laws in those states but because it is more difficult for criminals to get guns in the "strict law" states from sellers who do obey the gun laws. The well-established pattern of gun movement from weak gun-law states to strong ones demonstrates that regulating the legal market in guns affects the illegal market.

Looking at it from another perspective, the pattern of interstate movement also shows that the weak laws of some states undercut the effectiveness of the strong laws of other states. Criminals in New Jersey, New York, and Massachusetts would have a tougher time getting guns if the supply of trafficked guns from other states were reduced. Because guns cross state lines so easily, ultimately a federal solution is required.

A favorite argument of gun control opponents is that gun laws clearly don't work because places like Washington, DC, and Chicago, with their strong laws, have much higher homicide rates than places like Georgia and Montana, with their weak laws. This comparison is invalid on multiple levels.

First, it compares *cities* with *states*. Obviously, urban areas are plagued with particularly high concentrations of poverty, unemployment, family disintegration, poor housing, illegal drugs, substandard schools, and a myriad of other contributors to violent crime.[38] Indeed, no comparison of the effect of state gun laws could possibly be valid without controlling for the degree of urbanization in the states being studied. If *city* homicide rates are compared, it is manifestly *not* true that cities in states with strong gun laws generally have higher homicide rates than cities in states with weak gun laws. In 2009, for example, the homicide rate in New Orleans (in a state with notoriously weak gun laws) was over nine times the homicide rate in New York City (in a state with strong gun laws). The homicide rates in Atlanta and Memphis (in weak gun-law states) were substantially higher than in Boston (in a state with strong laws). On the other hand, it is also true that Newark (in a strong gun-law state) has a higher homicide rate than Phoenix (in a weak gun-law state).[39] The point is that the strength of a jurisdiction's gun laws is only one of many factors bearing on its homicide rate, and snapshot comparisons of cities prove nothing. Comparisons between cities and states prove less than nothing.

Apart from the obvious invalidity of comparing cities with states in this context, the comparison never includes the origins of the guns that are plaguing cities like Washington, DC. Only 4 percent of the guns used in crime in that city are originally sold by licensed gun dealers within its borders.[40] The murder rate in the District is not evidence of the ineffectiveness of its gun laws; indeed, as discussed above, if DC's gun laws had no effect on the criminal market, far more of its crime guns would be homegrown, not imported. DC's murder rate reflects a complex of socioeconomic and other factors, including the movement of guns across state lines ensuring that its crime will remain highly lethal.

THE CRIMINALS-WON'T-REGISTER ARGUMENT

What about gun laws that are directed at individual gun owners, not licensed dealers? Some states regulate transactions between individuals by requiring the buyer to present to the seller a license or permit to purchase issued by a government agency only after presentation of a valid identification and completion of a background check. In some states, such a licensing system is supplemented by a requirement that the seller register the sale with the government. At first glance, these seem to be gun laws destined for failure because criminals would be the last people who would ever obtain licenses or register their guns. As longtime pro-gun activist Joseph Tartaro put it, "There is little, if any, evidence that such registries would accomplish much" because "[m]ost criminals acquire their arms outside the legal, federally regulated commerce in firearms."[41] The "registration record" of a gun would, at most, be a record of transactions between law-abiding citizens, at least sufficiently law-abiding that they bothered to register. Our drive-by shooter would not be among them.

This analysis, however, misses the point of licensing and registration laws. Like the Brady Act and state one-gun-a-month laws, laws requiring that gun owners be licensed and gun sales be registered do not depend, for their success, on compliance by criminals. Rather, they seek to reduce access to guns by criminals by regulating gun sales by lawful gun owners.

Let's assume that the gun used by our drive-by shooter was initially sold by a licensed dealer to a law-abiding citizen. Call him Good Guy #1. He keeps the gun for two years, then sells it to another law-abiding citizen and license holder (Good Guy #2). Good Guy #1 registers the sale, providing the government the name of Good Guy #2. So far, so good. After keeping the gun for three years, Good Guy #2 decides to sell the gun. He is contacted by a prospective buyer who appears to be a solid citizen but has no license to buy a gun. The buyer is in fact a convicted felon and a member of a violent gang. We'll call him Bad Guy #1. Good Guy #2 has two choices. He can obey the law and refuse the sale, in which case Bad Guy #1 is denied the gun. Or he can sell the gun to Bad Guy #1, thinking no one will ever know. Let's assume he chooses to roll the dice and sells the gun to Bad Guy #1. Bad Guy #1 uses the gun in a drive-by shooting and then sells the gun to Bad Guy #2, a "black market" sale that goes unregistered. In a drug raid, the police arrest Bad Guy #2 on illegal-gun-possession charges and confiscate the gun.

Without registration, the police can trace the gun to Good Guy #1, the buyer from the retail dealer, but no further. With registration, the gun can be traced to Good Guy #2, who now can't account for what he did with the gun and is therefore exposed to criminal liability. He also is a potential source of valuable information about his buyer, our drive-by shooter, Bad Guy #1. Therefore, under a properly constructed licensing and registration system, either Bad Guy #1 is denied his gun or he is at far greater risk of apprehension for using it in the drive-by shooting.

Any pro-gun partisan worth his ammo will ask: Why wouldn't Good Guy #2 simply say the gun was lost or stolen? This loophole could be closed by adding to the licensing and registration system a further requirement that gun owners must report lost or stolen guns promptly to the authorities. Such a requirement exists for guns stolen from, or lost by, gun dealers.[42] Why shouldn't gun owners have the same obligation? The point is that gun owners should be accountable for what happens to their guns. If they sell them, the sale must be to a properly licensed individual and must be reported to the government. If the guns are stolen or lost, that must be reported to the government as well. As former ATF special agent William Vizzard has observed, "Registration records would allow investigators to track every gun to its last legal owner. This alone would deter most gun owners from making an illegal transfer. Even persons who routinely violate other laws would have reason to avoid illegal gun transfers. They do not welcome police attention and thus would have reason to avoid transferring guns registered to them."[43]

The objection that registration is doomed to fail because only law-abiding citizens will register presumes that people are easily and forever divided into the categories of "criminal" and "law-abiding citizen." Real-world experience shows that sometimes people who are convicted of violating the law actually registered their guns *before* they were convicted. (The NRA has a difficult time accounting for this, because its worldview assumes that every criminal has always been a criminal, whether he has been convicted yet or not, and that criminals, by definition, don't obey the law and register their guns.) If gun sales have been registered, authorities can identify gun owners who became legally prohibited from owning guns after they registered. In 2002, the California legislature enacted a statute directing state authorities to use the existing gun-sale registration records to identify persons who own guns, despite being prohibited by law from doing so. In the first three years the law was in effect, over four thousand firearms, including over one thousand assault weapons, were seized from felons and other prohibited persons.[44] Licensing and registration systems also make it more difficult to use "straw buyers" without detection. As we have seen, criminals who would fail a Brady background check frequently recruit people with clean records to serve as straw buyers. According to one Wisconsin gun dealer, straw buying sometimes happens "two, three times a day" at his store.[45] A straw buyer violates federal law because he must lie on the federal firearms-transaction form when it asks whether he is, in fact, the actual buyer of the gun. However, it is difficult to prove the violation unless the straw buyer and the prohibited real buyer made it obvious to the dealer that they were working as a team *and* the dealer is willing to testify against them. With licensing, registration, and theft reporting in force, a case can be made against the straw buyer simply because he no longer has the gun (having given it to the real buyer), yet has neither reported the sale of the gun nor its theft or loss. There is no need to prove that he was merely acting as the intermediary or agent for the real buyer. Of course, the straw buyer's obvious violation of his legal obligations under the licensing and registration laws also gives the authorities leverage to get information about the real buyer.

The efficacy of a properly constructed licensing and registration system does not, therefore, depend on compliance with the system by criminals. Rather, licensing and registration, by regulating the last *legal* sale of a gun, construct barriers to the flow of guns from the legal into the illegal market. Whereas the Brady Act and state one-gun-a-month laws regulate the last legal sale of a gun by a lawful dealer, licensing and registration laws regulate the last legal sale by a lawful owner.

An important study by researchers at Johns Hopkins University supports the idea that strong licensing and registration systems make it more difficult for criminals to acquire guns.[46] Using the crime-gun trace data from twenty-five of the communities that did comprehensive tracing through ATF, the study found that states with strong licensing and registration systems tend to import their crime guns from other states. The researchers divided the twenty-five cities into three groups: (1) those in states with gun licensing *and* registration, (2) those in states with *either* gun licensing *or* registration, and (3) those with neither gun licensing nor registration. In the five cities located in states with both licensing and registration, a mean of 33.7 percent of crime guns were first sold by in-state gun dealers, compared with 72.7 percent in cities that had either licensing or registration (seven cities) and 84.2 percent in cities without licensing or registration (thirteen cities). The cities with the lowest proportion of homegrown crime guns—Boston, Jersey City, and New York—were in the states with the toughest licensing and registration laws, requiring fingerprinting of purchase applicants and longer waiting periods, and that gave police greater discretion to deny licenses to buy guns. According to the Johns Hopkins team, "Our findings suggest that comprehensive gun sales regulations that include permit-to-purchase licensing and registration can affect the availability of guns to criminals."[47]

This conclusion is buttressed by a later study by Johns Hopkins researchers of the impact of repealing a state gun-licensing law. In 2007, Missouri rescinded its law requiring that all handgun buyers first obtain a permit from the local sheriff, whether for purchases from a licensed dealer or a private seller. After the repeal, private sales became unregulated, and sales by dealers no longer involved processing by the sheriff. One result was a sharp increase in the share of Missouri crime guns originating from Missouri gun dealers, accompanied by a decrease in the share of Missouri crime guns originating out of state. The researchers found this consistent with the hypothesis that the Missouri law had been preventing guns from being diverted to criminals.[48] The Johns Hopkins team also found that repeal of the Missouri permit-to-purchase law was associated with an additional fifty-five to sixty homicides per year for the first five years after repeal.[49] Missouri criminals were finding it easier to get homegrown crime guns, with tragic consequences for public safety in that state.

GUN CONTROL CATCH-22

Some have commented that the reason it is difficult to show the positive impact of gun control laws is that they have never been tried. There is much truth in this. Our gun laws are a hodgepodge, full of unexplainable gaps and bizarre distinctions. As we have seen, state laws inherently are subject to being undermined by the importation of guns from other states. Occasionally, Congress has been persuaded to pass national gun laws, but they invariably involve painful legislative compromises that result in gaping loopholes and irrational limitations. In this way, the gun lobby does its best to maneuver the country into a gun control catch-22. The NRA and its allies claim gun control laws don't work. When comprehensive controls are proposed, the NRA then works to ensure that they will be as weak and ineffective as possible. Then the NRA argues, once again, that gun control laws don't work.

We have seen this pattern with the Brady Act. The NRA has enthusiastically embraced a study by Philip Cook of Duke University and Jens Ludwig of the University of Chicago that found no evidence that the Brady Act has led to a reduction in homicide rates.[50] According to the authors, if Brady had a dampening effect on homicide, it would be seen most significantly in the states that did not have background-check systems before Brady, as compared to the states that did. Yet the post-Brady homicide trends in the two groups of states were quite similar. The authors acknowledged, however, that their methodology would not account for any disruptive impact of the Brady Act on the trafficking of illegal firearms into the states that already had background-check systems. At least one other study found that Brady has, indeed, substantially affected interstate gun-trafficking patterns.[51] Not only does the NRA never mention this limitation of the Cook-Ludwig study; it also neglects to note that the two professors attributed the limitations on Brady's effectiveness largely to the fact that its background checks apply only to sales of guns by licensed dealers, not to sales between unlicensed people in the so-called "secondary market." Because 40 percent of gun sales occur in the secondary market, exempt from Brady regulation, Cook and Ludwig refer to it as "an enormous loophole that limits the effectiveness of primary-market regulations" like Brady.[52] Later the professors wrote: "Some may argue that the regulation of gun acquisitions is futile. A more likely explanation for why the Brady Act did not do more to reduce gun homicide is that the act exempts the 30%–40% of all gun sales each year that do not involve a licensed dealer."[53] Of course, the NRA does not advocate that the loophole be closed by requiring background checks on *all* gun sales. It would prefer to use the limitations of the Brady Act to insist that gun control doesn't work.

THE MACHINE GUN STORY

There is one federal law, however, that stands as a powerful counterpoint to the "when guns are outlawed" argument. In 1934, President Franklin Roosevelt signed into law the National Firearms Act (NFA), the first significant federal statute regulating guns. The Roosevelt administration pushed for the new law as a response to the rise in gangsterism in the Roaring Twenties and into the 1930s.[54] The NFA was passed as an amendment to the Internal Revenue Code and was designed primarily as a taxation statute, imposing a tax on the manufacture and sale of machine guns and other "gangster-type" weapons and accessories, like sawed-off shotguns, short-barreled rifles, and silencers. Significantly, the statute also requires machine guns and other such weapons to be registered with ATF, as well as requiring buyers of the guns to be fingerprinted, submit to an extensive federal background check, and obtain the permission of their local police department.[55] The NFA, however, does not prohibit law-abiding citizens from owning machine guns. It is, in effect, a comprehensive registration, licensing, and taxation statute—but not a gun ban. (It should be kept in mind that the NFA applies to machine guns, which are fully automatic weapons that fire continuously as long as the trigger is depressed and there is still ammunition to be fired, as distinct from semiautomatic weapons, which fire one round for each trigger pull and automatically reload the next round.)

In 1986 Congress banned the future production of machine guns for sale to the civilian market as a last-minute addition to the infamous Firearm Owners' Protection Act, a Reagan administration–supported statute curbing the enforcement powers of the Bureau of Alcohol, Tobacco, and Firearms.[56] The act, however, did allow machine guns already legally owned to be bought and sold subject to the existing NFA registration and taxation requirements. To this day, therefore, it is still possible to legally own a machine gun, if it is properly registered.

The NFA stands as an eighty-year-old experiment in the comprehensive federal regulation of a specific kind of firearm. If the National Rifle Association is right about the futility of gun laws, the nation should continue to face a severe problem of machine gun crime, as it did in the days of Al Capone. After all, machine guns can certainly be valuable tools of the criminal trade. By definition, they can fire continuously until the ammunition magazine (which may contain scores of rounds) is exhausted. A machine gun can fire approximately thirty rounds in about two seconds,[57] an enormous advantage in a gunfight with police. Therefore, if it is true that the determination of criminals to be heavily armed will overcome any gun control laws, then machine gun–wielding criminals should be commonplace. Are they?

Plainly not, even according to some of the nation's strongest gun control critics. According to the National Center on Policy Analysis, a libertarian think tank sharply hostile to gun control, "Even the illegal use of machine guns by drug dealers and other violent criminals is extremely rare."[58] Pro-gun researcher Gary Kleck found that machine guns are far less of a threat to police officers than other firearms. Kleck found that of 713 police officers killed in the line of duty in the United States from 1983 to 1992, 651 were killed with guns but only four with fully automatic weapons.[59]

ATF crime-gun trace data confirms negligible use of machine guns in crime. Of the crime guns submitted for tracing by law-enforcement agencies, only three in one thousand are machine guns.[60] Of course, the evidence would be stronger if we had comparable data on the use of machine guns in crime for the pre-NFA period, but such data does not exist. Nevertheless, all sides in the gun control debate seem to agree that machine gun crime is not a serious problem after decades of tight controls, even though the value of these guns to criminals is obvious.

The apparent success of the NFA suggests that the solution to weaknesses in our gun laws is stronger gun laws. The NFA does not suffer from the same limitations and loopholes that affect other gun control laws. Although the Brady Act's background-check system has been invaluable in stopping over two million prohibited purchasers from buying guns from licensed dealers, it suffers from limitations that do not plague the NFA regulatory system. Unlike the Brady Act, the NFA regulates every sale of the guns covered by its provisions, not simply sales by licensed dealers. Unlike the Brady Act, the background checks for NFA weapons have no time limit. Incredibly, if a Brady background check is not completed within three working days, federal law allows the dealer to complete the sale anyway. These are known, in the background-check business, as "default proceeds." It is not uncommon for the FBI to determine, after a default proceed has occurred, that the buyer is, in fact, a convicted felon or falls into another of the categories of prohibited buyers under federal law. Justice Department figures show that this happened approximately 15,000 times in the period 2010–2014 alone.[61] It accounted for the sale of a gun to the shooter who, in June 2015, murdered nine parishioners at Mother Emanuel Church in Charleston, South Carolina. Fundamentally, the NICS system created by the Brady Act puts a premium on speed, to minimize inconvenience to gun buyers. It is, after all, the National *Instant* Criminal Background Check System. The premium on speed also means that only records that have been entered into a computer database can be checked, allowing sales to individuals like the Virginia Tech shooter, whose record of being adjudicated as mentally ill and dangerous had not been entered into the system. Under the NFA, in contrast, because there are no time limits for the background checks, there is not the same imperative that the records be computer accessible. The absence of time constraints makes checks of manual records possible. In short, under the NFA, background checks take as long as necessary to do them right.

Ironically, even the National Firearms Act was a victim of the NRA's catch-22. The bill originally proposed by the Roosevelt Justice Department included handguns among the weapons to be regulated. At the urging of the NRA and other gun groups, the bill was weakened in committee, and handguns were removed.[62] If, during the last eighty years, handguns had been subject to comprehensive NFA regulation, there is every reason to believe that countless lives would have been saved. Of course, there may be sound policy objections to imposing on handguns the same tight controls we impose on machine guns. But the "criminals will always get guns" argument is not one of them. Based on the machine gun regulatory experience, there should at least be a presumption that a strong, well-administered licensing and registration system can be as effective for other firearms as it has been for machine guns.

ARE "OUTLAWS" THE ONLY PROBLEM?

The argument that "when guns are outlawed, only outlaws will have guns" is based on two premises that are central to the argument against gun control laws. First, the world can be neatly divided into "outlaws" on one hand and "law-abiding citizens" on the other. Second, the gun violence problem is entirely one of criminals acquiring guns to undertake criminal activity. At this point in the discussion of the argument, these premises have gone unquestioned. We have taken for granted that the gun violence problem in America is largely a problem of intentional violence committed by people who are easily identifiable as criminals. Is this an accurate picture of gun violence? Or is the picture more complicated?

One obvious complication is that most gun violence has nothing to do with criminals. Most gunshot deaths and injuries in America are inflicted with guns owned by, in the NRA's parlance, "law-abiding citizens." These are, by definition, the people most likely to obey the law.

For example, more Americans die from gun suicides than from gun homicides.[63] In 2010, for instance, of 31,672 firearm deaths, 19,302 were suicides while 11,078 were homicides.[64] More people kill themselves with guns than by all other methods combined.[65] Several years ago, I was debating an NRA representative at William and Mary Law School, and I cited the figure that more than thirty thousand Americans lose their lives every year to "gun violence." During the Q&A session following the debate, one audience member took me to task because I did not disclose that most of those deaths were suicides. He thought it highly misleading that I would refer to gun suicides as "gun violence." In his view, the gun violence problem is strictly a problem of criminals using guns.

I suppose it is possible to simply define away a huge part of the problem by stipulating that gun violence means use of guns by criminals. Surely, however, this is a highly artificial approach. If the incidence of suicide can be reduced by public policies that limit access to guns by depressed teenagers or others at risk, then why shouldn't suicide be considered part of the gun violence problem? Obviously, the claimed determination of criminals to overcome any obstacle to gain access to guns is irrelevant to the suicide problem. We saw earlier that the use of guns in suicide attempts makes them far more likely to succeed than if other means are chosen. Can gun control laws make guns less accessible to the suicidal and, by doing so, save lives?

There is no question that some people are so determined to kill themselves that they are destined to succeed regardless of whether a gun is available. However, suicide often is an impulsive act, motivated more by a passing crisis than by severe mental illness. Dr. David Hemenway of the Harvard School of Public Health has summarized the striking evidence that suicide attempts do not often follow extensive deliberation and, if not fatal, may never be repeated. He writes:

> Many suicides appear to be impulsive acts. Individuals who take their own lives often do so when confronting a severe but temporary crisis. In one small study of men who survived self-inflicted intentional gunshot wounds to the face, few attempted suicide again. In another study of nearly lethal suicide attempts, 24 percent of attempters reported spending less than five minutes between the decision to attempt suicide and the actual attempt. In yet another study of self-inflicted gunshot wounds that would have been fatal without emergency treatment, none of the thirty attempters had written a suicide note, and more than half reported having suicidal thoughts for less than twenty-four hours. In two years of follow-up, none of the thirty attempted suicide again. As the lead researcher put it, "Many patients in our sample admitted that while they had originally expected to die, they were glad to be alive, and would not repeat the destructive behavior, despite the continued presence of significant medical, psychological and social problems."[66] [citations omitted]

Given that suicide attempts with guns are far more likely to be fatal than with other means, and that the suicidal impulse is often temporary, it stands to reason that access to guns will increase the risk of suicide. Put simply, with guns around, there is likely to be no second chance.

Sure enough, Hemenway reports that ten studies in the previous twenty years examined the relationship between gun ownership and suicide in the United States, "and all find that firearms in the home are associated with substantially and significantly higher rates of suicide."[67] In the last chapter we noted one of these studies, by Arthur Kellermann and his colleagues. Kellermann looked at over eight hundred suicides that occurred during a thirty-two-month period in two urban areas: Shelby County, Tennessee, a predominately poor black community, and King County, Washington, a predominately upper-middle-class white community. After controlling for several variables bearing on suicide risk, including alcohol consumption and use of medication for mental illness, the study showed that the presence of a gun in the home was associated with an almost fivefold increase in the risk of suicide. Kellermann also found that the association between guns in the home and suicide was even greater for persons with no history of depression or mental illness. Other studies have documented the tragic association between guns in the home and the risk of suicide by adolescents. The presence of guns is a particularly high suicide risk factor for adolescents with no apparent psychiatric disorder.[68] Is there much doubt that many lives, particularly young lives, have been lost to suicide because a gun was readily available to people who merely wanted to stop the intense, but temporary, pain of being spurned by a loved one, losing a job, failing in school, or some other passing trauma?

Of course, it is a separate question whether gun control laws can prevent suicide. But the research is encouraging. One study found that after the District of Columbia enacted its handgun ban in 1976, there was an abrupt 23 percent decline in firearm suicide, with no increase in suicide by other means.[69] Even far less extreme controls may have a preventive effect. Several studies have found that strict state gun control laws, none of which were as restrictive as the DC handgun ban, are nevertheless significantly associated with lower levels of suicide.[70] Indeed, one study found that such modest handgun restrictions as waiting periods, reporting of handgun sales to the government, and requiring permits to purchase handguns each were correlated with lower suicide rates.[71]

Particularly promising are laws designed to require gun owners to make their guns inaccessible to young people. Research shows that "safe storage practices"—storing household guns locked, unloaded, or separate from the ammunition—reduce the risk of suicide among adolescents and children.[72] As noted previously, eighteen states had enacted "child-access prevention" (CAP) laws to impose criminal penalties on gun owners who are negligent in their storage of guns. A study published in the *Journal of the American Medical Association* showed that CAP laws were associated with an 8 percent reduction in suicide rates for youth aged fourteen to seventeen, which translated into 333 suicides in that age group prevented since Florida enacted the first CAP law, in 1989.[73] This life-saving success, of course, did not depend on criminals obeying gun laws but on compliance by presumably law-abiding gun owners.

Perhaps the most striking study of suicide and guns was done by Garen Wintemute of the University of California–Davis and his colleagues and published in the *New England Journal of Medicine*.[74] Wintemute looked at death rates among the 238,292 persons who purchased a handgun in California in 1991, compared to death rates in the general population. He found that in the first year after the purchase of a handgun, handgun purchasers were over four times more likely to commit suicide than persons in the general population and that this increased risk was entirely attributable to an increased risk of suicide with a firearm. This increased risk of suicide for handgun buyers persisted for at least six years. He also found that *in the first week after the purchase of a handgun, the rate of suicide by firearm was fifty-seven times as high as the suicide rate in the general population.* This is the best evidence yet developed to indicate that some people buy handguns with the intention of killing themselves.

In 1991, California had a fifteen-day waiting period for handgun purchases (it has since been shortened to ten days, applicable to all gun purchases). Given the temporary nature of suicidal impulses in many individuals, Wintemute's findings suggest that the waiting period alone likely saves lives, although obviously we can't count the number of potential suicides that never occur because the desire to buy a handgun was temporarily frustrated. A "cooling-off" period to prevent suicides and impulsive homicides was part of the original justification for proposals for a federal mandatory waiting period. However, as finally passed into law, the Brady Act included no such waiting period. For the first five years after enactment (1993–98), law-enforcement authorities had five business days to conduct a background check on handgun buyers, but this was not a true waiting period because the purchase could be completed if the check took less than five business days to complete. In 1998, the "permanent provisions" of the Brady Act kicked in and the National Instant Criminal Background Check System became applicable, not just to handguns but to all firearms. Under NICS, the FBI has three business days to complete the background check, but 95 percent of the checks are completed within two hours.[75] Obviously, there is no "cooling-off period" under federal law; indeed, a major rationale for NICS is to ensure that the background checks are done, as the name makes clear, "instantly." The suicide evidence suggests that there is life-saving value in a waiting period, not simply to ensure a high-quality background check but also to make it more difficult for someone with passing suicidal thoughts to get access to the most lethal means of converting those thoughts into action.

Apart from suicides, unintentional shootings are another category of gun violence that appears to have little to do with criminals (although, I suppose, it is possible for criminals, as well as law-abiding citizens, to make mistakes with guns). Gun accidents would appear inherently more preventable than gun suicides or homicides, even though, of course, gun suicides and homicides often can be prevented too. Unintentional shootings are, by definition, not subject to any substitution effect; that is, unlike suicides and homicides, there is no basis for saying that if the perpetrator of an unintentional shooting had been denied access to a gun, he would have unintentionally hurt himself or someone else by some other means. The causal connection between the gun and the infliction of injury is therefore far more direct in unintentional shootings, there being no doubt that the injury would not have been inflicted if the shooter did not have access to a gun.

Although unintentional shootings represent a far smaller percentage of gun deaths than homicides or suicides, they nonetheless account for a significant loss of life. From 2005 to 2010 almost 3,800 people in the United States died from unintentional shootings; 1,300 of them were under twenty-five years of age.[76] For every person who dies in a gun accident, about thirteen are injured seriously enough to be treated in hospital emergency rooms.[77] These figures likely understate the number of deaths and injuries from unintentional shootings. As experts have pointed out, medical examiners in some states typically classify as homicides or suicides all shootings when the shooter intentionally pulls the trigger, regardless of whether the shooter intended to harm the victim.[78] In instances in which the shooter inflicts injury because he did not know his gun was loaded, the incident is nevertheless not classified as "unintentional" or "accidental."

Gun accidents often victimize children. Data from the Centers for Disease Control shows that between 2007 and 2011, an average of sixty-two children age fourteen and younger died each year in unintentional shootings.[79] This is almost surely a significant undercount. A *New York Times* review of hundreds of child firearms deaths found that accidental shootings occurred roughly twice as often as the records indicate, "because of idiosyncrasies in how such deaths are classified by the authorities."[80] An analysis of cases of unintentional firearm deaths of children age fourteen and younger for sixteen states from 2005 to 2012 also found significant misclassification, arriving at an estimate of 110 such deaths in the United States annually.[81] (The undercounting of accidental deaths should be born in mind when gun advocates compare child gun deaths with child deaths in swimming pools, etc.) In other industrialized countries, these child gun tragedies are virtually nonexistent. Even without considering US undercounting, the unintentional gun-related death rate for children aged five to fourteen in the United States is over twelve times greater than the combined rates for twenty-two other high-income countries.[82]

In arguing against gun control laws, the NRA and the gun industry often point out, quite correctly, that the accidental firearm death rate has been decreasing over time. The NRA attributes the decline to its own "voluntary firearms safety training, not government intrusion,"[83] while offering no evidence that a higher percentage of gun owners receive such training now than in earlier periods or that such training is more effective now than before. Harvard's David Hemenway cites other likely factors, including a rising American standard of living, improvements in emergency medicine, increasing suburbanization, and a sharp decline in the number of hunters, particularly young hunters, who are at highest risk for accidental shootings.[84] Perhaps the most significant factor is the parallel trend toward fewer households with guns, from a peak of 54 percent in 1977 to 32 percent in 2014.[85] Whatever the reasons for the decline in accidental shootings, the trend is hardly a good reason to oppose policies that will accelerate the trend and save even more lives. Should the government not have required cars to have air bags because mandatory installation of seat belts had already reduced auto deaths?

If the NRA is right and "voluntary" safety training accounts for the decline in accidental gun fatalities, wouldn't even more accidents be prevented if the training were mandatory for every gun owner? If cars are sufficiently dangerous to require safety training in order to drive, then aren't guns sufficiently dangerous to require such training of prospective gun owners? Mandatory gun training that included a "safe storage" component could be especially important in reducing the risk of gun accidents involving young people. Operator manuals provided by manufacturers with new guns typically advise gun owners to store their guns locked and unloaded, with the ammunition stored separate from the gun. Research shows that compliance with this advice substantially lowers the risk of unintentional shootings involving adolescents and children.[86] Why shouldn't safe storage be part of mandatory gun-safety training?

Child-access prevention laws, shown above to be an effective strategy against teen suicide, also are promising in their potential to prevent accidental shootings by children and teens. During the first eight years it was in effect, Florida's CAP law was associated with a 51 percent decline in the rate of unintentional firearms deaths to children under fifteen years old, which translates to fifty-two young lives saved.[87] Although this dramatic effect has not been observed in other CAP-law states, that may be due to Florida's stiffer penalties for violations (felony versus misdemeanor), its far higher rate of unintentional firearm deaths of children before the law was passed, and the unique publicity given the law because it was the first of its kind in the nation.[88] The Florida experience suggests that CAP laws can save lives by communicating a serious message, backed by serious penalties, that storing a gun accessible to a child is very dangerous behavior. Again, the success of these laws requires compliance by law-abiding gun owners, not criminals.

Required safety training and CAP laws seek to prevent unintentional shootings by altering the behavior of gun users. Injury-prevention specialists teach us, however, that more deaths and injuries from a dangerous product can be prevented by changing the product itself. In this regard, the most illustrative success story has been the automobile. Until the 1950s, public policy toward auto accidents consisted of trying to instill good driving habits in the general population and punishing bad drivers. The focus was entirely on the driver, not the car. This orientation reflected the influence of the auto industry, which sought to deflect attention from its own lack of interest in making its cars safer by promoting the idea that injuries from auto accidents were entirely due to bad driving. Research into auto design by engineers and physicians began to change that perspective. This led to a series of design innovations, including padded dashboards, shatterproof windshields, collapsible steering columns, additional brake lights, seat belts, and air bags. In the second half of the twentieth century, the number of motor-vehicle fatalities per mile driven has dropped more than 80 percent. (In 2015, for the first time in more than sixty years, firearms and automobiles killed Americans at an identical rate, due largely to the sharp decline in auto deaths.)[89] There appears to be little evidence that drivers have gotten significantly more careful. Rather, the dramatic drop in auto deaths appears largely related to safety improvements in cars.[90]

Similarly, safer guns likely would save more lives and prevent more injuries than an exclusive focus on the behavior of the gun user. If guns truly were regulated as consumer products, and safety features were made mandatory, unintentional shootings could be prevented. One study sought to assess the percentage of unintentional shooting deaths (and shooting deaths in which the intent was undetermined) that would be preventable if certain safety devices were placed on guns.[91] The researchers studied three possible safety improvements: loaded chamber indicators, magazine safeties, and "personalization" technology. A loaded-chamber indicator alerts the user of a pistol that the gun is loaded but is included in only about 10–20 percent of new pistol models. A magazine safety prevents a pistol from being fired when its ammunition magazine is removed, but many pistols do not have this feature. This device is designed to prevent unintentional shootings that occur when a user thinks he has unloaded the gun by removing the magazine, forgetting that there may be a round left in the gun's firing chamber. A personalized gun can only be fired by an authorized user, thus preventing use by children, teenagers, and others. The study found that of the shooting deaths examined, 20 percent were preventable by a loaded-chamber indicator, 4 percent by a magazine safety, and 37 percent by personalization.[92] The researchers emphasized that the deaths would not *necessarily* have been prevented, but they *could* have been prevented with these design changes. Again, if these devices were required by law, their risk-reducing benefits would depend on compliance with the law not by criminals but by gun manufacturers, who, the gun industry constantly assures the public, are absolutely law abiding.

. . .

We have seen that expanding the concept of gun violence beyond the use of guns by "outlaws" both changes the debate and the range of policy options for preventing gun deaths and injuries. If the objective is reducing the number of gun suicides and accidents, the debate over whether gun laws can prevent access to guns by hardened criminals is transparently irrelevant. Moreover, if the gun violence problem were defined as a problem of "gun death and injury," as opposed to a problem of "gun crime," it would dramatically alter our beliefs about who is at the greatest risk of gun violence and where they live. Most Americans assume that gun violence in America is a problem largely of California and the urbanized states of the East and Midwest, with rural states in the West and South largely exempt. Which state has the higher rate of guns deaths (that is, deaths per one hundred thousand residents, not simply total deaths)? New Jersey or Montana? New York or Mississippi? Massachusetts or Alaska? The truth is completely counterintuitive. Montana's gun-death rate is three times higher than New Jersey's. Mississippi's is over four times higher than New York's. Alaska's is six times higher than Massachusetts'.[93] (See appendix 2.) How can this be true? Because there is a largely ignored gun-suicide epidemic in rural America. Indeed, in many rural counties, the incidence of suicide with guns is greater than the incidence of murder by guns in major cities.[94] "Americans in small towns and rural areas are just as likely to die from gunfire as Americans in major cities," says Charles Branas of the University of Pennsylvania School of Medicine. "The difference is in who does the shooting."[95]

It will also come as a shock to gun control opponents that the ten states with the highest gun death rates in the nation are rural states with among the weakest gun control laws, whereas the six states with the lowest gun death rates are urban states with among the strongest gun control laws.[96] This is not to say that weak gun laws necessarily mean higher gun-death rates, or that strong laws necessarily means lower death rates. As with city-by-city comparisons, state-by-state comparisons reflect many factors other than gun laws. But state comparisons do illustrate that framing the gun violence issue as purely one of criminal conduct with guns has a profoundly distorting impact on the debate. The NRA benefits greatly from the widespread assumption that communities with the worst gun violence problems also have the strongest gun control laws. That assumption is destroyed as soon as "gun violence" is redefined to include all gun deaths and injuries, not just those inflicted by criminals. As we have seen, there is substantial reason to believe that background checks, waiting periods, CAP laws, mandatory safety training, and consumer-protection regulations can reduce "gun violence" as so defined.

Alas, however, our elected officials are a long way from viewing the gun violence problem as anything but a gun-crime problem. In the fall of 2004, Congress passed new legislation to prevent youth suicide, which takes about 750 young lives every year.[97] Named for Garrett Lee Smith, the twenty-one-year-old son of Senator Gordon Smith (R-Oregon) who killed himself in his college dorm room, the new law expands counseling services and other efforts to identify kids at risk for suicide. As Dorothy Samuels of the *New York Times* lamented, however, nothing in the legislation addresses the need to protect suicidal kids from access to guns. "Fear of the gun lobby is such," she wrote, "the subject never came up."[98] Although political cowardice was no doubt an important factor, I suspect that even those few in Congress who are willing to stand up to the NRA would have regarded a debate over guns to be out of place when the subject is teen suicide. Even when policymakers summon the courage to discuss gun violence, the equation of "gun violence" with "gun crime" continues to frame the issue.

ARE GUN CRIMINALS ALWAYS "OUTLAWS"?

We have seen that a fundamental premise of the argument that "when guns are outlawed, only outlaws will have guns" is that the gun violence problem is entirely one of criminals acquiring guns to undertake criminal activity. We also have seen that this premise works only by artificially excluding from the "gun violence" problem any mention of suicides and unintentional shootings. Even if we narrowly define the problem to be one of "gun crime," however, the argument depends on a second, and equally artificial, premise: the world can be neatly divided into "outlaws," on the one hand, and "law-abiding citizens," on the other.

Of course, it is trivially true that anyone who commits a gun crime is an "outlaw," in the sense that they, by definition, have defied the law. Gun control opponents seek to prove something more: gun criminals are "outlaws" in the sense that they are so determined to be armed, so defiant of our criminal laws, and so easily able to dip into the vast pool of illegal guns, that gun control laws can have no effect on their behavior or their access to guns. Much energy, therefore, has been invested in trying to show that because violent gun criminals, particularly murderers, have long criminal records, they are fundamentally different than the rest of us and, essentially, incapable of being deterred by gun laws. Self-described "criminologist" Don Kates, for example, has made a career of debunking what he calls "the myth that ordinary people murder."[99]

According to some studies, most homicide offenders have serious prior criminal records. One Justice Department study showed that 67 percent of homicide defendants in the largest urban counties have at least one felony arrest; 54 percent have at least one felony conviction.[100] A later study, published in the *Journal of the American Medical Association*, of Illinois arrest records for a ten-year period showed that although persons arrested for homicide were far more likely to have previous felony convictions than the general population, nevertheless only 42 percent of homicide arrestees had prior felony convictions in the previous ten years.[101] Even if a majority of those arrested for homicide had a previous serious criminal record, it is unclear how such facts support a critique of gun control laws. Indeed, if it is true that murderers commit other crimes before they kill, this would support a policy of ensuring that every gun purchase, whether from a licensed dealer or a private citizen, be preceded by a criminal-background check. As we have seen, there is strong evidence that such a policy of universal background checks, supplemented by required registration of gun transfers, would prevent substantial numbers of violent criminals from obtaining guns.

There is, of course, a flip side to the data showing that a majority, or near majority, of gun homicides are committed by offenders who already have a criminal record. It means that many gun homicides are committed by people who have *no* criminal record until they pull the trigger. These are not the hardened career criminals who are most likely to have multiple potential illegal sources to acquire guns. Rather, they are people who were able to arm themselves only by exploiting weaknesses in existing gun laws because they had no ready access to the illegal market. Absent those weaknesses, they might have committed a violent act, but it would not have been with a weapon of the same lethality as a gun.

The school shootings in recent years that so horrified the nation were not committed by hardened criminals with ready access to a pool of illegal guns destined to be unaffected by strong gun laws. We have already seen that the Columbine killers armed themselves by exploiting the loophole allowing guns to be sold at gun shows with no questions asked. A year earlier, thirteen-year-old Mitchell Johnson and eleven-year-old Andrew Golden killed four girls and a teacher, and wounded eleven others, at their middle school in Jonesboro, Arkansas, with guns they had taken from Golden's grandfather, a wildlife-conservation officer. They took rifles displayed in a gun rack hanging on the wall, pistols that were "hidden all over the house," according to the grandfather, and boxes of shells stacked on top of the kitchen refrigerator.[102] However, when they broke into Golden's father's house, they were unable to get the high-powered rifles locked in his safe and had to be satisfied with three guns that weren't locked up.[103] The guns that were secured were not used. The guns that weren't secured ended up being murder weapons. Arkansas had no Child Access Prevention Law to require that guns be secured away from kids. There is no federal or state requirement that guns have internal locks or be otherwise "personalized" to bar use by juvenile thieves and other "unauthorized" users. Had such laws existed, Johnson and Golden might well have acted out their violent fantasies, but likely not in a way that inflicted mass carnage on their classmates. The guns they used were easy targets of opportunity. The opportunity was created by the too-casual storage of guns by a law-abiding father and grandfather, and by the failure of gun manufacturers to make design changes to reduce the risk of misuse.

"When guns are outlawed, only outlaws will have guns" is, then, fallacious on several levels. Taken literally, it is simply irrelevant to a range of policy proposals that dominate the public debate over guns but do not "outlaw" guns. To the extent that it expresses the view that gun laws cannot be effective because they will not be obeyed by criminals, it is fallacious because the success of gun laws in limiting access to guns by criminals does not depend on the willingness of criminals to obey them. Finally, the argument is supported by two implied premises, both of which are untrue. The first premise, that gun violence is a problem only of criminals using guns in criminal activity, is contradicted by the evidence that most gun deaths involve shootings by law-abiding citizens in suicides and accidents. The second premise, that the world can be neatly divided into law-abiding citizens (who obey gun laws but are not the problem) and "outlaws" (whose access to guns is unaffected by gun laws), is both untrue and unpersuasive as an argument against gun control. It is untrue because some who use guns in violent acts are not "outlaws" until they pull the trigger, and their access to guns is made possible by the weaknesses in our gun laws. It is unpersuasive because even if every gun crime *were* committed by a hardened criminal with a long rap sheet, this would argue for, not against, a system by which every gun transfer is subject to a criminal-background check and registration of the transfer, a system that has been working since the Depression to limit criminal access to machine guns.

CHAPTER THREE

GUN CONTROL IS A SLIPPERY SLOPE TO CONFISCATION

Although this argument may never be bumper-sticker ready, it is as ubiquitous as "Guns don't kill people . . ." and "When guns are outlawed . . ." No gun control debate would be complete without the assertion, by opponents of gun laws, that to endorse whatever proposal is under discussion is to take the first step down a "slippery slope" toward more Draconian gun restrictions and, ultimately, toward confiscation of all guns.

There may be no other public policy issue where the slippery-slope argument is as frequently used. For example, Wayne LaPierre of the NRA invoked the argument as a key reason to oppose a waiting period for handgun purchases:

> This brings us back to the real intent behind waiting periods. Waiting periods are only a first step. Regardless of what they promise to do or not to do, they are nothing more than the first step toward more stringent "gun control" measures.
>
> Some people call it "the camel's nose under the tent," some call it "the slippery slope," some call it a "foot in the door," but regardless of what you call it, it's still the same—the first step.[1]

Six years after the passage of the Brady Bill (which, as we have seen, never did actually enact a waiting period), the NRA made it clear what was at the bottom of the slippery slope—the end of private ownership of firearms: "The plan is now obvious to all who would see: First Step, enact a nationwide firearms waiting period law. Second Step, when the waiting period doesn't reduce crime, and it won't, enact a nationwide registration law. Final Step, confiscate all the registered firearms."[2]

The NRA asserts that waiting periods are a bad idea for many reasons, for example, they may interfere with the legitimate exercise of self-defense, and they don't curb gun violence. In contrast to these arguments, the slippery-slope argument asserts that a proposed policy change (e.g., waiting periods) should be resisted, not because the policy change is itself a bad idea but rather because it will lead to the adoption of some other policy (e.g., confiscation of all guns) that *is* a bad idea.

WHY THE NRA NEEDS THE SLIPPERY SLOPE

Although slippery-slope arguments are commonly used in other public policy debates, they are especially important to the gun lobby for several reasons.

First, because it is so obviously difficult for the pro-gun forces to persuasively argue that many reasonable and popular measures—such as waiting periods, background checks, licensing and safety training, registration of gun sales, curbs on large-volume gun sales, and mandatory consumer-safety standards—are objectionable in their own right, it becomes essential to argue that these measures will ultimately lead to policies that have far less popular support and may be more difficult to justify. For example, given the reality that gun traffickers buy large numbers of guns from dealers and that few law-abiding gun owners really need to buy more than one handgun per month, the benefits of a national law restricting large-volume sales appear to substantially outweigh any inconvenience to gun owners uninterested in criminal activity. For this reason, the NRA's strategy is to suggest that the real problem with such laws is that they set a dangerous precedent that would lead to far greater restrictions in the future. Thus, the NRA argues that "one gun a month" could be changed to "one per year," "one per lifetime," or "none ever."[3]

Second, the NRA must sell the slippery-slope argument to convince gun owners and sportsmen that they have an important stake in the gun control fight. As noted previously, polls consistently show that gun owners, and even NRA members, actually support gun control proposals that are anathema to the gun lobby's leadership. This must be quite discomfiting to the NRA. If the NRA's core constituency does not view gun control as a threat to gun ownership, the foundation of the organization's political power will weaken. It is essential to the NRA's long-term viability that any gun control proposal be viewed by millions of Americans as an attack on a valued personal possession. Indeed, the NRA's strategy is to go even further—to portray even modest gun control as an attack on a way of life for which the gun is both an important tool and, more importantly, a powerful symbol.

As one NRA leader put it some years ago, "You would get a far better understanding if you approached us as if you were approaching one of the great religions of the world."[4] This is not a frivolous comparison. There is an unquestionably religious fervor about the beliefs of many pro-gun partisans. It is grounded in various articles of faith that form the catechism of the NRA: that law-abiding citizens are under constant risk from attack by predatory criminals, that the safety of every person and family depends on the ability of individuals to defend themselves with firearms, that the government cannot be trusted to provide security to individuals and families, that democratic institutions cannot be counted on to protect our liberties as Americans, that those institutions are at constant risk of subversion by tyrannical elements, and that tyranny is kept at bay only by the potential for insurrection by an armed populace intent on maintaining liberty. In the NRA's world, these are eternal truths. They are not themselves proper subjects for empirical testing or debate, but rather are *a priori* verities according to which the world is interpreted and understood.

Frequently gun control is referred to—alongside issues like abortion and gay rights—as a "cultural" issue. Describing it in such terms immediately elevates the stakes in the gun debate because it suggests that gun control proposals may be seen as attacks on a set of core beliefs that define many Americans, particularly Americans in rural areas for which guns symbolize important values of self-reliance and personal liberty. For the gun lobby, it is strategically critical to raise the stakes in this way. If the gun debate is seen as addressing only the efficacy of specific, practical proposals to reduce death and injury, then the NRA is on shaky ground because, as noted, even its own members do not have strong objections to many such proposals. However, if the gun debate is seen as fundamentally about larger issues involving the value systems of millions of gun-owning Americans, then the NRA is able to radicalize and mobilize those Americans who see their values as under attack. Gun control is then seen as an attack on gun-owning Americans and how they live their lives.

One of Charlton Heston's strengths when he was the NRA's president was his ability to frame the gun issue as part of a larger cultural struggle. In an angry, theatrical oration at Harvard Law School in 1999, he exclaimed: "As I have stood in the crosshairs of those who target Second Amendment freedoms, I've realized that firearms are not the only issue. No, it's much, much bigger than that." He went on to declare that "a cultural war is raging across our land."[5] The speech then turned into a rant against political correctness, the rights of transvestites, bilingual education, black separatism on college campuses, violent song lyrics, grade inflation, sexual harassment laws, and other grievances that made the "cultural struggle" worth fighting. The real audience for the speech was not Harvard Law students but conservative gun owners everywhere. Heston's message was that the NRA cause was about defending the values of ordinary Americans against attack by Eastern elitists. He was showing them that he was willing to take their cultural war right to the heart of the enemy.

For the gun lobby, then, the gun debate needs to be cast as a grand cultural struggle about banning all guns. The slippery-slope argument is the NRA's primary means of achieving this goal. As writer Osha Gray Davidson put it, "The religious fervor of many gun owners when it comes to firearms restrictions also has its roots in a less mystical and more pragmatic concern: the fear that all gun-control laws lead inexorably to the complete confiscation of all firearms."[6] We have already seen that one of the NRA's great successes has been to associate the words "gun control" in the public mind with the idea of banning gun possession. This is the power of the slippery-slope argument. It is not an overstatement to say that the future of gun control in America likely will turn on how slippery Americans believe that slope to be.

WHEN IS A SLIPPERY SLOPE REALLY A FLIGHT OF STAIRS?

The metaphor of the slippery slope suggests that, once we are committed to supporting one, presumably desirable, policy (the top of the slope), we will inevitably end up supporting another, presumably objectionable, policy (the bottom of the slope). The slipperiest of slopes would be those with which the endorsement of the desirable policy at the top leaves us with no rational basis to oppose the undesirable policy at the bottom. Once we step onto the slope, logic leads us inexorably to the bottom because all the possible brake points turn out to be completely arbitrary. This style of slippery-slope argument typically raises the question "Where do you draw the line?" as a way of suggesting that, once we are on the slope, any line drawing is arbitrary.

As I have noted, in the core slippery-slope argument of the gun lobby, the bottom of the slope is a ban on gun ownership, or at least handgun ownership. It should be immediately clear that the alleged slippery slopes that lead to a broad gun ban are not "logical slippery slopes"; that is, it is not difficult to find logical distinctions between a gun ban and the policy being proposed. I earlier quoted the NRA as claiming a slippery slope from a national waiting period, to registration of all guns, to eventual confiscation of the registered guns. But it should be immediately obvious that there is a logical distinction between a waiting period and registration, and between registration and confiscation. It is perfectly rational for a policymaker to endorse a waiting period and registration of gun sales because, for the reasons discussed in chapter 2, those policies will reduce gun deaths and injuries, and yet oppose confiscation of guns as an extreme governmental intrusion on the individual choice of law-abiding citizens to own a product they obviously value. The path from a waiting period to gun confiscation seems more like a staircase than a slippery slope. Once we take the "first step," we are not logically and inexorably committed to take any further steps. Rather, we realize that each step requires its own individual assessment of risks and benefits, and we are free to consider them before taking the next step to a new and different policy.

For some alleged slippery slopes, the apparent arbitrariness of possible lines drawn at various points on the slope incorrectly suggests that there is no rational distinction between the proposal at the top of the slope and the proposal at the bottom. This is the fallacy of the NRA's objection to "one gun a month" laws. According to the NRA, once the government imposes a limit on handgun purchases of one per month, that limit could easily be "one per year" or "one per lifetime" or "none ever." It is true that the line between "one per month" and "one per forty-five days" seems arbitrary. The line between "one per forty-five days" and "one per sixty days" seems equally arbitrary. Does this mean that there is no rational basis to endorse "one per month" and oppose "one per sixty days," or for that matter, "one per year" or "one per lifetime"? Clearly not. The point of restrictions on large-volume sales is to disrupt gun trafficking, while preserving the ability of legitimate buyers to purchase handguns. Whereas "one per month" interferes with legitimate gun purchases only to the extent necessary to achieve the anti-trafficking objective, "one per sixty days" arguably imposes an additional burden on legitimate gun purchasers (although a small one) not necessary to diminish gun trafficking.

Although reasonable people can disagree about where to draw the line, certainly a reasonable line can be drawn. It is fallacious to argue that because there is an element of arbitrariness between any two lines along the slope, no restrictions on large-volume sales should be imposed and gun trafficking should continue unabated. It would be similarly fallacious to argue that no waiting periods should be imposed on handgun purchases to deter suicides and allow time for effective background checks, because there is no rational distinction between a waiting period of five days versus six days, or six days versus seven days, and so on. If the NRA's arguments were valid, our roads would be without speed limits, since a speed limit of 55 mph could not be defended as materially different than one of 56 mph, and one of 56 mph is not materially different than one of 57 mph. The arbitrariness of any particular speed limit does not render irrational the task of setting a speed limit and should not mean that we must tolerate the deaths and injuries that would result from the absence of any speed limit.[7]

This is not to deny that there are some very slippery slopes in the gun control debate. For example, it may be claimed that once we recognize the necessity of mandatory background checks on people buying guns from licensed gun dealers, then there is no rational basis for not extending those background checks to purchases of guns through gun shows and elsewhere from unlicensed sellers. If the objective is to prevent the sale of guns to criminals, it should not matter whether the seller is a licensed dealer or an individual at a gun show claiming to be selling only his "personal collection." Indeed, in California, the background check requirement was limited to licensed dealers until 1991, when a new statute went into effect requiring even private sales to be handled by licensed dealers as a means of extending background checks to those sales.

Arguably, the NRA itself stepped on the background-check slippery slope in the early '90s when, as a ploy to slow the Brady Bill's gathering momentum in Congress, the organization endorsed the concept of a computerized "instant check," as an alternative to the Brady Bill's provision of five business days to conduct the background checks on gun-dealer sales. Of course, at the time the NRA came up with this idea, a computerized "instant check" was no check at all because the records to be checked had not been computerized.[8] But once the NRA conceded the desirability of background checks at licensed dealers (thereby undercutting its claim that "criminals don't buy guns at gun stores"), it became more difficult for the gun lobby to argue against background checks for other sales. Indeed, the NRA arguably stepped on the background-check slippery slope when it first claimed to support laws barring sales of guns to convicted felons. If it makes sense to deter gun sales to felons by making them a criminal offense, then would it not make even more sense to do criminal-background checks to prevent the sales in the first place?

Although the background-check slope may be treacherous, it clearly does not function in the way users of slippery-slope arguments intend. It does not make us oppose the proposal at the top of the slope, whether that be banning gun sales to convicted felons or requiring background checks at licensed dealers. Why? Because the proposal at the bottom of the slope—background checks for all gun sales—does not seem undesirable at all, especially if you think banning gun sales to felons or requiring background checks at licensed dealers are good ideas. Since the NRA needs the debate to be about banning guns, if the slippery-slope argument does not lead to a broad ban on guns at the bottom of the slope, then the argument is not of much use to the gun lobby. The dilemma for the NRA is this: the logical slippery slopes in the gun debate don't lead to a gun ban. And the path from modest gun control measures to a gun ban is more akin to a staircase than a slippery slope.

FACTUAL SLIPPERY SLOPES

To this point in the discussion, we have considered only what I have called "logical slippery slopes," that is, arguments to the effect that support of the proposal at the top of the slope logically compels support for the proposal at the bottom. There is, however, another category of slippery-slope argument. In this second category, the opponent of a proposal maintains that it should not be adopted because to do so would increase the likelihood that the next step would be taken, which would make a third step more likely and so on. I call these "factual slippery slopes" because they amount to factual predictions about what proposals will be adopted. Here the "flight of stairs" metaphor seems more appropriate than the "slippery slope," because each proposal on the slope can be logically distinguished from the others and a rational basis can be given for refraining from taking the "next step." But, it is claimed, because each step increases the likelihood of the next step, ultimately leading to an undesirable last step, the first step should not be taken at all.

To gun control opponents, the most fearsome factual slippery slope usually involves government registration of guns as a key element. Recall that the NRA objected to a waiting period for handgun purchases because it would lead to registration, which would, in turn, lead to confiscation of the registered guns. The idea here is that once the government has records of who owns what guns, confiscation of those guns from the registered owners will be made far easier. Pro-gun advocates, anxious to dispel the notion that the "knock on the door" fears of some gun enthusiasts reflect only their own paranoia, have sought to carefully explain just how gun registration can "lead to" gun confiscation.[9]

It is important to realize, however, that factual slippery slopes are inherently susceptible to the *post hoc* fallacy.[10] In offering examples of factual slippery slopes in action, it is not enough to be able to point to a succession of gradual reforms through time. The factual slippery slope is one in which each incremental reform has some causal connection to the incremental reform that followed it. Each reform must have an impact that increases the likelihood that the next reform will be undertaken, such as, for example, by removing a barrier to further reform. The causal connections between the incremental reforms are not established simply by evidence that one reform followed the other in time. Absent these causal connections, presumably the undesirable reform at the bottom of the slope would have occurred regardless of whether less radical reforms had been implemented or not.

For example, pro-gun writers frequently invoke the history of British gun laws as an example of how moderate gun laws can "lead to" an eventual handgun ban.[11] In 1997, Britain passed legislation banning the possession of virtually all handguns. The statute was enacted as a direct result of the massacre in the Scottish town of Dunblane a year and half before, in which a gunman used handguns to kill sixteen schoolchildren and their teacher. Under the new law, handgun owners would receive compensation for the guns they turned in and face prosecution for the guns they kept.

It is true that this handgun ban was preceded by a licensing and registration system. However, the British licensing and registration system had been in place since 1920, *over seventy years before the handgun ban was enacted.* Although other gun laws were enacted in the interim, the only guns that were banned during that period were short-barreled shotguns and machine guns. These "gangster" weapons were banned in 1936, two years after America had cracked down on these guns by passing the National Firearms Act. Would Britain have banned handguns in 1997 if the licensing and registration system had not been in place? Or would the Dunblane massacre have brought about the ban even if the prior gun laws had never been enacted? Given that Britain had licensing and registration for over seventy years before it banned handguns, it is highly speculative to argue that such a system eventually "led to" or "caused" the 1997 handgun ban. The fact that a handgun ban eventually followed licensing and registration in Britain does not itself demonstrate that such controls make gun banning "more likely."

Even if a causal connection could be established in Britain, other examples could be cited in which licensing and registration have not lead to a handgun ban or gun confiscation. The NRA cites New York City as another example of "registration leads to confiscation," but actually New York's gun laws prove the opposite. The city adopted a licensing and registration law governing rifles and shotguns in 1967, under Mayor John V. Lindsay.[12] Confiscation allegedly arrived in 1991, but even the NRA's own description of the 1991 law makes it clear that it only applied to "certain semiautomatic rifles and shotguns," that is, assault weapons.[13] The New York City assault-weapons ban required registered assault-weapons owners to surrender their weapons, render them inoperable, or move them out of the city. It would appear that the police were in pretty good position to enforce the ban against continued possession, given that the guns already were registered.

As explained earlier, however, legislation restricting assault weapons was passed only because its proponents were successful in arguing that assault weapons are fundamentally different than conventional firearms in terms of their greater firepower, which makes them a greater threat to public safety in the hands of criminals, as well as inappropriate for self-defense in the home. The question for the NRA is this: If there is such a slippery slope from registration to confiscation, why hasn't New York City banned continued possession of *all* the rifles and shotguns that are registered, instead of just the small minority of them that qualify as assault weapons? (During the early 1990s, ATF estimated that about 1 percent of the guns in circulation were assault weapons.) To the extent that the New York City experience teaches anything, it is that the registration of guns does *not* necessarily lead to their confiscation.

Many other examples can be offered of registration laws that have been on the books for decades without having prompted any move toward banning civilian gun possession or confiscating guns. The State of Pennsylvania, for example, has maintained records of handgun sales since 1931.[14] The Pennsylvania State Police currently maintains a database of persons who lawfully purchase handguns in Pennsylvania. Although in theory Pennsylvania's database would make it "easier" to confiscate guns should the state enact such radical legislation, nothing about Pennsylvania's registration of handgun sales has moved the state even close to doing so.

Other states with some form of registration include New Jersey, Massachusetts, Michigan, Maryland, and California.[15] Not one of those states has banned or tried to confiscate all handguns or long guns. Despite the fact that the authorities in those states have a pretty good idea of who owns the guns, all have been able to resist the temptation to demand their surrender.

On the other hand, examples can also be cited of gun bans that were enacted without being preceded by any registration system whatsoever. The federal assault-weapons ban, in effect for ten years beginning in 1994, banned an estimated two hundred types of pistols, rifles, and shotguns. None of those guns was subject to a federal registration system at the time they were banned. Thus, registration appears neither necessary nor sufficient to bring about an eventual gun ban.

The machine gun registration system created by the National Firearms Act raises particularly interesting slippery-slope issues. Under the NFA, since 1934 the federal government has had a record of every legal owner of a machine gun. As noted above, the NFA remained in undisturbed form until 1986, when Congress passed the NRA-supported Firearms Owners Protection Act, which severely weakened federal gun laws (more on that later) but featured one redeeming provision. Gun control forces in Congress were able to add an amendment, known as the "machine gun freeze," which banned the future manufacture of machine guns for the civilian market, as well as prohibiting the transfer and possession of machine guns not already legally owned when the act went into effect.[16] The amendment served to freeze the number of machine guns in circulation, while continuing to subject the "grandfathered" machine guns to the licensing, registration, and taxation provisions of the NFA.

Notice what did *not* happen in 1986. Even though the NFA enabled the government to know the identity of every legal machine gun owner, Congress did not move to confiscate those registered weapons nor bar their continued possession in any way. Even today, *over eighty years after the beginning of machine gun licensing and registration*, the government has done nothing to confiscate registered machine guns. As long as you comply with the licensing, registration, and taxation provisions of the NFA, it is entirely legal to buy, own, and sell a machine gun made before May 19, 1986, when the machine gun freeze went into effect.

Pro-gun law professor Eugene Volokh has described some of the "mechanisms" by which gun-registration laws may make gun bans more likely to be enacted.[17] In addition to making confiscation "easier," Volokh suggests that registration may alter public attitudes about gun ownership, discourage gun ownership itself, and thus reduce the natural constituency to oppose confiscation, create political momentum for confiscation, and make confiscation seem less radical a step. Volokh's speculations are all quite plausible, but they are speculations nonetheless. It is just as plausible that registration will have none of these effects. Instead, gun registration, like auto registration, may simply be regarded by the public as an appropriate regulatory and law-enforcement tool applied to a dangerous product, with no tendency to generate support for banning the product itself. Other than speculation of the Volokh variety, all we have to guide us is real-world experience. As we have seen, the US experience has been that gun-registration systems have *not* been precursors to gun bans or confiscation, both because registration has not led to gun bans and because gun bans have not been preceded by registration.

That brings us to the most potent argument against the pro-gun slippery-slope argument. We have seen that the factual slippery slope consists essentially of raw speculation that gun restrictions will lead to a gun ban, with little real-world evidence of such a causal effect. That speculative fear, however, is used by the gun lobby to argue against gun control measures *that have benefits that are not speculative at all.* If Congress had agreed with the NRA argument that the Brady Bill should be defeated because it is the "first step" toward a gun ban, during the last decade, over two million convicted felons and other illegal-gun buyers would have been able to buy guns over the counter. For those who oppose a general gun ban, the real slippery-slope question posed by the Brady Bill is this: Was the risk that the Brady Bill might eventually lead to a gun ban so concrete and severe that we should have been willing to tolerate the continued sale of guns to many thousands of criminals every year? In other words, allowing the slippery-slope argument to dictate gun policy has a cost, and it likely is a cost in death and serious injury from gunfire.

There is, in fact, a close connection between the slippery-slope argument and the argument that gun control is ineffective. It is fair to say that the persuasive power of the slippery-slope argument to a policymaker will depend, in large part, on her beliefs about the effectiveness of licensing, registration, and other proposals in treating the gun violence problem. If she is convinced that licensing and registration will save countless lives, she is likely to respond to a slippery-slope argument with a demand for much more than mere speculation that such life-saving measures will eventually lead to a gun ban. Thus, the more success the gun control movement has in convincing the public and policymakers that even moderate controls can be highly effective, the less they will be willing to forgo those benefits because of the inherently speculative threat that they may pave the way for a gun ban.

The slippery-slope argument, however, has functioned to intensify the gun control catch-22 that has ensured so many loopholes and weaknesses in our gun laws. When a gun control proposal is met with the charge that it is the first step toward confiscation of all guns, the frequent response is to point out how modest the proposal really is, emphasizing its limitations and allowing its opponents to then raise questions about its likely effectiveness. This, in turn, feeds the public's skepticism about whether gun laws really make a difference.

Whatever form the slippery-slope argument takes, then, it is critical that it be exposed as a misguided rationale for opposing gun restrictions that are easily justifiable in their own right.

If the argument is that supporting limited gun control measures like licensing and registration will, by force of logic, dictate support for a far-reaching gun ban, then the argument falls of its own weight. There is an obvious logical distinction between proposals like licensing and registration, which still permit law-abiding citizens to make the choice to own guns, and gun bans, which substitute the judgment of the government for that of the individual on the issue of gun ownership.

If the argument is that the adoption of limited gun control measures will operate to increase the likelihood that a broad gun ban eventually will be adopted, then it fails for lack of historical evidence that when modest gun restrictions are adopted, they actually have the predicted causal impact.

In the final analysis, the slippery-slope argument asks policymakers to forgo the life-saving benefits of sensible gun control policies because it is possible to dream up some hypothetical scenario in which such policies may increase the likelihood of a gun ban. This is sheer folly. In no other area of policymaking would we allow such rank speculation to defeat proposals that have concrete and demonstrable benefits.

The fact is that virtually all progress toward alleviating societal ills is incremental in nature. Seldom does the "first step" turn out to be sufficient. Instead, it often simply reveals the necessity for the "next step." Taken to its logical conclusion, the fear of the slippery slope would have a paralyzing effect on policymaking on a wide range of issues. Surely the automotive industry could have argued (and likely did argue) that once the federal government starts mandating safety features in cars like padded dashboards and shatter-resistant glass, it is taking the first steps on a slippery slope toward a host of expensive safety mandates that someday would make cars unaffordable for most American families. If policymakers had been persuaded by such an argument, the "next steps," like seat belts and air bags, never would have been taken, and many thousands of lives would have been lost. With guns as well, the fear of slipping down the imaginary slope is simply too costly, in needless deaths and shattered lives, to allow it to block movement toward sanity in our gun laws.

HAS THE SUPREME COURT FLATTENED THE SLIPPERY SLOPE?

We have seen that the slippery-slope argument, in all its forms, never made sense as a reason to oppose sensible gun laws that will save lives. Does it make even less sense after the Supreme Court rulings in *Heller* and *McDonald?* In *Heller*, the Court erected a constitutional barrier to any federal law banning the possession of guns in the home for self-defense. In *McDonald*, the Court held that the right recognized in *Heller* also applies as a restraint on state and local legislation; *McDonald* thus bars state and local handgun bans.

Since these rulings were handed down, gun advocates have continued to try to frame gun control as a cultural issue, portraying gun control activists as elitists who have nothing but contempt for gun owners and their values. While campaigning in 2008, Barack Obama made a comment at a San Francisco fund-raiser about "bitter" people who "cling to guns" to "explain their frustrations," which became an instant hit as an NRA T-shirt ("I'm a Bitter Gun Owner and I Vote"). No doubt the search for evidence that advocates of reasonable gun restrictions "really want" to ban all guns will continue.

Nevertheless, it would appear that the Supreme Court decisions protecting handgun ownership give gun control advocates an additional response to the slippery-slope argument. The rulings have erected a new constitutional barrier to a general gun ban by declaring individual gun ownership a constitutional right. Even if the gun control agenda included a ban on guns for law-abiding citizens, it would be an agenda that is now, in Justice Scalia's words, "off the table."

Heller and *McDonald* also stand as an additional barrier to the effective use of logical and factual slippery-slope arguments against modest gun laws. Before these rulings, it was already easy to draw a logical distinction between regulating guns and banning them. After the two rulings, an additional distinction emerges, based on the new meaning given the Second Amendment. Moreover, the gun lobby's examples of factual slippery slopes—gun regulation leading to gun bans—become even less relevant. Even if it were true that it occurred in places like New York City (which it did not), in none of those cases did the courts recognize a constitutional barrier to banning guns.

Even prominent gun advocates occasionally have acknowledged the impact of the new constitutional right on the slippery-slope argument. In a revealing discussion on public radio in Los Angeles a few days after the *Heller* ruling, lawyer Chuck Michel, who has represented the NRA and other gun groups, was asked about *Heller*'s effect on gun registration and licensing. He responded this way:

> "The problem has always been that registration and licensing led to confiscation and I . . . still think registration and licensing is . . .

problematic in multiple respects . . . , but I think that now . . .
there are a lot of people in the gun control movement who are
really gun . . . banners. They're in favor of civilian disarmament.
These folks are never going to get their way now as a result of this
[*Heller*] opinion, so *I think licensing and registration is . . . going to
be . . . tougher to criticize* [emphasis added]."[18]

Michel was suggesting that because *Heller* has taken a general gun
ban "off the table," what some gun control advocates "really want"
has become less relevant, making it more difficult for the NRA to
successfully argue against licensing and registration.

At this point in the history of gun control after *Heller* and *Mc-
Donald*, it is surely difficult to discern concrete ways in which the
decisions have affected the use of the slippery-slope argument. It
continues to be employed with great passion by pro-gun advocates,
who appear to be far from secure that the slim 5–4 majorities in both
cases are sufficient protection against a slide toward gun confiscation. It may be possible, however, that slippery-slope argumentation
will prove somewhat less persuasive to elected officials and policymakers as a result of the Court's rulings, although the real impact
will take many years to assess. For now, it is worth observing the
paradox that the two greatest gun-rights victories in our constitutional history may, in the long run, end up strengthening the effort
to pass sensible gun laws by undercutting one of the core gun-lobby
arguments against those laws.

CHAPTER FOUR

An Armed Society Is
a Polite Society

This venerable slogan uses a dose of sarcasm to express a bedrock principle of gun control opponents: if law-abiding citizens are armed, they will collectively deter crime because criminals will not risk a confrontation with an armed defender. "Self-defense works," writes Wayne LaPierre of the NRA, because "criminals fear armed citizens. . . . The survival instinct is not exclusive to law-abiding citizens, it is just as basic to criminals."[1]

Unlike the arguments we have previously dissected, the "armed society" argument is not only *against* gun control; it also is *for* guns. It unambiguously claims that the more law-abiding citizens are armed, the lower will be the incidence of crime, including violent crime. Thus, gun ownership by the law abiding is seen as a social good. To the extent that gun control laws function to discourage gun ownership, they are seen as crime enhancing. Under this theory, public policy should encourage private gun ownership, including permitting gun owners to carry their guns in public places in order to maximize the purported deterrent and protective effects of guns. For many years, Kennesaw, Georgia, was infamous for taking this idea to its logical limit by requiring its adult citizens to own guns, until its law was struck down as a violation of the right *not* to bear arms.[2]

JUST HOW POLITE ARE WE?

By its terms, the argument makes a societal claim: societies with a well-armed populace will be more "polite"—that is, experience less crime and violence—than societies that have fewer legal guns. From the outset, the argument faces a formidable problem. American society is quite well armed, but not very polite. As gun control advocates have long and effectively pointed out, if guns made us safe, we would be the safest nation on Earth. We are far from it. Although, as we have seen, the violent-crime rate in America is not dramatically different from that in other Western democracies, it is definitely higher than average.[3] As we also have seen, violent crime in America is far more lethal than in other countries. If we look at the least "polite" crime of all—homicide—in the United States the homicide rate is over seven times the combined rate of twenty-two other populous high-income nations, which is driven by a firearm-homicide rate that is over twenty-five times higher.[4] (See appendices 3 and 4.)

Yet, by any measure, the United States has the highest rate of gun ownership in the industrialized world.[5] If "an armed society is a polite society," how can this be? In the gun lobby's simple world of "good guys" versus "bad guys," it should necessarily be true that the more gun-saturated a society, the greater the deterrent effect on criminals and the lower the incidence of crime. According to the NRA's account, criminals prey on the unarmed because they want to reduce the risk of getting shot. The greater the likelihood that any prospective victim will be armed, the less likely the criminal will attack at all. The United States, the nation that presents its criminals with the greatest risk of encountering a prospective victim who is armed, should have the lowest crime rate in the world. It seems clear that an armed society is not necessarily a polite society at all.

Perhaps because the homicide rate in the United States is so dramatically high versus that of other high-income nations, gun advocates consume much energy to prove that nations can have lots of guns and still be relatively free of crime, or can have few guns and lots of crime. According to pro-gun lawyer Don Kates, for example, "Norway, with the highest gun ownership rate in Western Europe, has the lowest murder rate—far below England's."[6] And "Holland, with Western Europe's lowest rate of gun ownership, has a 50 percent higher murder rate than Norway."[7] I have no doubt that numerous other country pairings could be made to illustrate the point that the incidence of gun ownership in a country does not necessarily correlate with the incidence of violent crime. The proposition that greater gun availability necessarily means greater violence, or even lethal violence, is a straw man that gun advocates like Kates take great pleasure in knocking down, again and again. The central policy issue is whether the enactment of specific restrictions on firearms will prevent violence. Whether violence necessarily increases with the number of guns available in a society provides little guidance on that central issue. This is shown by briefly examining the NRA's two favorite examples of countries where legal ownership of guns is common and crime is low—Switzerland and Israel.

WHAT SWITZERLAND AND ISRAEL HAVE IN COMMON

In his book *Guns, Crime, and Freedom*, the NRA's Wayne LaPierre claimed that Switzerland "has a higher rate of firearms possession than the United States" and, yet, in 1990 had only thirty-four firearm-related homicides.[8] According to LaPierre, this shows "that there is no causal effect between firearms possession and crime. Indeed, just the opposite seems to be the case: a thoroughly armed people is relatively crime free; it is the ultimate deterrent to crime."[9]

In this brief passage, LaPierre managed to commit multiple errors, both factual and logical. First, it is not true that Switzerland has a higher rate of firearms possession than the United States, although it appears to have a higher rate of gun possession than other European countries, with the possible exception of Finland.[10] Second, LaPierre refutes the idea that "firearms possession causes crime," even though the case for sensible gun control laws has never turned on a showing that there is a causal link between gun possession per se and crime. For the gun control issue, the critical gun/crime causal link, as we saw in chapter 1, is between gun use in crime and the lethality of crime, not between gun possession and crime. Gun laws that reduce the use of guns in crime will save lives, whether the incidence of gun ownership is relatively high or relatively low. Finally, and of greatest importance, LaPierre confidently asserts that Switzerland's low number of homicides is due to the deterrent effect of a well-armed society, without accounting for Switzerland's strong gun laws. Pro-gun advocates repeatedly misrepresent the circumstances of gun ownership in that country. If you believed their accounts, you would think that the Swiss government issues a machine gun to every citizen for his or her personal use. In fact, Switzerland has a functioning militia system (of the kind originally contemplated by the framers of our Second Amendment) in which every able-bodied male citizen is enrolled for required military training from the ages of twenty to forty-two. Privates and lower-ranking noncommissioned officers are issued a 5.56 assault rifle, while officers and higher-ranking noncommissioned officers are issued semi-automatic handguns. The army stopped issuing ammunition for home storage in 2008.[11] Although these weapons are to be kept in the homes of the militiamen, they are intended only for military use, as defined by the government. The weapons are required to be stored under lock and key. The guns must be presented for regular inspections, and failure to store them securely is severely punished by the military justice system.[12] In describing the Swiss system, LaPierre makes much of the fact that fully automatic rifles are supplied by the government "free of charge," without mentioning that they are subject to government regulation that goes much further than registration and actually makes Swiss citizens subject to regular government inspections of the guns.[13] Can you imagine the fury of the NRA's opposition to any suggestion that guns in the homes of US citizens be subject to government inspection?

The Swiss can also possess their own private firearms, but they are subject to a licensing system of a kind the NRA would surely denounce as totalitarian. Prior to 1997, the system was implemented by agreement of the Swiss cantons, which are comparable to American states. Anyone wishing to acquire a handgun had to obtain a license, which would be denied not only if the applicant has a criminal record but also if he "gives cause to believe that he might become a risk to either himself or a third person."[14] This was a highly restrictive system in which the government had discretion to deny a license even to those who, in the NRA's world, are "law-abiding citizens." In

1997, the Swiss Parliament adopted a federal licensing law that went into effect in 1999 and incorporates the same restrictive standards of the earlier canton laws. The federal law applies to purchases of both handguns and long guns from a gun dealer. Subsequent transfers between private citizens have to be documented, and the paperwork must be retained by the parties for ten years.[15]

Wayne LaPierre asserts that the Swiss experience proves that "a thoroughly armed people is relatively crime free,"[16] when it may prove only that a society can be well armed and crime free *only if its guns are tightly controlled.* He does note that Great Britain and Switzerland have similar homicide rates, despite the fact that they have vastly different rates of gun ownership[17] (which, of course, undercuts the argument that more guns make a nation safer), but he omits to mention a salient similarity: *they both have restrictive gun laws.*

Few would think Switzerland and Israel have much in common, but to the gun partisans, Israel also qualifies as a crime-free utopia due to its well-armed populace. It is true that the homicide rate is lower in Israel than in the United States, but its civilian gun-ownership rate also is well below that of the United States.[18] As in Switzerland, Israel has a system of near-universal military service in which nearly every adult—male and female—serves in the armed forces at one time or another.[19] Much of the population is armed in connection with active or reserve military service. Nevertheless, as CNN Jerusalem bureau chief Walter Rodgers noted, "Israel has incredibly strict gun control laws. Try to buy a handgun, and you'll face perhaps a 3-month waiting period, police, medical and psychological checks and hard-to-win approval from the Interior Ministry."[20] Licenses are given on a "show-need, case-by-case basis."[21] As in Switzerland, far from gun ownership being a citizen's "right," it is the government that gets to decide who is to own a handgun. Such a system would be anathema to the NRA. Finally, although gun advocates can point to some instances where armed civilians have stopped terrorist attacks in Israel, it is absurd on its face to argue, based on that nation's experience, that an armed populace necessarily deters violence. Israel is, for unique political reasons unrelated to gun ownership, a society plagued by acts of horrific violence committed by persons obviously undeterred by the prospect of armed response.

The key point obscured by the pro-gun commentators is that in both Switzerland and Israel, the government has a pervasive role in the private possession of guns. It is beyond strange that the pro-gun advocates choose these two countries to make their case that "more guns means less crime," because their experience just as persuasively demonstrates that "more gun control means less crime."

DO MORE GUNS = LESS CRIME?

International comparisons, therefore, do little to bolster the theory of "gun ownership as crime deterrence." America's infatuation with guns has not made it a noticeably polite society, when stacked against other high-income nations. But, the gun advocates may respond, that's because gun control laws prevent law-abiding Americans in high-crime areas from owning more guns. Where gun control laws are weak, and law-abiding people own lots of guns, so the pro-gun argument goes, crime is low because criminals know their potential victims likely are armed. According to the NRA's Sandra Froman, "As lawful firearm ownership increases in a community, violent crime decreases. Criminals still prefer to prey on the weak, and they don't like armed victims."[22]

Does this theory have even a remote resemblance to the facts? Let's look first at the relationship between gun ownership and homicide rates. Researchers at the Harvard School of Public Health looked at this relationship in all fifty states and found that people living in "high-gun states" were *more likely* than those in the "low-gun states" to become homicide victims.[23] Although these results were due primarily to higher gun-related homicide rates in states with higher rates of firearm ownership, non-gun-related homicide rates were also higher in states with more guns.[24] This association remained strong even after the researchers controlled for other factors that could affect homicide rates, such as poverty rates, urbanization, unemployment, per capita alcohol consumption, and violent crimes other than homicide.

The relationship is striking if you look at the states with the highest rates of gun ownership versus the states with the lowest. Residents of the extreme "high-gun states" (Louisiana, Alabama, Mississippi, Wyoming, West Virginia, and Arkansas) were more than *2.5 times* more likely to become homicide victims than those in the extreme "low-gun states" (Hawaii, Massachusetts, Rhode Island, and New Jersey).[25] In the NRA's world, Arkansans must be safer than residents of the Garden State because Arkansas criminals are cowering in fear of law-abiding Arkansas gun-owners, whereas Jersey criminals have little to fear because New Jersey gun control laws have disarmed the law-abiding population. The facts show the opposite.

The Harvard study made no claim that higher rates of gun ownership "cause" higher rates of homicide, only that there is a positive association between the two. The researchers acknowledged they could not rule out "reverse causation," that is, the possibility that higher homicide rates in states like Arkansas may have led to increased gun acquisition in such states.[26] But even assuming that such "reverse causation" could be shown, what would this mean? It certainly would provide no support for the Wayne LaPierre view that "more guns" means "less crime." If LaPierre were correct, then the association between high homicide rates and high gun ownership could not exist for long, because murderous criminals would begin, at some point, to be deterred from crime by the realization that they were increasingly likely to be confronted by law-abiding gun owners. The Harvard study shows, rather, a strong association between high levels of gun ownership and high homicide rates over a nine-year period. If the question is whether a well-armed populace deters criminals from engaging in lethal violence, the statistical evidence provides a compelling reason to believe the answer is no.

In a later study, the same Harvard team found significant reason to doubt the "reverse causation" possibility.[27] Using survey evidence to measure state firearms-ownership levels, they found that higher rates of household firearm ownership were associated with significantly higher homicide victimization rates, but not with non-firearm homicide rates. They also found that rates of robbery and aggravated assault were not associated with household firearm prevalence. These findings militate against the possibility that high firearm prevalence was an effect of, not a cause of, high homicide rates.

What about crimes other than homicide and other violent crimes? If criminals fear law-abiding gun owners, then areas with a high incidence of gun ownership should experience fewer property crimes like burglary. The first systematic evidence on this question, assembled by economists Philip Cook and Jens Ludwig, actually found that residential burglary rates tend to *increase* with the prevalence of guns in a community.[28] Their study controlled for various nongun factors bearing on burglary rates, such as per capita income, prisoners per capita, the poverty rate, and alcohol consumption.[29] Not only did widespread gun ownership not have a net deterrent effect, but a 10 percent increase in gun ownership actually increased burglary rates by 3 to 7 percent. According to Cook and Ludwig, the most plausible explanation for this effect is that guns are extremely valuable loot for burglars.[30] But isn't it possible that the prospect of being confronted by an armed citizen may lead burglars to avoid homes when they are occupied, thus reducing the risk of violence arising from burglaries? Pro-gun researchers have long been excited by figures purporting to show that the percentage of "hot" burglaries (meaning those of occupied homes) is far higher in Canada and some European countries than in the United States, which the gun enthusiasts attribute to differences in gun-possession rates.[31] Cook and Ludwig find these comparisons "entirely unpersuasive" because they fail to control for other obvious differences between the countries that could also account for the lower percentage of hot burglaries in the United States.[32] For instance, when burglars are arrested in this country, they are subject to more certain and severe punishment than in other countries—another potent incentive for burglars to avoid contact with victims.[33] In any event, the analysis by Cook and Ludwig of US data from the National Crime Victimization Survey shows that hot-burglary victimizations tended to increase, not decrease, with gun prevalence. They conclude: "If anything, residences in a neighborhood with high gun prevalence are at greater risk of being burglarized, hot and otherwise."[34]

There is, therefore, not much in the way of statistical evidence to support the theory that criminals are deterred by the prospect of confrontation with armed citizens. The deterrence theory also poses a logical conundrum. The theory says that criminals avoid prospective targets who are armed due to the fear of being shot. If this is true, then why aren't armed criminals deterred from attacking other armed criminals? Why do armed drug dealers have anything to fear from other armed drug dealers? Why do armed gangs have anything to fear from other armed gangs? Indeed, why isn't being an armed criminal a relatively safe way to make a living? Gary Kleck reports studies showing that street-gang members are 8.8 times more likely to own handguns than other youths, and 19 times more likely to be homicide victims.[35] Drug dealers are 3.7 times more likely to own a handgun and 6 times more likely to be homicide victims.[36] Why doesn't their gun possession deter attacks on these criminals? Does the deterrence theory suggest that criminals fear armed law-abiding citizens more than other armed criminals? If it does, there seems to be something quite wrong with the theory.

Rather than being deterred from criminal acts by the potential of confronting armed victims, it seems at least as likely that criminals will simply ensure that they are better armed than their potential victims. In one prisoner survey, 62 percent of respondents who used a gun to commit the crime for which they were incarcerated reported that the possibility of encountering an armed victim was "very important" or "somewhat important" in their decision to employ a gun.[37] The proliferation of guns in a community does not cause criminals to choose another line of work; rather, it causes an arms race in which the criminals make sure they are not left behind.

Surveys show that most people do not believe they would be safer if there were more guns in their community. As to non-gun owners, over 80 percent say they would feel less safe if more people in their community acquired guns; only 8 percent would feel more safe.[38] Even more striking, for gun owners, about half would feel less safe with more guns in their community.[39] Obviously there are gun owners who may think their own gun makes them safer, but are less than comfortable about their neighbors owning guns.

I sometimes wonder if advocates of the deterrence theory really believe it themselves. If the NRA really believes in the crime-deterring effect of gun possession, then why does it repeatedly have its annual meeting in convention centers that don't allow guns? Why would the NRA put its members at a greater risk of crime in this way? And when NRA-supporting legislators vote to ease restrictions on carrying concealed weapons, they typically do so after walking through metal detectors that prevent the law-abiding public from bringing guns into legislative offices. How could the NRA's elected true believers subject themselves and their staffs to such an unsafe environment? The answer can't be that it is important to keep out the armed bad guys. The premise of the NRA's argument is that the bad guys will always find ways around efforts to separate them from their guns, but will be deterred from using them by fear of the armed citizenry.

The fact is that when our society really wants to ensure that a particular group of people, place, or event is safe and secure, we do everything we can to keep the guns out. The greater our fear of violence, the greater are our efforts to exclude guns. The best illustration of this is from the gun industry itself. Several years ago, the National Shooting Sports Foundation (NSSF), an industry trade association ironically headquartered in Newtown, Connecticut, began a program it called "Project Childsafe," which involved a van touring the country handing out free gun locks. The NSSF started the program as an image booster after manufacturers were targeted by lawsuits charging that they had failed to incorporate locks in their guns to prevent access by children. On the door of the van could be found these words: "This vehicle contains NO firearms."[40] In other words, the NSSF advertised the fact that its van was a "gun-free zone." The premise of the deterrence theory is that criminals will avoid potential victims who might be armed, but will search out victims they know are not armed. If the theory is right, the NSSF was issuing an engraved invitation to criminals to attack the Project Childsafe van and its occupants. In reality, the legend on the van means that even the gun industry itself understands that when complete safety is the goal, the guns must go. It also is an obvious admission that, if the van carried guns, they would be far more likely to be stolen than to be used to fend off a criminal.

The NSSF also sponsors the largest industry trade show—the annual SHOT (Shooting, Hunting, Outdoor Trade) Show. One of the NSSF's rules for attendance at the SHOT Show is "Personal firearms and/or ammunition are not allowed."[41] If guns carried by law-abiding citizens into restaurants, movie theatres, sports stadiums, and shopping malls make us all safer, as the gun lobby insists, why does this principle not apply to gun trade shows as well? The deterrence theory will be debated for years to come, but it will always be somewhat detached from reality. There are some radical pro-gunners who actually are consistent in arguing that we need more guns in schools, bars, courthouses, churches, airplanes, and pretty much everywhere else. For most of us, however, such views are the reductio ad absurdum of the deterrence theory.

CHAPTER FIVE

The Only Thing That Stops a Bad Guy with a Gun Is a Good Guy with a Gun

Even if law-abiding gun ownership is not much of a deterrent to crime, it may still prevent individual crimes. According to the NRA's Wayne LaPierre, the lesson of the Newtown shooting was "The only thing that stops a bad guy with a gun is a good guy with a gun." Another arresting slogan destined for bumper-sticker stardom, this phrase expresses multiple pro-gun themes: (1) the world is neatly divided into two permanent and easily identifiable groups of "bad guys" and "good guys"; (2) it is futile to try to stop "bad guys" from getting guns; and (3) the only recourse for "good guys" is to be armed and prepared to defend themselves.

We have already seen that the neat categorization of every person as either "bad guy" or "good guy" is a gross oversimplification that misses the reality that some people appear to be "good" until they become "bad." We also have seen that nations comparable to our own also have "bad guys" but have strong laws that deny them guns. As to the assertion that guns need to be widely available for self-defense, let's begin by asking: How often do "good guys" with guns actually stop "bad guys"?

If you ask any delegate to the NRA's convention how many times Americans use guns each year for self-defense, you will get the same answer every time: 2.5 million.[1] They may not know the source of the figure or how it was derived. But they know it like they know there are twenty-four hours in a day.

The number is, in fact, mythical. It is based on a 1993 telephone survey done by Gary Kleck and his Florida State colleague Marc

Gertz. They surveyed five thousand individuals, asking each if he had used a firearm in self-defense and, if so, under what circumstances and with what effect. They reported only fifty-three incidents of self-defensive gun use and, from those fifty-three incidents, they extrapolated to estimate 2.5 million defensive gun uses each year in the general population.[2]

Thus, in Kleck's survey, slightly more than 1 percent of the respondents reported a defensive gun use. The fact is that such a tiny percentage of the population will say just about anything. Researcher David Hemenway of Harvard gives an amusing illustration. In a random telephone survey like Kleck's, more than 1,500 adults were asked, "Have you yourself ever seen anything that you believe was a spacecraft from another planet?" Ten percent said "yes." These 150 people were then asked, "Have you personally ever been in contact with aliens from another planet or not?" Six percent, or 9 people, said "yes."[3] If we extrapolate to the entire US population, as did Kleck, we could conclude that 1.2 million American adults have seen ET! I am not suggesting that defensive uses of guns are figments of the imagination, only that it is risky business to estimate millions of annual defensive uses based on a handful of positive answers to a survey, particularly, as we will see, given the built-in incentives for a falsely positive response.

There is far more reliable data that enables us to determine just how far off Kleck is. The National Crime Victimization Survey (NCVS), conducted by the US Bureau of the Census for the Justice Department, twice every year surveys a nationally representative sample of 59,000 households to estimate the incidence of crime in the United States. That's 59,000 households surveyed twice every year, as opposed to Kleck's 5,000 individuals surveyed once. Residents of each of the households aged twelve or older are interviewed over a period of three years. Respondents who report an attempted or completed victimization answer detailed questions about the incident, including whether they did or tried to do anything about the incident while it was going on. Victims who say they took action are then asked to describe what they did. The survey then follows up with an additional question: "Did you do anything (else) with the idea of protecting yourself or your property while the incident was going on?" Victims who respond "yes" are again asked to describe their activities.[4] The questioning certainly gives crime victims every opportunity to volunteer their use of guns in self-defense.

The NCVS paints a picture radically different than Kleck's. Estimates for defensive uses for other years based on the NCVS have ranged as high as 120,000 per year.[5] A far cry from Kleck's 2.5 million.

Finding the flaws in Kleck's estimate has become a growth industry for gun violence scholars. The first problem they note is the nature of the question asked in Kleck's survey. The question was whether, within the past five years, the respondent or a member of his household "used a gun, even if it was not fired, for self-protection or for the protection of property at home, work, or elsewhere." If the answer was yes, the respondent was then asked whether any of the incidents happened in the past twelve months. Unlike those surveyed for the NCVS, Kleck's respondents were not first asked whether they had been victimized by a criminal act. The Kleck question is far more open-ended and allows the respondent to resolve the obvious ambiguity in the phrase "used a handgun for self-protection." This ambiguity creates a serious risk of "false positives," that is, reports of self-defensive gun use that involved something other than the legitimate use of a gun to repel a criminal attack. As researchers have pointed out, "Persons who have used firearms to settle arguments might believe that they have prevented assaults."[6] After all, in a survey of prison inmates, 63 percent of those who fired guns during crimes described their actions as self-defense.[7]

There is an obvious potential for gun owners to give biased and inaccurate claims of self-defensive gun use. Particularly for handgun owners, who are far more likely to have bought their guns for self-protection than for sport, the claim of successful self-defense is the ultimate justification of their purchase. This natural bias is enhanced by the intense admiration the gun culture, as well as the general public, bestows upon those who use guns against criminals.

For example, consider the story of Susan Gaylord Buxton, an Arlington, Texas, grandmother who used her .38 pistol to confront a "bald-headed, muscle-bound burglar crouching in her front-hall coat closet," as the incident was described by the *Dallas Morning News*.[8] The 911 tape of the incident captured Ms. Buxton screaming in the background, "How dare you come in my house, you lousy son of a bitch!" When the burglar tried to grab her gun, she shot him in the thigh. "If you can't protect your own home" she told the *Morning News*, "then life's not worth living."[9] Grandma Buxton became an instant star in the gun culture, with the NRA's talk-show host, Cam Edwards, using her story to show how the gun is the "equalizer" for senior citizens against the criminal element.[10]

I am not here intending to minimize Ms. Buxton's actions, which apparently were carried out with considerable intestinal fortitude. I offer this incident only as an example of the kind of positive public reaction to reports of gun use against criminals that could easily encourage gun owners to exaggerate their own self-defense achievements when asked. Scholars have noted that, in any survey designed to show the incidence of a relatively rare event, even a small percentage of respondents giving falsely positive responses can produce estimates far in excess of the actual incidence of the event. Kleck surveyed five thousand people and found only fifty-three reported incidents of firearm self-defense. As David Hemenway has put it, Kleck's search is "for a needle in a haystack."[11] Only a few respondents need exaggerate their gun use to yield a huge overestimate of defensive gun use.

Kleck claims that the NCVS systematically underestimates defensive gun uses because the NCVS surveyors make it clear they are government employees and respondents may fear that they will be putting themselves in legal jeopardy by describing their gun use to the government.[12] This would be true, of course, only if the respondents fear that their gun use or possession is, in fact, illegal. It would not be a reason to believe that the NCVS undercounts defensive gun uses by law-abiding citizens, only that it undercounts such uses by law violators. Putting aside for a moment the interesting question of whether illegal defensive uses of guns should "count," the fear of legal jeopardy would have to be pervasive among gun owners to reconcile Kleck's data with the NCVS results. "To preserve the 2.5 million self-defense gun estimate," writes David Hemenway, "Kleck and Gertz are forced to claim that nineteen of every twenty people with a genuine self-defense use do not report it to the NCVS (and virtually no one without a genuine self-defense use in the time frame does report one)."[13] This seems improbable, especially since, as Hemenway also points out, there is no reasonable basis to believe that information given the NCVS could be used to prosecute someone for a crime. The Census Bureau interviewers are not permitted to report the information received to other authorities, nor has it been reported to other authorities, nor has any respondent ever been subjected to punishment for the answers given.[14]

Kleck's survey data yields absurd results that, as researcher Douglas Weil puts it, "bear no resemblance to what we know about the real world."[15] For example, Kleck's survey estimates that about two hundred thousand criminals are shot each year by their intended victims, though we know from other data that the total number of shootings of *all* kinds is less than two hundred thousand per year.[16] We also know that, according to the FBI, there are only between two hundred and three hundred justifiable self-defense firearm homicides by civilians every year.[17] Given the inherent lethality of firearms, is it plausible to believe that civilians use guns in self-defense 2.5 million times per year, but less than three hundred attackers die?

Telephone surveys may be fine for sampling public opinion, but they appear utterly unreliable for estimating the frequency of a comparatively rare event, like the use of guns in self-defense.

Finally, by his own admission, Kleck said his survey "made no effort to assess either the lawfulness or morality" of the respondents' reported defensive uses of guns.[18] It turns out that a high number of claimed self-defensive gun uses likely are reckless and illegal. Researchers from the Harvard School of Public Health did their own telephone surveys and then had the individual reports of firearm self-defense analyzed by a panel of courtroom judges. The judges found 51 percent of the claimed self-defense uses to be "probably illegal."[19] Just as revealing, three respondents accounted for 58 percent of the total defensive uses, claiming fifty, twenty, and fifteen self-defense incidents each in the previous five years.[20] A single eighteen-year-old male reported six incidents in which he used a gun in self-defense. It seems that there are more than a few "make my day" defensive gun uses being counted. Somewhat understating the matter, the Harvard researchers observed that "[m]any reported self defense gun uses from a respondent creates a suspicion that the uses may be aggressive rather than defensive."[21]

For Kleck, the calculation of defensive gun uses is but the prelude to his clincher statistical argument: guns are used to defend against crimes far more often than to commit them. Based on his estimate that there are about "500,000 to 700,000 incidents in which criminals used guns to commit crimes," he reaches the startling conclusion that guns are used defensively by crime victims four to five times more often than they are used by offenders to commit crimes.[22]

The Kleck-Gertz survey was conducted in the spring of 1993 and, according to the Justice Department, there were over 1 million violent crimes committed with guns in 1993, not 500,000–700,000, as estimated by Kleck.[23] Using the Justice Department figure, the Kleck-Gertz survey means that guns are used defensively by crime victims more than twice as often as guns are used to commit violent crimes. Whatever the exact ratio, it is now accepted wisdom in pro-gun circles that guns are used far more often in self-defense than in crime. When conservative ABC News reporter John Stossel set out on *20/20* to explode the "myth" that "guns are bad," he confidently asserted that "guns are used twice or three times as often for defensive uses as they are to commit crimes."[24]

If this were true, it would mean criminals are even dumber than we thought. Apparently, they frequently commit crimes with weapons less lethal than guns and are met with resistance by gun-wielding victims. Assuming that this situation persists year after year (and Kleck does not suggest otherwise), it must mean that criminals do not respond to this risky situation by starting to pack heat. Obviously, if criminals started to use guns in greater numbers, then the ratio of self-defense to criminal use would move closer to 1:1. Nor does it mean that criminals turn away from crime, because we have already seen that a well-armed citizenry does not deter crime. Instead, criminals apparently continue to assume the risk that their knives or fists will encounter their victims' guns. Kleck's estimates suggest that there are many criminals who actually are bringing a knife to a gun fight. And these are the same criminals the NRA says are so clever and resourceful that they will always find ways to get guns?

What is the true ratio of criminal use to self-defensive use of guns? The most methodologically sound way to measure would be to use the same survey to estimate both the number of gun crimes and the number of self-defense uses of guns (something Kleck did not do). Based on the NCVS, University of Maryland researchers determined that, during the period they studied (1987–1990), *guns were used in crime ten times more often than they were used for protection.* Using their own 1996 telephone survey for both gun crimes and self-defense uses, Harvard's David Hemenway and Deborah Azrael estimated that *the number of gun crimes exceeded the number of self-defense uses by a ratio of between 4:1 and 6:1.* In short, the available evidence indicates that guns are used in crime far more often than they are used to defend against crime.

GOOD GUYS VS. BAD GUYS IN THE HOME

For gun advocates, the debate over gun ownership begins and ends with the question "If a criminal is coming through your sliding glass door, what would you do?"[25] Call 911? Threaten him with a kitchen knife? Hit him with a baseball bat? In this way, the issue is framed in a way that seems to guarantee victory for pro-gun advocates. If we confine ourselves to the scenario in which a home-invasion crime is in progress, the argument for having a gun for self-defense becomes quite persuasive. An NRA poster published some years ago asked women: "Should you shoot a rapist before he cuts your throat?" The question, of course, supplies the answer. If the gun control issue is framed in this way, it compels the conclusion that the primary goal of our public policy should be to avoid interfering with the ability of that prospective victim to shoot the rapist before he cuts her throat. There is now an established body of research into how guns kept in homes are actually used. Instead of using surveys, this research uses the alternative approach of studying official reports of crimes and shootings that actually occurred. This technique has been used by public-health researchers, who have uncovered some remarkable results. The studies establish that the "criminal coming through the sliding glass door" is not the only scenario for gun use to be considered; indeed, it is a far less likely scenario than others in which the gun plays a far less salutary role.

First, good guys seldom use guns to defend against bad guys in the home. In one study, a team of researchers, headed by Arthur Kellermann of Emory University, worked with the Atlanta police department to review every case of unwanted home entry in that city during a three-month period. They found that in only 1.5 percent of the cases (3 out of 198) was a firearm used at all in self-defense.[26] Two individuals brandished the gun but did not fire; the third fired, but missed. None of the three defenders suffered injury; one suffered a property loss. There also were three cases in which the gun kept in the home was stolen by intruders who left undetected, and another in which the victim lost the gun during a scuffle with the intruder.[27] The study suggests that many guns kept for self-defense are simply not used for that purpose, even when the need arises. Gun partisans would insist that even if the statistics are true, they mean only that too many gun owners are listening to the advice of safe-storage advocates (and, for that matter, gun manufacturers) and are locking away their guns and making them insufficiently accessible. The trouble is that the gun kept loaded and unlocked in the nightstand may be more accessible for use in self-defense, but it also is more accessible for use in other scenarios most gun owners would dearly love to avoid.

In a separate study, Kellermann and his colleagues examined all fatal and nonfatal gunshot injuries involving guns kept in the home during a specific time period in Memphis, Seattle, and Galveston, Texas. For every time a gun in the home was used in a self-defense or legally justifiable shooting, there were four unintentional shootings, seven criminal assaults or homicides, and eleven attempted or completed suicides.[28] Thus, guns kept in the home were used to injure or kill twenty-two times more often in criminal assaults, accidents, and suicides than to injure or kill in self-defense. For fatal shootings alone, the ratio rises to 43:1.[29] Clearly, the issue is not as simple as "What will you do when the bad guy is coming through the sliding glass door?" Other questions are equally relevant: What will you do when your curious ten-year old finds your gun in a box under your bed? What will you do when your depressed teen is able to unlock your gun rack? Will you be tempted to get the upper hand in an angry argument by reaching for the gun yourself?

Other work by public-health researchers has attempted to determine whether the mere fact of having a gun increases the risk of homicide in the home. Arthur Kellermann and his colleagues investigated this question using the "case-control" method.[30] They obtained lists of persons killed in their homes in three urban counties in Tennessee, Washington State, and Ohio (the "cases") and compared them with persons of the same sex, race, and approximate age living in the same neighborhood (the "controls"). Since the households with homicide victims more commonly contained an illicit-drug user, a person with prior arrests, or someone who had been involved in a fight in the home, the researchers controlled for those factors. They found that "keeping a gun in the home was strongly and independently associated with an increased risk of homicide" and that "[v]irtually all of this risk involved homicide by a family member or intimate acquaintance."

Much of the debate over Dr. Kellermann's work concerns whether it proves that a gun in the home actually causes an increase in the risk of homicide, or whether it simply means that people who are exposed to a high risk of homicide tend to acquire guns. Gary Kleck has argued, for instance, that "virtually all known factors that increase the risk of homicide victimization could also increase the likelihood that persons exposed to those factors would acquire a gun for self-protection."[31] But Kellermann did control for a number of independent risk factors for homicide and still found that the homes of homicide victims were substantially more likely to have guns. Other case-control studies have yielded similar results. One found that keeping a gun in the home is associated with an increased risk of homicide for women, particularly at the hands of a spouse, an intimate acquaintance, or a close relative.[32] Another found that the purchase of a handgun is associated with an increased risk of homicide victimization.[33] A third case-control study found that individuals in possession of a gun (whether in the home or elsewhere) were over four times more likely to be shot in an assault than those not in possession of a gun.[34] The authors suggested a number of plausible reasons for this result, including that a gun may empower a person to instigate conflicts or enter dangerous environments, or that individuals may bring a gun to an otherwise gun-free conflict only to have it wrested away.

Regardless of whether the case-control method demonstrates that gun ownership causes an increased risk of homicide, one conclusion is clear: gun ownership does not reduce the risk of homicide. Just as gun-owning nations and states are not more polite, neither are gun-owning households. If the "criminal coming through the sliding-glass door" is the only relevant scenario and a gun in the home is an effective defense, then homicide victims should be less likely to have a gun in the home, not more likely, as Kellermann found.

The best available evidence, therefore, tells us that a gun in the home (1) does not reduce the risk of homicide or burglary; (2) can be used for self-defense but is rarely used for that purpose, even in cases of home invasion; and (3) is far more likely to victimize those who live in the home, or their acquaintances, than to be used to shoot intruders. It can therefore be said, with some confidence, that bringing a gun into the home is usually a very bad idea. These facts do not necessarily lead to the conclusion that our public policy should bar gun ownership. As with consumption of alcohol, it may be that the government should allow individual citizens to make their own mistakes. But our public policy should at least ensure that people know the truth about guns in the home, just as the risks of consuming alcohol should be widely known. And we blind ourselves to the truth by insisting that the only relevant risk is that of being unarmed as a criminal approaches in a darkened bedroom.

The NRA has done its best to blind us to the truth about the dangers of guns in the home. When researchers began to publish studies in prestigious, peer-reviewed journals showing that guns actually increase risk, the gun lobby's solution was to shut down the research and suppress the truth. In the mid-1990s, under pressure from the NRA, Congress took the $2.6 million budgeted by the Centers for Disease Control and Prevention for firearm-injury research and earmarked it for traumatic brain injury.[35] Congressional Republicans also included language in CDC-appropriations legislation directing that no injury-research funding could go to research that could be "used to advocate or promote gun control." Although the language was ambiguous, the message received by the CDC was not. The CDC's support of gun violence research ended, and research resources devoted to gun violence are minuscule compared to other public-health issues like tobacco use, cancer, or HIV.

The NRA has even gone so far as to work for state laws limiting what doctors can say to their patients about the risks of guns in the home. Pediatricians have long counseled parents about the danger to children of guns in the home, just as they have advised them on the dangers of household poisons, unsupervised swimming pools, and riding bikes without safety helmets. In response, the NRA has worked for restrictive state laws, such as one enacted in Florida, that limit what doctors can say to their patients about guns by threatening the loss of a physician's medical license for the offense of "unnecessarily harassing a patient about firearms ownership during an examination," whatever that means. Apparently the NRA's devotion to the First Amendment does not match its enthusiasm for the Second.

GOOD GUYS VS. BAD GUYS ON THE STREETS

If guns in the home deter crime and enable resistance to criminal attack, as the NRA insists, then it stands to reason that gun carrying by law-abiding citizens in public places would deter even more crime and allow more good guys to shoot bad guys. After all, crime frequently victimizes people outside the home. Thus, the logical extension of "more guns means less crime" is to encourage the legal carrying of guns in public places.

Indeed, pro-gun advocates have responded to the recurring American nightmare of mass shootings in public places by arguing that they typically occur in "gun-free zones" where carrying of guns is legally prohibited, like Sandy Hook elementary school, which shooters select because they need not fear the presence of a "good guy with a gun." In fact, there is no correlation whatsoever between the location of mass shootings and the legal status of guns in that location. One analysis of 110 mass shootings (using the FBI's definition of an incident in which at least four people were shot) between January 2009 and July 2014, showed that, of thirty-three mass shootings that happened in public spaces, at least eighteen occurred where concealed guns could be lawfully carried, with only thirteen occurring in so-called "gun-free zones."[36] It is fanciful to believe that those intent on mass killing carefully choose the site of their attack by analyzing the relevant gun laws and the probability that they will be confronted by a gun-wielding good guy.

The circumstances of the Tucson, Arizona, shooting in which six were killed (including a nine-year-old girl) and thirteen were wounded, including Democratic representative Gabby Giffords, provide a particularly compelling illustration of how the NRA's "good guys" versus "bad guys" view of the world is divorced from reality. That shooting occurred outside a Safeway grocery store where there were no restrictions on concealed carry. Indeed, Arizona had become one of the few states to allow concealed carry of guns in public places without any permit at all. Not only was the shooter, Jared Loughner, not deterred by the prospect of being confronted by a "good guy," *in the NRA's world, Loughner himself was a "good guy with a gun" until he actually pulled the trigger.* Arizona's gun laws are so nonexistent that it was entirely legal for Loughner to be carrying his Glock pistol outside that Safeway until the moment he started shooting. Loughner's community college had expelled him because he was thought to be too dangerous to be in class, but his threatening conduct did not disqualify him from legally possessing guns or legally carrying them concealed. Even if his community college had reported his behavior to the Tucson police, under Arizona law there was nothing the police could have done to prevent Loughner from carrying a concealed weapon.

As it turned out, there actually was a "good guy with a gun" on the sidewalk in front of the Safeway. His name is Joseph Zamudio, and he, like Loughner, was legally carrying a concealed weapon that day. He has said he got to the shooter only after someone else had grabbed the gun from Loughner's hands. Zamudio added that he was prepared to "shoot the person with the gun" and initially thought the hero who had grabbed the gun was, in fact, the shooter. Thankfully, Zamudio showed sufficient caution that he did not shoot an innocent person. But his gun did no one any good that day and came dangerously close to adding to the carnage.

There is, of course, a self-evident distinction between guns in the home and guns in public. As we have seen, the risks from the decision to bring a gun into the home are borne largely by those who live there. This, of course, does not mean that the public has no legitimate interest in that decision. A gun in the home can victimize visitors to the home as well as residents. Bullets have been known to penetrate external walls and injure those in attached or nearby homes. Almost by definition, however, the public has a more direct interest in gun carrying in public. The risk from an individual's decision to carry a gun in public is borne almost entirely by strangers who had no say in that decision and, if the carrying is concealed, have no knowledge of the decision. No one shopping at the Tucson Safeway that day or talking with Representative Giffords at her "Congress on Your Corner" event, knew of the danger they were about to confront, nor were they in a position to protect themselves from that danger.

The risk of guns in public is not limited to intentional misuse. Take the case of Kelli McCormack Brown and Dawn Larson, two Minnesota health educators who were out for dinner with college friends at an Indianapolis restaurant. Little did they know that another diner, Thomas Neuman, had a loaded .32 caliber derringer concealed in his shirt pocket. Neuman's valid Indiana concealed-weapons permit proved no insurance against carelessness. When he bent over to retrieve a broken necklace, the gun fell out of his pocket, struck the floor, and discharged a single bullet that struck Ms. Brown's hand before it penetrated Ms. Larson's arm.[37] One bullet. Two injuries. Obviously it could have been much worse. To add a measure of heavy irony to the incident, the two women were in Indianapolis to attend the annual meeting of the American Public Health Association.

The distinction between guns in private homes and guns carried in public places, until recently, has been reflected in state concealed-weapon laws. Traditionally, states have imposed far greater restrictions on the carrying of concealed weapons in public than on the ownership of guns per se. Until the 1990s, in fact, most states either banned the carrying of concealed weapons, or at least had very restrictive permitting systems. Most states vested law-enforcement authorities with great discretion to deny permits to carry concealed weapons, even for applicants who had no criminal record. Such discretionary systems recognize that a clean criminal record is no guarantee that an applicant is a responsible, law-abiding person (Jared Loughner, for example). One Massachusetts police chief told a local newspaper that it is important to be able to weed out applicants who may have clean criminal records but are closely associated with gangs and may be involved in buying weapons for them.[38] For the NRA, however, allowing police this kind of discretion is an unacceptable limitation on the right of self-defense in public places and an open invitation to criminals to victimize law-abiding citizens without fear of retaliation. As noted previously, the NRA embarked on a nationwide campaign to push "shall is- sue" concealed-weapon laws in which authorities would be forced to issue concealed-weapon permits to anyone without a criminal record who wanted them. The campaign was regrettably successful, and now the vast majority of states have adopted "shall issue" CCW (carrying a concealed weapon) permit laws or, like Arizona, have no permit requirement at all.

The CCW issue is a singular illustration of the NRA's power over state legislatures in utter defiance of the popular will. A May 1995 poll of Louisiana voters found that 60 percent opposed legisla- tion to weaken that state's CCW law.[39] A year later, Louisiana be- came a "shall issue" state. A February 1995 Texas poll found that 62 percent of Texans were opposed to legislation allowing law-abiding citizens to carry concealed weapons in public.[40] Texas enacted just such a law that same year. A November 1994 Michigan poll found 76 percent opposition to relaxing that state's CCW law.[41] After several failed attempts, the NRA finally succeeded in ramming a "shall issue" bill through the Michigan legislature in 2001. And in April 1999, the NRA suffered a humiliating public repudiation of its CCW campaign when Missouri voters defeated an NRA- sponsored referendum to enact a "shall issue" law. The NRA spent $4 million on the issue in Missouri, nearly five times the amount spent by its opponents, and still lost. Only four years after Missouri citizens made their views clearly known (by voting, not by answer- ing a pollster's questions), the Missouri legislature passed the very statute the voters had rejected. The deciding vote was cast by a state senator serving in the Army National Guard in Guantanamo Bay, Cuba, who was able to fly back to Missouri for the vote.[42] He was later reprimanded by the military.[43] When it comes to twisting arms in a state legislature, the gun lobby is not to be trifled with.

In recent years, the NRA has taken its concealed-carry cru- sade to Congress, where it has worked for legislation that would force states to recognize the concealed-carry permits of visitors from other states. Under this legislation, states could enforce their concealed-carry restrictions on their own residents but not against visitors from other states with less restrictive laws. For example, Arkansas bars concealed carry by those who have voluntarily committed themselves to a mental-health institution or who are chronic alcohol abusers. If the NRA's bill were to become law, Arkansas could enforce those restrictions against its own residents but not against out-of-state visitors who have licenses to carry from states that lack the same restrictions. Some of the strongest supporters of this legislation in Congress also are traditional advocates of states' rights against federal encroachment. Yet, to please the gun lobby, they are willing to support a federal bill that would make their own state laws unenforceable against concealed carriers from other states.

If you take a seat in a movie theatre, ready to see the latest blockbuster, would it make you feel more or less safe to know that several of your fellow law-abiding citizens are packing heat? How about in a restaurant? In a bar? In a stadium during a football game? In church? At your doctor's office? At your son's little league baseball game? Surveys show that most people take a dim view of being in places where others have hidden handguns in their clothes, purses, or cars. A national survey by the Harvard Injury Control Research Center asked, "Some states have recently changed their laws concerning gun carrying. . . . If more people in your community begin to carry guns, will that make you feel more safe, the same, or less safe?" Sixty-two percent said "less safe," with only 12 percent saying "more safe."[44] Another Harvard survey asked whether "regular citizens should be allowed to bring their guns into (a) restaurants, (b) bars, (c) college campuses, (d) hospitals, (e) sports stadiums, and (f) government buildings." Generally *more than 90 percent of the respondents answered "no" to each location.*[45] Yet the NRA's "shall issue" CCW laws are designed to ensure that greater numbers of ordinary citizens will carry hidden handguns in those locations. Even when the survey question made explicit reference to allowing only law-abiding citizens who have passed safety-training courses to carry concealed weapons, the respondents still disliked the idea. A survey by the National Opinion Research Center asked, "Do laws allowing any adult to carry a concealed gun in public provided that they pass a criminal background check and gun safety course make you feel more safe or less safe?" Fifty-six percent of respondents replied "less safe," and 36 percent said "more safe."[46]

The public's instincts on the concealed-carry issue are borne out by experience. The NRA claims that its opponents have been discredited on the CCW issue because, according to the NRA, they hysterically claimed there would be "blood in the streets" and "Dodge City gunfights" in "shall issue" states, when nothing of the kind has occurred. It's not clear how much blood would have to flow to impress the NRA, but it is not difficult to find case after case of mayhem, and near mayhem, involving the "good guys" who were legal concealed carriers like Jared Loughner.

One of the most infamous cases in recent history was the shooting of unarmed teenager Trayvon Martin by Florida concealed-carry permit holder George Zimmerman. Zimmerman was a neighborhood-watch captain who had called police around 7:30 on the night of February 26, 2012, to report a "suspicious person" in his gated community. In defiance of neighborhood-watch guidelines, Zimmerman was carrying a concealed, loaded pistol. He was told by a police dispatcher to wait for patrol officers but ignored their counsel, followed Martin in his car, and then got out of his car, leading to a confrontation with Martin. Martin was returning from a convenience store to purchase snacks for his stepbrother and was armed only with a bag of Skittles and an iced tea. During the confrontation with Martin, Zimmerman fatally wounded the teenager. Zimmerman was charged with second-degree murder and manslaughter but was acquitted of those charges in June 2013.

Although much about the case stoked public controversy, one conclusion seems clear: if Zimmerman had not been armed, there is every reason to believe that no fatality would have occurred. It is improbable that an unarmed Zimmerman would have left his vehicle to follow a man he deemed suspicious enough to warrant a call to the police. And even if he had followed and confronted Trayvon Martin, the absence of a gun would have made a lethal outcome far less likely.

I could probably devote the next twenty pages to describing additional similar incidents involving CCW-license holders, but restraint is clearly called for. Permit me, however, to share a few examples—my own version of the NRA magazine's longtime feature, "The Armed Citizen."

- US Army Major Nidal Malik Hasan shot and killed thirteen people, almost all soldiers, and wounded over thirty others in the Soldier Readiness Center at the US Army base in Fort Hood, Texas. Some years before, after completing his official "NRA Personal Protection Course," Hasan was issued a concealed-weapons permit in Virginia.[47]
- Concealed-carry permit holder George Sodini attacked an LA Fitness center in suburban Pittsburgh armed with multiple handguns loaded with high-capacity ammunition magazines, murdering three women, wounding nine others, and then killing himself.[48]
- Richard Poplawski, a concealed-carry license holder, opened fire on police officers responding to a domestic-disturbance call placed by his mother. Wearing a bulletproof vest and armed with an assault rifle and two other guns, Poplawski killed three Pittsburgh police officers. He had previously been discharged from the Marine Corps during basic training, and a girlfriend had filed a protection-from-abuse order against him.[49]
- Michael McLendon killed his mother, drove twenty miles to shoot five members of his extended family, then randomly fired at cars, stores, police officers, neighbors, a man walking down the street, a woman at a store, and a passing motorist. Armed with a handgun, a shotgun, and two assault rifles, he killed ten people during his rampage. The police reported he was licensed to carry handguns.[50]
- Tulsa, Oklahoma, resident Harold Glover, who became a CCW permit holder shortly after that state's law went into effect, shot and killed Cecil Herndon at a day-care center, as

250 children looked on. Glover and Herndon were arguing about who would take their four-year-old grandson home, when Glover pulled out his .357 magnum and shot Herndon in the chest. Glover claimed that Herndon had threatened him with a pocketknife, but authorities determined that Herndon was not acting in a "life-threatening" manner.[51]

- Seventy-six-year-old Clay "Junior" Wallace, an Arkansas CCW permit holder, shot and killed Robert Qualls, sixty-five, after an argument over new sewer service for the town of Black Oak. The two men had been arguing inside Vera's Café and went outside to settle the argument with fists. After being knocked to the ground twice, Wallace pulled out a .38 caliber revolver and shot Qualls twice in the stomach, killing him.[52]
- One day after his wife filed for a protective order against him after months of domestic abuse, Carlton Evans of Seattle applied for, and was granted, a Washington State concealed-weapons permit. Less than two months later, Evans killed his wife and baby.[53]
- Robert Herndon, a Florida CCW holder, gunned down popular Aventura, Florida, surgeon Bradley Silverman outside the doctor's office. Florida's concealed-weapons statute allowed Herndon a permit even though he had been twice charged with assault (the charges were either dropped or reduced to a misdemeanor), had threatened his neighbors with a gun, and had voluntarily committed himself to a mental institution.[54]
- Naveed Afzal Haq, who had been issued a concealed-carry license despite his history of mental illness and a pending charge of lewd conduct, opened fire at the Jewish Federation of Greater Seattle, killing one woman and wounding five others.[55]

Remember, these are the people who, according to the NRA, are supposed to be making this a more polite society by lawfully carrying hidden handguns in public. These are the "good guy" permit holders whom we can count on to shoot the "bad guys." How could "good guys" cause such havoc? According to Wayne LaPierre, "Good people make good decisions. That's why they're good people."[56] Of course, it is obvious that some people we thought were "good" do, in fact, make bad decisions. When they make those decisions with guns in public places, there is big trouble.

Of course the proponents of concealed carry can no doubt cite their own list of instances where truly law-abiding citizens thwarted a criminal attack with a hidden handgun. The issue, however, is not whether concealed weapons can be successfully deployed in self-defense in public places. After all, the "may issue" states, which allow law enforcement discretion to deny permits even in the absence of an applicant's criminal record, recognize that some concealed carry of firearms can be justified. The issue is whether it is good public policy to require the police to issue CCW permits to anyone who can pass a criminal-background check, or whether the police should have the freedom to assess the risk that the permit applicant will be subject to violent attack before issuing the permit, as well as the risk that the applicant himself will misuse the gun.

Accurately separating the "good guys" who should get a license from the "bad guys" who should be denied has proven to be challenging. A *Los Angeles Times* exposé showed that, in the first five years the Texas "shall issue" law was in effect, more than four hundred people were licensed despite prior criminal convictions, and more than three thousand other licensees had been arrested.[57] It took some digging for the *Times* to uncover these facts. Texas authorities do not release the names of licensees who run afoul of the law. The South Florida *Sun-Sentinel* obtained the database of Florida CCW holders just before the effective date of a new law sought by the NRA barring disclosure of those names. When the newspaper compared the names to available criminal records, it found the CCW holders included over 200 people with active arrest warrants and 128 people with domestic-violence restraining orders against them.[58] Among the "law-abiding" citizens whom the State of Florida issued licenses to carry concealed weapons were the following:

- Adel Ahmad, a Tampa pizza deliveryman, who kept his CCW license for four years even though he was wanted by police for shooting and killing a teenage boy over a stolen order of chicken wings.
- Lyglenson Lemorin of Miami, who was a valid CCW holder when he was arrested with six other South Florida men on terrorism conspiracy charges involving a plot to blow up buildings in Miami and Chicago, including the Sears Tower.
- Nathaniel Ferguson of Lake Mary, who still had a concealed-weapons license after he pleaded no contest to attempted manslaughter charges for shooting a woman in a parking lot outside a Seminole County bar.
- Barry Cogen of Sunrise, who was arrested for aggravated stalking *the day after he obtained his concealed-weapons permit.*
- Robert Rodriguez of Tampa, a bar owner who held a CCW permit in 2005 *despite having been arrested twenty-two times between 1960 and 1998.*

The underlying premise of "shall issue" laws is that there is a public benefit to increasing the number of citizens without criminal records who carry guns because prospective criminals will be deterred by the prospect of armed resistance and legal concealed carriers will be able to intervene to stop criminal acts. Given that the number of "high-risk" licensees will always be a minority of the total number of licensees, it may be that the deterrent effect of all those law-abiding people carrying loaded handguns will outweigh the added risk from sometimes putting guns in the hands of dangerous people and turning them loose on the streets. We have seen, however, that the available evidence provides no support for the deterrent value of gun ownership per se. Nevertheless, there have been some dramatic claims of crime deterrence made on behalf of "shall issue" concealed-carry laws. That brings us to John Lott.

MORE GUNS, A LOTT OF CRIME

The August 2, 1996, edition of *USA Today*, with the headline "Fewer Rapes, Killings Found Where Concealed Guns Legal," reported the results of a new "comprehensive" study showing that "shall issue" concealed-carry laws were associated with substantial decreases in homicides, rapes, and aggravated assaults. The study, by economists John Lott and David Mustard, was imposing indeed; it analyzed crime statistics in the nation's 3,054 counties from 1977 to 1992. The Lott-Mustard study made the remarkable claim that had all states adopted "shall issue" laws by 1992, 1,500 murders would have been avoided annually, along with 4,000 rapes, 11,000 robberies, and 60,000 aggravated assaults.[59] Lott then published a book based on his study, audaciously entitled *More Guns, Less Crime*.

The Lott study was an adrenaline shot for the NRA's concealed-weapons campaign. For the first time, the gun lobby and its allies could give a quasi-scholarly veneer to its claim that criminals would be deterred by the fear of gun-carrying law-abiding citizens. From the beginning, other researchers found Lott's work deeply flawed. As with Kleck's estimate of defensive gun uses, there has been a feeding frenzy of scholarly criticism. More than a dozen researchers have attacked Lott's methodology and his conclusions.[60]

Lott's study is essentially a comparison of crime rates in the states that adopted "shall issue" laws between 1985 and 1992 with those in the states that did not. As multiple scholars have pointed out, the core problem with the study is that the ten states Lott studied that enacted "shall-issue" laws during those years were states like Maine, West Virginia, Mississippi, Montana, and Virginia, which are more rural than the states that did not adopt those laws, like New York, New Jersey, California, and Illinois. Lott's study also encompasses a period when a wave of violent crime, particularly homicide, was sweeping the nation. This wave, most criminologists agree, was fueled by the crack-cocaine epidemic, and it was concentrated among adolescents and young adults in urban areas. That crime wave peaked in 1993 (with, as we have seen, gun crime peaking in 1994).

If we look at later years, when the urban crime wave receded and violent crime began to plummet nationally, we see a very different story emerge about the "shall issue" CCW states. Lott's study period ended in 1992. From 1992 to 1998, violent crime began an impressive decline nationally, and the violent-crime rate in the states that did not adopt "shall issue" laws fell twice as fast as in the "shall issue" states.[61]

The work of Stanford University economist John Donahue is perhaps the most devastating to Lott. Donahue simply extended Lott's statistical model through 1997, a period during which thirteen additional states, relying in part on Lott's study, adopted "shall-issue" laws. Donahue found that "shall-issue laws were uniformly associated with crime *increases*."[62] This helps to explain why, during a period of generally decreasing violent crime in the 1990s, the states with "shall-issue" laws lagged behind the other states in fighting crime. Donahue and Yale Law School's Ian Ayres later extended the data analysis through 2006 and found not only that "shall issue" laws did not reduce crime; they actually were associated with an increase in the rate of aggravated assault.[63]

It's safe to say that the research community has left Lott's study in tatters, but not before it was cited in state after state to support the NRA's successful campaign to loosen concealed-carry restrictions. Even today, the gun lobby continues to use Lott's bogus study to push its high-risk strategy of fighting crime through the proliferation of guns. More guns in more homes. More guns on more streets. More guns in bars and on college campuses. More guns anywhere people gather. There is no sound social science supporting this strategy. Its most prominent public defender has been thoroughly discredited.

The nations with more guns are not safer. The states with more guns are not safer. The homes with more guns are not safer.

In an armed society, people are not more polite and the "good guys" are not safer. They are simply more fearful, and with very good reason.

CHAPTER SIX

WE DON'T NEED NEW GUN
LAWS. WE NEED TO ENFORCE
THE LAWS WE HAVE.

This is a relative newcomer to the gun lobby's parade of myths and fallacies. It was first unveiled during the Clinton administration following the NRA's stinging defeats in Congress on the Brady Bill and the assault-weapons ban. The slogan was designed to communicate the message that President Clinton was a hypocrite on the gun issue because he supported new gun laws but cared nothing about enforcing them once they were enacted. Because the slogan was not nearly as useful for the NRA when its guy was in the White House, it was rarely heard during the Bush years. During the Obama administration, it made a comeback. As discussed earlier, the NRA has always taken the view that the panacea for criminal gun violence is to severely punish gun criminals after the fact. If the problem is criminals committing violent crimes with guns, the solution is to lock them up for those crimes and throw away the key. For the NRA, punishment is prevention. The gun lobby has long assailed the criminal-justice system, including its "bleeding-heart, criminal coddling judges and prosecutors," in the words of Marion Hammer, the NRA's Florida lobbyist.[1] So what was new about the NRA's call for "enforcing current laws" instead of passing new ones?

SUPPORT ENFORCEMENT—DESTROY THE ENFORCERS
The new wrinkle was that the NRA's attack involved the alleged failure to enforce *federal* gun laws. The NRA was calling for stronger *federal* enforcement of gun laws by the Clinton administration. What's wrong with this picture? In his 1994 book, *Guns, Crime, and*

Freedom, Wayne LaPierre assailed the Bureau of Alcohol, Tobacco, and Firearms—the agency that enforces federal gun laws:

> If I were to select a jack-booted group of fascists who were perhaps as large a danger to American society as I could pick today, I would pick BATF. They are a shame and a disgrace to our country.[2]

LaPierre was actually quoting Congressman John Dingell, who was an NRA board member at the time he made the statement. Dingell said it in 1982. For years, the NRA had been attacking the ATF—*not for its failure to enforce the law, but for enforcing the law too aggressively.*

The NRA's attack on the Clinton administration and ATF for overly aggressive enforcement reached a fever pitch after the raid on the Branch Davidian compound in Waco, Texas, by ATF and other federal law-enforcement agents in February of 1993. ATF acted based on evidence that David Koresh and his followers had illegally amassed dozens of machine guns, unlawfully converted by the Davidians from semiautomatic assault weapons. The feds were attempting to serve a lawful search warrant on Koresh when his followers opened fire, killing four federal agents and wounding sixteen others. Agents later found forty-eight illegal machine guns in the compound, along with sixty-one AK-47 assault rifles, thirteen shotguns, two .50-caliber rifles, and millions of rounds of ammunition.[3] As is well known, the initial exchange of gunfire was followed by a fifty-one-day siege, ended by the final operation against the Davidians by federal authorities on April 19, 1993, during which the compound erupted in a horrific fire, killing scores of those inside.

Obviously much could be criticized, and was, about the tactics of federal agents during the Waco operation. But supporters of strong enforcement of federal gun laws could be expected to at least recognize the importance of enforcing the federal machine gun ban, particularly against a group suspected of building an arsenal of illegal machine guns. The NRA, on the other hand, would have been quite content to allow Koresh and his followers to flout federal law and continue to stockpile illegal machine guns. According to Wayne LaPierre, the Branch Davidians were simply a "religious cult of men, women, and children, who grew their own food, taught their own children, and pretty much stayed to themselves."[4] The Davidians, LaPierre wrote, were being investigated for "technical violations" of federal gun laws.[5]

LaPierre apparently was untroubled by the murder of federal agents. His message: they brought it on themselves.

> The government agents in charge knew there were firearms in the compound—the "alleged" type of firearms is what the charade was all about. Did they expect to charge the farm house and not a shot be fired?[6]

The plain meaning of this statement is that the NRA would not condemn the murder of federal agents by persons suspected of violating federal gun laws. In the NRA's view, if the ATF tries to enforce the law against armed violators, it does so at its own risk. This is the same NRA that says we need to more vigorously enforce federal gun laws.

The ugliness of the NRA's post-Waco rhetoric is now the stuff of legend. It called ATF an "unchecked, renegade federal power."[7] It warned that federal "agents clad in ninja black" were launching "[h]eavy-handed raids against law-abiding citizens,"[8] using "reckless, storm-trooper tactics."[9] It ran full-page ads in the *Washington Post* and *USA Today* calling ATF a "rogue agency" with "a tyrannical record of misconduct and abuse of power" that "deserves public contempt." The NRA told its members that ATF agents were engaged in "brutal misconduct" and threatened ATF to back off or be destroyed—"We plan to challenge its existence."[10]

NRA supporters were whipped into an ATF-hating frenzy. On NRA electronic bulletin boards, its members lashed out. NRA board member Harry Thomas sent this threat of violence to Attorney General Janet Reno: "If you send your jackbooted, baby-burning bushwhackers to confiscate guns, pack them a lunch. The Branch Davidians were amateurs. I'm a professional."[11] Another post on the NRA's electronic bulletin board stated, "If the Republicans will not disband the ATF or demand the head of Reno, it might be time for armed conflict over the desecration of the Bill of Rights."[12] The electronic bulletin board featured a recipe for building a homemade bomb with baby-food containers and shotgun shells.[13]

In a now-infamous fund-raising letter from April 13, 1995, Wayne LaPierre warned his members about murderous federal agents:

> Jack-booted government thugs [have] more power to take away our Constitutional rights, break in our doors, seize our guns, destroy our property, and even injure or kill us. . . . [I]f you have a badge, you have the government's go-ahead to harass, intimidate, even murder law-abiding citizens. . . . Not too long ago, it was unthinkable for federal agents wearing nazi bucket helmets and black storm trooper uniforms to attack law-abiding citizens. Not today, not with Clinton.[14]

Six days later, as NRA members found the fund-raising letter in their mail, Timothy McVeigh bombed the Murrah Federal Building in Oklahoma City. McVeigh acted on the second anniversary of the fire at the Branch Davidian compound. The Murrah Building housed the offices of ATF agents, as well as other federal agencies. When he was apprehended that same day, McVeigh had in his possession a plain white envelope packed with articles on the Waco siege. The articles referred to federal agents as "Gestapo" or "Terrorist Goon Squads,"[15] strikingly similar to the Nazi references in LaPierre's fund-raising letter. It is chilling to read the passage in LaPierre's 1994 book condoning the violence against federal agents at Waco, knowing of the violence to come in Oklahoma City.

Later it was discovered that McVeigh had written his congressman complaining about "firearm restrictions" in a letter stamped with an "I'm the NRA" logo.[16] During the siege of the Branch Davidian compound, he traveled to Waco, where he passed out bumper stickers condemning gun control and the enforcers of gun control laws. The bumper stickers featured such slogans as "Fear the government that fears your gun" and "When guns are outlawed, I will become an outlaw."[17] At gun shows, he wore and sold ATF baseball caps, punctured with two bullet holes.[18] McVeigh had completely absorbed the NRA ideology that saw gun control laws as tyrannical and ATF, the laws' enforcers, as the agents of tyranny. When he committed the worst terrorist act up to that point in United States history, McVeigh was acting out the hate-filled anti-ATF rhetoric of the NRA.

McVeigh also was acting out the NRA's long-held but utterly perverse "insurrectionist" view of the Second Amendment, in which the Constitution, the charter of our government, guarantees a right to destroy the government.[19] As an NRA field representative once told the *New York Times,* "The Second Amendment . . . is literally a loaded gun in the hands of the people held to the heads of government."[20] The NRA long had asserted the right to use violence as a tool of political dissent. Timothy McVeigh, tragically, took the gun lobby's constitutional theory to its lethal extreme.

The NRA's incendiary antigovernment rhetoric, followed by mass murder at the hands of a rabid pro-gun true believer, was too much for some loyal NRA supporters to bear. President George H. W. Bush, who had threatened to veto the Brady Bill in 1991, resigned his life membership in the organization, calling the NRA's statements against federal law enforcement a "vicious slander on good people" and a "broadside against federal agents [that] offends my own sense of decency and honor."[21]

WHICH GUN LAWS SHOULD WE ENFORCE?

Barely two years after savaging ATF for enforcing federal gun laws, the NRA launched its new campaign to savage the Clinton administration for not enforcing federal gun laws. The same Wayne LaPierre who in 1995 pledged to challenge the existence of ATF, in 1997 wrote:

It's a moral crime for Bill Clinton, Al Gore and Janet Reno and a host of Federal officers and prosecutors to fail to enforce the law. It's evil. And when innocent blood flows, it's on their hands.[22]

How can LaPierre believe it is a "moral crime" to fail to enforce the law, when he so easily dismissed the Branch Davidians' illegal machine guns as "technical violations" of the law? It turns out that the NRA is quite selective about the gun laws it wants enforced.

In its zeal to attack the Clinton administration, the NRA focused on the administration's record prosecuting felons caught in possession of firearms. It had long been a criminal violation for a felon to possess guns. Wayne LaPierre charged that President Clinton and Attorney General Janet Reno had "blood . . . on their hands" for failing to prosecute these cases:

> Almost uniformly, the Clinton Administration has refused to use the powerful, existing Federal firearms laws to arrest and prosecute armed, convicted, violent felons.
>
> The result of that refusal to enforce existing Federal law against violent career criminals has created a horrible waste of innocent lives. Thousands of our citizens have been robbed, maimed or murdered because Bill Clinton and Janet Reno have not met their duty to enforce the law.[23]

LaPierre also accused the Clinton administration of failing to prosecute the felons who try to buy guns from dealers but are denied because of Brady background checks. "Under the Brady Act, [Bill Clinton] turns criminals away. He doesn't arrest them."[24]

The critique of the Clinton administration for failing to bring cases based on Brady purchase denials was heavy with irony. It is true that any prospective gun purchaser turned away because of a Brady background check could potentially be prosecuted for falsely claiming on a federal form that he was not a felon or member of any other prohibited class of gun buyers. However, it is only because of the Brady Act (or state background-check laws) that those potential criminal cases are even identifiable. Before Brady, those felons and other prohibited buyers would have lied on the federal form and the authorities would never know. The NRA, of course, fought tenaciously to defeat the Brady Bill and mourned its passage. "When Bill Clinton signed the Brady Bill," the NRA wrote, "a drop of blood dripped from the finger of the sovereign American citizen."[25] After the bill became law, the NRA gave financial support for multiple lawsuits seeking to strike down the new law, ultimately filing a brief in the US Supreme Court expressly asking the Court to void the entire statute.[26] Yet, without apparent embarrassment, the NRA accused the Clinton administration of having "blood on its hands" because it failed to bring federal prosecutions *that only the Brady Act made possible.*

Thus, when the NRA says we should "enforce existing gun laws instead of passing new ones," it really means that the feds should prosecute more criminals caught lying by the Brady Act, and more cases of felons caught with guns, instead of passing new laws. When it comes to enforcement of other gun laws, the NRA's enthusiasm wanes. We have seen, for instance, that the NRA was not bothered by the manufacture of illegal machine guns by the Branch Davidians. Indeed, when gun owners defy laws the NRA has opposed, far from expressing outrage at the law breakers, it characterizes the illegality as "civil disobedience." Thus when relatively few California gun owners registered their assault weapons as required by that state's landmark assault-weapons law, the NRA ran a cover story in its magazine *America's 1st Freedom* asking, in bold type, "Is Massive Civil Disobedience at Hand?"[27] The article stated, "Through confusion or conscious decision, observers say, tens or even hundreds of thousands of Californians . . . may be quietly disobeying" the assault-weapons law. It asked, hopefully, "Could this be the most massive act of civil disobedience in our country's history?" The article assured readers that "ignoring the law of the land is never the advocated position of the National Rifle Association."[28] *Advocated* position?

In the NRA's world, one can be a "law-abiding citizen" and still violate a criminal law, as long as it is a gun control law that the NRA does not like. The NRA is not a proponent of respect for the law, only for the laws it supports.

And what about gun-law enforcement after President George W. Bush took office in 2000 with the strong support of the NRA? It turns out that federal prosecutions of gun buyers for lying on the federal gun-purchase form increased all of 0.1 percent from 2000 to 2003. During those years, 566,000 potential buyers falsely claimed on the federal form that they had clean records and were blocked from buying a gun by the Brady law. Only 2,126, or far less than 1 percent, were charged.[29] During the Clinton administration, the failure to prosecute such people drew charges that the president and Janet Reno had "blood on their hands" because they "turn criminals away" instead of arresting them. When over 99 percent of these criminals felons were "turned away" and not arrested by the feds during the George W. Bush administration, what was the NRA's response? Silence. No charges that President Bush was "evil," or that he had "blood on his hands," or that he had committed "moral crimes" against the American people.

During the Obama years, the NRA again found its voice on the enforcement issue. In January, 2016, its magazine *America's 1st Freedom* quoted Wayne LaPierre decrying the fact that, in 2010, eighty thousand legally prohibited gun buyers attempted to buy a gun (it is a felony for them to even make the attempt because they would have had to lie on the federal form), but only forty-four of them were prosecuted. Again, this low number of prosecutions is exactly what was happening during the Bush years. Of course, LaPierre doesn't mention that, had the NRA prevailed in the Brady Bill battle many years before, all eighty thousand of those prohibited buyers would have left the gun shop with a gun in 2010.

When the Justice Department's inspector general looked at the dearth of Brady Act prosecutions during the Bush years, he concluded that charges were rarely brought because convictions are difficult to obtain. According to the IG, among other factors, it is "difficult to prove that the prohibited person was aware of the prohibition and intentionally lied" to the dealer.[30] (This no doubt also explains why there were so few such prosecutions in the Clinton and Obama years.) Did the NRA respond by urging that the proof standard be changed to put more criminals behind bars? Of course not. The issue obviously is too politically useful to the gun lobby when the Democrats are in charge.

SUPPORT ENFORCEMENT, WEAKEN THE GUN CONTROL ACT

As we have seen, the gun laws the NRA actually wants to be enforced are few. As to the gun laws it doesn't like—the vast majority—the NRA not only seems untroubled by defiance of those laws; it also has devoted itself to weakening the laws and making them less enforceable.

The NRA's greatest victory in this arena was its campaign in the 1980s to weaken the 1968 Gun Control Act, which culminated in a set of amendments labeled the "Firearm Owners' Protection Act of 1986" (FOPA). The statute actually protects gun dealers, not gun owners, particularly dealers inclined to break the law.

FOPA, for example, created an extraordinarily high standard for ATF to prove criminal violations of the Gun Control Act, as well as to revoke the licenses of law-breaking gun dealers. For both, the government must show a "willful" violation of the law, which requires proof not only that the conduct was intentional, but also that the violator had knowledge that his conduct was unlawful.[31] Before FOPA, courts had interpreted federal law to require only a showing that the defendant or miscreant dealer had "knowingly" violated the law.[32] Although this required proof that the law violator "knew what he was doing" and thus precluded enforcement against a violator making merely inadvertent mistakes, the "knowing" standard did not demand evidence that the dealer knew his conduct was illegal. In practice, this has meant that ATF has been able to revoke the licenses of rogue gun dealers only rarely, and then only after years of multiple violations of the law.

FOPA also helped protect law-breaking dealers by reclassifying violations of federal firearms record-keeping laws as misdemeanors rather than felonies. Although "record-keeping" sounds inherently unimportant, actually these laws are crucial to ATF's law-enforcement function. We have noted before that ATF helps to solve crimes by using the unique serial numbers on guns to trace guns used in crime to identify the first retail purchaser. Of course, this can only be done if the dealer has complied with the record-keeping provisions of federal law. In addition, a failure to comply with record-keeping laws may be the only avenue to prosecute dealers suspected of selling guns "off the books" to criminals. In a survey of its own trafficking investigations, ATF found that "[f]ailure to keep required records was found in almost half of the trafficking investigations involving [federal firearms licensees], and the FFL making false entries in the records was found in just under a fifth of these investigations. These violations are primarily misdemeanors, despite being associated with investigations involving a high volume of trafficked firearms."[33] Since it is difficult to convince a federal prosecutor to bring misdemeanor cases, dealers caught violating federal law by ATF inspectors routinely escape criminal prosecution. And since "willfulness" is the standard for license revocation, scofflaw dealers often are able to both escape criminal prosecution and continue to sell guns. Congress made the situation even worse beginning in 2004 by annually attaching a rider to ATF appropriations bills preventing ATF from requiring that licensed dealers conduct annual inventories. In any other retail business, such inventories would be regarded as an essential business practice.

FOPA also made it less likely that record-keeping violations will be uncovered, by limiting ATF to a single, unannounced inspection every twelve months.[34] Thus, once a dealer has been inspected in a given year, he knows he is "free and clear" for another twelve months. ATF has told Congress that this limitation "enables unscrupulous licensees to conceal violations of the law and is an impediment to ensuring compliance with the provisions of the Gun Control Act."[35] Just as crippling to ATF's enforcement efforts has been the bureau's chronic problem of underfunding, a direct result of the NRA's influence over congressional appropriations. In 2004, the

Justice Department's inspector general found that "most [licensed dealers] are inspected infrequently or not at all," a record "due in part to resource shortfalls."[36] The inspector general concluded that, with ATF's limited manpower, "it would take the ATF more than 22 years to inspect all [federal firearms licensees]."

One of the great oddities of federal gun laws is that the federal record documenting gun sales by licensed dealers is, except under certain limited circumstances, *not in the possession of the federal government at all.* The federal Firearms Transaction Record (Form 4473), which reflects the name and address of the purchaser, along with his sworn declaration that he is not legally prohibited from buying firearms, generally remains in the gun shop. This is akin to a requirement that tax returns remain in the possession of taxpayers, but not the government.

Limiting access to the federal government's own gun records is, of course, the handiwork of the NRA. Its paranoia about anything approaching gun "registration" led to language appearing in every ATF appropriations bill since 1979 prohibiting ATF from maintaining and centralizing gun-purchase records.[37] FOPA also included a provision preventing ATF from establishing a database of firearms sales records.[38] In the digital age, tracing a gun using its serial number should take seconds. Instead, crime-gun tracing is far more cumbersome and time consuming, because the NRA-inspired restrictions make it necessary for ATF to ask the dealer for the information on Form 4473 to complete the trace. In addition, since gun dealers are the custodians of these vital records, physical inspection of gun shops is an especially critical part of ATF's enforcement program, and FOPA's limits on such inspections are that much more objectionable.

FOPA also was responsible for making gun shows an enforcement nightmare for ATF. Before FOPA, dealers had to have a federal firearms license for each location where they sold guns. This effectively barred dealers from selling at temporary locations like gun shows. FOPA lifted this limitation and allowed dealers to sell at gun shows within the dealer's state. According to ATF, this has led to "a wide range of criminal activity by [federally licensed dealers] . . . and felons conspiring with [gun dealers] at gun shows."[39] In addition to allowing sales by licensed dealers at gun shows, FOPA made it easier for sellers at gun shows (and elsewhere) to avoid the licensing requirements altogether. The Gun Control Act had required anyone "engaged in the business" of selling firearms to obtain a federal license. FOPA created a new definition of "engaged in the business" that allowed unlicensed sellers to sell their "personal collection" of firearms, no matter how large, without obtaining a license and without doing the Brady background checks on buyers.[40] This new loophole has created a new class of "gun show cowboys" (like Timothy McVeigh) who go from gun show to gun show, always claiming to sell guns from their "personal collections." As we have seen, the Columbine killers exploited this loophole to obtain their guns. According to ATF, the effect of the loophole "has often been to frustrate the prosecution of unlicensed dealers masquerading as collectors or hobbyists but who are really trafficking firearms to felons or other prohibited persons."[41] ATF's gun-trafficking investigations reveal gun shows to be the second-largest source of guns trafficked to criminals (second only to corrupt dealers).[42]

FOPA, then, was a disaster for enforcement of the Gun Control Act and, to this day, handcuffs ATF. For this, we have the NRA to thank, the same NRA that said President Clinton had "blood on his hands" for failing to enforce federal gun laws. As I have noted, FOPA had one salutary provision; its opponents did succeed in adding a Floor amendment banning manufacture and sale of new machine guns to civilians. This was the provision David Koresh and his followers violated when they converted their semiautomatic assault weapons into fully automatic rifles. As soon as FOPA passed, the NRA sought repeal of the machine gun freeze[43]—the one provision in FOPA that did not weaken enforcement of federal gun laws.

SUPPORT ENFORCEMENT, WEAKEN THE BRADY ACT

As we have seen, the NRA, without embarrassment, sought to overturn the Brady Act in court and then accused the Clinton administration of malfeasance in allegedly failing to enforce that very statute. After failing to destroy the statute in court, the gun lobby has done everything in its power to weaken it.

If the subject is NRA hypocrisy on enforcement issues, the gun lobby's vehement opposition to the Brady Act is particularly instructive. The lesson of the Brady Act is this: *sometimes it is necessary to pass new laws in order to enforce existing laws.* Before Brady was enacted, it already was illegal for felons to buy guns at gun stores. As we have seen, though, that law was difficult to enforce because felons would simply lie about their criminal history and buy their guns. The Brady background check is, in the final analysis, an enforcement tool. It allows the government to enforce the preexisting law against felons buying guns from dealers. For this reason, the Brady Bill was supported by every national police organization. When he gave the bill a huge boost by announcing his support, former president Ronald Reagan aptly described it as a new "enforcement mechanism" that "can't help but stop thousands of illegal gun purchases."[44] If the NRA had prevailed, "lie and buy" would still be mocking the legal bar on gun sales to criminals.

Having failed to defeat the legislation in Congress, or have it overturned in court, the NRA has resorted to weakening the Brady Act as an enforcement tool. This is another case where the NRA's paranoia about gun records trumps any pretended concern about strong law enforcement. Under the Brady Act's National Instant Criminal Background Check System (NICS), once the background check is completed and no disqualifying record is found, the statute requires that "all records of the system relating to the person or the transfer" be destroyed.[45] This record-destruction requirement itself was a concession to the gun lobby's friends in Congress, who sought to vanquish any hint of gun "registration" from the Brady Act. (Of course, the provision was not enough to satisfy the NRA, which opposed the bill anyway. Another example of the gun control catch-22.) The statute does not, however, specify *when* the background-check records must be destroyed. When the Clinton administration quite reasonably adopted the FBI's recommendation that the records be preserved for six months to allow for proper audits of NICS, the NRA charged off to court, seeking an order that the records be destroyed immediately upon completion of the background check, because anything less would be equivalent to "registration."[46] The US Court of Appeals for the District of Columbia rejected the NRA's argument, and the Supreme Court denied review.[47]

Though not legally required to do so, on its own initiative, the Clinton Justice Department then shortened the record-retention period from six months to ninety days.[48] This, of course, was not good enough for the gun lobby and its friends in the incoming Bush Justice Department. Under Bush attorney general John Ashcroft, the Justice Department instead proposed that the background-check records on allowed sales be destroyed *within twenty-four hours of the sale*, citing the need to protect "the privacy interests of law-abiding citizens."[49] Since 2004, the twenty-four-hour rule has been included as a rider to the appropriations bills governing the Justice Department (which includes ATF).

There is no question that the twenty-four-hour rule has helped to arm criminals. Before the new rule went into effect, the General Accounting Office did a study of its likely effect. During the first six months of the Clinton administration's ninety-day retention policy, there were 235 cases in which prohibited gun buyers erroneously cleared the NICS background checks and were allowed to buy guns.[50] Because the records of these erroneous "approvals" had been retained, the FBI was able to discover the errors and retrieve the firearms. According to the GAO, *had the twenty-four-hour record destruction rule been in effect during the period examined, 97 percent of the prohibited buyers would have evaded detection and retained their guns.*[51] Chances are, some of those people would have committed violent crimes with their guns.

The Justice Department's inspector general also found that the twenty-four-hour rule would make it more difficult for the FBI to detect fraud by corrupt dealers to cover up their sales to criminals.[52] Dealers could provide the FBI with a different name than that of the actual buyer to get NICS approval, and then complete the sale to the actual prohibited buyer. Destroying the records within twenty-four hours, said the inspector general, would make such a scheme nearly impossible to detect.

The NRA's concern for the rights of "law-abiding citizens" has even extended to suspected terrorists. Federal law does not preclude known terrorists from buying firearms unless they already have been convicted of a felony or fall into another category of prohibited gun buyers. From 2004 to 2014, persons on the FBI's consolidated terrorist watch list—typically placed there because there is "reasonable suspicion" that they are a known or suspected terrorist—attempted to purchase guns from American gun dealers at least 2,233 times. In 2,043 of those cases—91 percent of the time—they succeeded.[53] The NRA has opposed proposals to strengthen the Brady Act to prevent persons on the terrorist watch list from buying firearms. Wayne LaPierre explained that such proposals are "aimed primarily at law-abiding American gun owners."[54] The US Senate defeated such a proposal in December 2015, the day after the San Bernardino terrorist gun attack.

A FALSE CHOICE

Putting aside the NRA's selectivity, inconsistency, and outright hypocrisy in arguing for stronger enforcement of federal gun laws, does its core argument make sense? Even if we could strengthen enforcement of existing federal gun laws, is that a good reason to oppose new federal gun laws?

Public-opinion surveys suggest, at first glance, that the NRA has struck a chord with its call for stronger enforcement instead of new laws. From 2000 to 2012, Gallup polls have consistently shown greater public support for "enforcing current gun laws more strictly and not passing new laws" versus "passing new gun laws in addition to enforcing the current laws more strictly."[55] These poll results likely reflect the NRA's genius in framing its message, rather than the public's actual belief that stronger enforcement is a sensible substitute for good laws. Notice that the NRA's theme is "we need to enforce the laws we have, not pass *new* laws." It seems very likely that the polling results would be quite different if the choice presented were stronger enforcement versus "stronger" or "stricter" laws, rather than "new" laws. The public is understandably less than enthusiastic about passing "new" gun laws for their own sake. The application of a different adjective suggesting that the new gun laws would bring about some desirable change (i.e., "stronger" laws or "stricter" laws) likely would yield a higher level of support for the "enforcement plus laws" alternative.

Sure enough, when the National Opinion Research Center at the University of Chicago posed the same issue using different language, it got a different result. To the question "Which of the following options would be most effective in reducing gun violence?," 54 percent of those surveyed said "passing *stricter* gun control laws and strict enforcement of both the current and new laws," while only 33 percent preferred only "strict enforcement of the current gun laws."[56]

The NRA's "enforcement, not new laws" theme also benefits from deep public ignorance about the current state of our gun laws. A Yale University survey in 2014 showed that 41 percent of Americans incorrectly believed that universal background checks are already required by federal law, whereas 47 percent correctly reported that a federal background check is required only for some gun purchases and 12 percent believed that no federal background checks are required. The survey also showed that correct information about existing laws predicted support for stricter gun laws.[57] For people who incorrectly believe that we already have in place popular laws like universal background checks, it makes sense to favor stronger enforcement of those laws over enacting new gun laws.

Giving the NRA credit for its inspired use of effective messaging, however, does not make its argument valid. The fatal fallacy in the NRA's claim is that it poses a false choice, i.e., between strong enforcement of current laws and the enactment of new laws. The NRA has never been able to answer the question "If enacting new gun laws would save lives, why can't we have strong enforcement of current laws *and* enact new laws as needed?" It may well make sense for the feds to prosecute more Brady Act cases and felon-in-possession cases and to seek longer sentences for those gun crimes. Even if this is so, why is it a reason to oppose stronger gun laws? Let's take a specific example. We have seen that gun trafficking into the illegal market is regularly fed by dealers who make sales of multiple handguns to "straw purchasers" for gun traffickers. By prohibiting multiple sales, state "one gun a month" laws can disrupt gun trafficking; a federal law would be even more effective. Assuming, for the sake of argument, that US attorneys could prosecute more felon-in-possession cases than are now being brought, is this a sufficient reason to oppose the enactment of a federal law banning multiple handgun sales? Whether or not the feds are currently prosecuting the optimal number of felon-in-possession cases has nothing to do with the wisdom of a curb on multiple sales. Indeed, our experience with state "one gun a month" laws suggests that, by disrupting gun trafficking into the illegal market, those laws will prevent felons from acquiring guns in the first place.

The NRA's argument really amounts to the proposition that the solution to criminal gun violence is to increase federal prosecution and punishment of criminal offenders *instead of* enacting federal laws to prevent access to guns by criminals in the first place. What if our nation had applied this logic to the issue of airline security? Many years ago, airliners were plagued by frequent hijackings. From 1968 to 1972, there were 364 hijackings worldwide.[58] One solution could have been to simply impose harsher punishments on hijackers of American airplanes. An alternative was both to punish hijackers severely and require the airlines to do security checks on passengers to prevent them from bringing weapons aboard airplanes. The NRA's logic would have supported a policy of increasing penalties *instead of* implementing new preventive policies. Our nation followed a different course. In 1973, the Federal Aviation Administration issued an emergency rule making inspection of carry-on baggage and scanning of all passengers by airlines mandatory. In 1974, Congress required the same in new legislation.[59] As a result, the number of

American airplane hijackings has been sharply reduced. To the extent our preventive policies have failed (as in the 9/11 disaster), our response has been to tighten them, not abandon them in favor of a "punishment only" response.

When the NRA insists on greater enforcement of existing laws instead of enacting new laws, it also raises the question "How much more enforcement is enough?" Regardless of the number of prosecutions, more could be brought. Regardless of the level of punishment, it could always be increased. For the NRA, however, it is quite clear that *no degree of enforcement or punishment is enough to justify considering new gun laws.* In response to a group of mayors calling for enactment of new "common-sense gun legislation" to stem the flow of guns to criminals, Wayne LaPierre was quoted as saying, "You can have press conferences all day. Until you provide 100% enforcement of the existing laws, [criminals are] going to laugh at you, and . . . go about their business."[60] What is "100% enforcement"? Does it mean that we shouldn't consider enacting new federal gun laws unless every felon with a gun is caught and put in a federal prison? The NRA is clearly playing games here.[61]

Thus, the premise of the NRA's argument—that our nation must choose between strong enforcement and stronger laws—is simply wrong. The "choice" is a phony one. We should strongly enforce current laws, but not ignore the need for new laws that also make us safer. Indeed, sometimes new laws are needed to strengthen the enforcement of existing laws. I mentioned earlier that the Brady Act is a prime example of such a law. It was needed in order to enhance enforcement of the law as it existed before Brady, i.e., the law against gun dealers selling guns to felons and other prohibited purchasers. The NRA opposes these enforcement-enhancing new laws, *even if they help us enforce the law against those who have actually used guns in violent crime.* The best examples are laws promoting technology that helps catch perpetrators after their crimes have been committed.

. . .

As explained earlier, among available weapons that criminals could use in their activities, guns have lots of advantages. They also have one very big disadvantage: they leave evidence behind at crime scenes, namely bullets and cartridges. Unfortunately for criminals, every firearm leaves unique, reproducible markings on each bullet and cartridge case it fires. These markings are often referred to as "ballistic fingerprints." By comparing the markings on bullets and cartridges left at various crime scenes, trained forensic examiners can determine whether the same gun was used to commit multiple crimes. In the DC-area sniper case, during the fall of 2002, police used ballistic-identification analysis to establish that the multiple sniper shootings had been committed with the same gun. This kind of analysis can be done quickly using the federal computerized database of digital images of cartridge cases and bullets recovered in criminal investigations, known as the National Integrated Ballistic Information Network (NIBIN). The NIBIN system shortens and simplifies the ballistic-identification process for participating police agencies. Once the snipers had been arrested and their rifle taken into police custody, investigators also could test-fire the rifle and compare the ballistic fingerprints left by the rifle with those on the bullets at the crime scene. By doing so, they were able to connect the snipers' gun with those bullets and cartridges.

However, although police investigators could determine that the same gun had been used in multiple sniper attacks, before the sniper suspects had been arrested, the authorities had no way to determine which particular gun had been used. Why? Because there is no database of ballistic fingerprints of guns sold, only of some guns associated with crime. If gun manufacturers were required to test-fire every gun before it was shipped into commerce and transmit the digital images of the cartridge and bullets to a central federal database, law enforcement would have a powerful new investigative tool. Based on a spent cartridge at a crime scene, police could determine the serial number of the gun used in a shooting and then trace the gun to the person who bought it from a licensed dealer. In states with gun registration, police could extend the trace to subsequent buyers. Crimes with guns would be solved faster, criminals apprehended faster, and other crimes prevented. Indeed, such a ballistics database could actually deter some criminals from selecting guns as their weapons of choice, precisely because they would leave such a strong evidentiary trail. As we have seen, reducing the use of guns in crime reduces the lethality of crime.

Also promising is an even newer technology known as "microstamping." This involves the use of lasers to make microscopic engravings on the firing pin or breech face of a gun. When the gun is fired, these engravings are transferred to the discharged cartridge and can identify the make, model, and serial number of the firearm. This would permit the gun to be traced based on the spent cartridges left at a crime scene, but without the need for a database of ballistic fingerprints of all guns sold. California now requires all new semiautomatic pistols manufactured or sold in the state to be equipped with microstamping technology. Obviously, a federal law imposing such a requirement would be far superior to any state law.

The gun lobby constantly assures us it is in favor of severe punishment of gun criminals. Since it is difficult to punish criminals without catching them first, surely the NRA would support ballistic fingerprinting and microstamping as crime-fighting tools, right? Wrong. The NRA calls ballistic fingerprinting a "scheme" for "national gun registration"[62] and decries microstamping as "ammunition registration."[63] Of course, neither system need involve the registration of gun owners or gun sales. Under both systems, only gun owners associated with guns used in crime would be revealed to the authorities, in the same way that their identities are revealed to the authorities by crime-gun tracing as it's currently done. The advantage of these new systems is that a crime-gun trace can be done without police having custody of the gun used in the crime. The NRA's knee-jerk objection to these new technologies as "registration" reveals, once again, that the gun lobby is not really interested in punishing criminals. It opposes new gun laws, even if they help put gun criminals behind bars.

The NRA's slogan supporting "enforcement of existing laws" instead of "new laws" is the gun lobby at its cynical worst. A product of pollsters and focus groups, carefully constructed by the "messaging" gurus of the right wing to attack the Clinton administration and then the Obama administration, it should be admired for its success in helping to fend off additional gun control initiatives.

Its long-term impact is questionable though, for several reasons. First, the message has the wrong messengers. The NRA does not really believe in enforcing the laws we have; it actually despises most of those laws. Hypocrisy can remain hidden only for so long. Second, most people can understand that "enforcing current law" is a sufficient policy against gun violence only if "current law" is sufficient for the task. Where strong enforcement is difficult precisely because the law is so weak, the case for "new laws" is made. Finally, there is no reason why our national policy toward gun violence should be subject to an artificial "choice" between strong enforcement and strong laws. Ultimately, the message manipulation of the gun lobby will likely yield to the conclusion required by common sense: strong laws *and* strong enforcement of those laws.

CHAPTER SEVEN

Is Budweiser Responsible for Drunk Drivers?

This rhetorical question invokes a simple, and effective, analogy that helped to give the NRA and the gun industry one of their most important legislative victories in recent history. The analogy was used to oppose liability lawsuits against the gun industry and to argue in favor of the ill-named Protection of Lawful Commerce in Arms Act, signed into law by President Bush in 2005, to protect the industry from those lawsuits. When over two dozen urban municipalities filed suit against major gun manufacturers in the late 1990s, seeking to recover some of the crushing public cost of gun violence, the industry responded by arguing that just as the beer industry should not be legally responsible for drunk driving, gun manufacturers should not be legally responsible for the misuse of guns. "You can't sue the manufacturer of a firearm, any more than you can sue Budweiser when someone gets involved in a drunk-driving accident," explained attorney Larry Keane of the National Shooting Sports Foundation.[1]

Makes sense, doesn't it? The victim of gun violence should pursue legal remedies against the person who pulled the trigger, so the argument goes, not against the manufacturer of the gun. To impose liability on the manufacturer is to shift responsibility from the party who inflicted the harm to another party who had nothing to do with the harm. Years later, during his presidential campaign, Democratic senator Bernie Sanders (Vermont) tried to defend his vote ten years before in favor of the Commerce in Arms Act by similarly characterizing lawsuits against the gun industry: "If somebody has a gun and it falls into the hands of a murderer, and that murderer kills somebody with the gun, do you hold the gun manufacturer responsible? Not anymore than you would hold a hammer company responsible if somebody beat somebody over the head with a hammer."[2]

The argument would be sound if the only asserted basis for the industry's legal responsibility was that its products are used in crime. No accepted legal doctrine would support the idea that a gun's use by a criminal is a sufficient reason to hold the manufacturer or seller of a gun legally accountable for the crime. The problem with the Budweiser analogy is that the lawsuits attacked by the gun lobby have not been based on the simplistic and indefensible idea that the gun industry should be legally responsible simply because some people use guns to cause harm. The Budweiser analogy is yet another example of the gun lobby constructing an elaborate "straw man" and knocking it down. Yet this "straw man" framed the national debate over the legal liability of the gun industry. Taking advantage of years of spending by corporate America to demonize plaintiffs' trial lawyers under the banner of "tort reform," it was not difficult to sell the idea that lawsuits against the gun industry were the trial lawyers' latest outrage, after they were finished suing McDonald's for selling excessively hot coffee. A Gallup poll in July 1999 asked a national sample of adults: "Would you favor or oppose allowing local governments to sue gun manufacturers in order to recover the costs incurred because of gun violence in their areas?" Sixty-one percent were opposed.[3] The question, however, said nothing about the rationale for such lawsuits. During my career as a lawyer representing gun violence victims, I filed my share of lawsuits against the gun industry. But if I were asked by a pollster whether gun manufacturers should be sued simply because people commit violent acts with guns, I would certainly answer "no."

In fact, there are powerful arguments supporting the legal responsibility of gun manufacturers and sellers for much of the gun violence that plagues our nation. Gun manufacturers and sellers have made choices, in the way guns are designed and sold, that increase the risk of injury and death. When that risk becomes reality, those responsible should be held accountable in our courts.

AREN'T GUNS SUPPOSED TO BE UNSAFE?

Consider this tragic scenario, versions of which are repeated over and over again in gun-owning households across America: Two bored and curious teenage boys are at home, looking for something to do. One of the boys, wanting to impress the other, remembers his father's semiautomatic pistol, stored unsecured, with loaded ammunition magazines, in his parents' bedroom. He's been told time and again to never touch the gun without a parent being present, but he retrieves it anyway. He takes the loaded magazine out, thinking he has unloaded the gun. What he doesn't know, and what the gun's design conceals from him, is that there is a round remaining in the firing chamber. Wanting to demonstrate his prowess with a real gun, he playfully points the gun at his friend and pulls the trigger. In an instant, two young lives are shattered. One suffers death or serious injury; the other a lifetime of guilt and shame.

In chapter 2, I made mention of various laws that could prevent such a tragedy. A child-access prevention (CAP) law could have deterred the parent from leaving a loaded pistol accessible to the teenagers. If guns were regulated as other consumer products, the government could have required the pistol to have additional safety features, such as a load indicator, which could have alerted the teen that the gun was still loaded, or a magazine disconnect safety, which would have prevented the pistol from firing after the magazine had been removed, or a personalization system, which would have allowed only the parent to fire the gun. Leaving aside, for a moment, the issue of what laws could prevent such shootings, there is the separate question of how our legal system should allocate responsibility when a shooting occurs. We have a civil-justice system that functions to award damages to innocent persons injured by the wrongdoing of others. When it's working as it should, the system compensates injured persons and deters similar wrongdoing by others. In the teen shooting scenario, who, if anyone, should be required to pay damages to the victim or his family?

There is certainly enough blame to spread around. The boy who pulled the trigger was certainly irresponsible in ignoring his parents' instructions, along with every rule of safe gun handling. But liability need not be confined to a single party, even if he was more responsible for the injury than anyone else. It is commonplace for our legal system to attach responsibility to multiple parties whose irresponsibility may have contributed to a single injury. We don't want to let a negligent party off the hook simply because others also were negligent in causing the injury. Therefore, in addition to the teen shooter, the adult gun owner arguably should be accountable for failing to take proper precautions to prevent access to the gun by his underage son. For example, a Louisiana court held that a gun owner could be liable for a shooting by a nine-year-old, even though the gun had been stored on a high shelf in a closet and the child had been instructed not to go into the closet. The court found that possession of a loaded gun carried with it a duty of "extraordinary care" that was not met by a "simple warning . . . that the pistol was off-limits and the placing of the pistol on a closet shelf."[4] But, in our teen shooting scenario, what about the manufacturer of the gun? Is there any basis to hold the manufacturer legally responsible for the shooting? After all, the gun wasn't "defective" in the ordinary sense of the word. The gun, unfortunately, operated exactly as it was designed to operate. The child pulled the trigger. The gun fired.

A strong case can be made, though, that the shooting could have been prevented had the manufacturer chosen to incorporate feasible, low-cost safety mechanisms in the gun. A magazine-disconnect safety, for example, would cost the gun maker less than thirty cents to install but would block discharge of a round if the magazine is out of the gun. Some pistols have them; most do not. Moreover, gun manufacturers know that this kind of accident happens *over and over again.* They know it happens, and they know that a feasible, low-cost design change could save lives. Given these facts, why should the manufacturer of the gun in our teen shooting scenario escape all responsibility?

The concept of "defect" in product-liability law is far broader than the ordinary meaning of "defect" as a malfunction of the product. The Ford Motor Company was held liable because the placement of the fuel tank in its Pinto model caused fires in rear-end collisions. Even though the fuel tank's placement did not cause the car to malfunction, the car's design was "defective" because it created an unreasonable risk that passengers would be incinerated following a collision. A product also can be defective in design because it lacks feasible safety mechanisms, even if it was perfectly manufactured and operated exactly as intended. For example, the Ohio Supreme Court held that the manufacturer of a disposable lighter could be liable for failing to "child-proof" its products to prevent children from using them. The court wrote: "[A] product may be found defective in design . . . where the manufacturer fails to incorporate feasible safety features to prevent harm caused by foreseeable human error."[5] Manufacturers can be liable even though human errors contributed to the injury—the error of the child in misusing the lighter to start a fire and the error of the adult in leaving the lighter accessible to the child. The key to liability is the "foreseeability" of the errors to the manufacturer of the product. In the disposable lighter case, the Ohio Supreme Court cited statistics showing that 5,800 residential fires, 170 deaths, and almost 1,200 injuries occur each year from children under five playing with lighters. "Lighters are commonly used and kept around the home," the Court wrote, "and it is reasonably foreseeable that children would have access to them and attempt to use them."[6]

Substitute "guns" for "lighters" and the statement is just as true. Because it is foreseeable to gun manufacturers that gun owners will leave guns accessible to minors and that minors will misuse them, gun manufacturers should also be held to a duty to design their products to prevent such misuse. As we have seen, thousands of kids die or are injured in gun accidents every year. Even though major gun manufacturers typically include warnings urging gun owners to store their guns unloaded, locked, and with gun and ammunition inaccessible to children, studies show that millions of gun owners disregard those warnings. One survey found that 20 percent of all gun-owning households—and 30 percent of handgun-owning households—had a loaded, unlocked gun in the home.[7] An estimated 2.6 million children live in homes where at least one gun is stored either unlocked and loaded, or unlocked with the ammunition at the same location as the gun.[8] In one study of eighty-eight California children under the age of fifteen who were unintentionally shot by other children or by themselves, "[t]he most common case history was of children playing with a gun that had been stored loaded, unlocked, and out of view; the shooting often occurred in the room where the gun was stored."[9] Gun makers need not have to read academic surveys to know that kids have access to guns in the home and use them to kill and injure other kids. The constant and depressing drumbeat of headlines reporting the individual tragedies establishes the "foreseeability" of these accidents. The Ohio Supreme Court, the same court that recognized the potential liability of manufacturers of disposable lighters for fires caused by children, four years later found that gun makers could be similarly liable for failing "to incorporate feasible safety features to prevent foreseeable injuries."[10]

Other courts have made similar rulings. In one New Jersey case, a police officer had left his house one morning, leaving behind his fully loaded Glock semiautomatic in its holster, completely unsecured.[11] Tyrone Hurst, the fifteen-year-old son of the officer's girlfriend, found the gun and showed it to his teenage friend as they prepared to walk to school together. Tyrone removed the magazine from the pistol and put in on the kitchen table. Thinking it was unloaded, his friend picked up the pistol, pointed it at Tyrone, and pulled the trigger, hitting him in the head. In finding that Glock could be liable (in addition to the police officer and Tyrone's friend), the court noted the testimony of experts that patents for magazine-disconnect safeties had been granted as far back as 1910 because of the well-recognized danger of accidental firings after removal of the magazine from the gun.[12] Lest there be any doubt about the foreseeability of such accidents, the court quoted from an NRA magazine in 1957, noting "accidents caused by people thinking they have unloaded the gun when they have merely removed the magazine and left a cartridge in the chamber."[13]

Even in "gun friendly" states, courts have recognized the legal liability of gun makers for failing to build safety into their products. For example, in 2001, the New Mexico Court of Appeals decided that Bryco Arms, a notorious manufacturer of cheap, low-quality but highly concealable "Saturday Night Special" handguns, could be liable for failing to install magazine-disconnect safeties in its guns.[14] Like so many others, the case involved teenage boys fooling around with a handgun they thought they had unloaded by removing the magazine. Recognizing a gun manufacturer's "duty to consider risks of injury created by foreseeable misuse" of its products,[15] the court allowed the teenaged victim, who had survived being shot in the face by his friend, to proceed with his lawsuit against Bryco. Incredibly, Bryco officials testified in the case that in making and selling the J-22 handgun involved in the shooting, they "did not consider additional safety devices for the J-22; that no product analyses were conducted on the J-22; that no one reviews Bryco products to see if they can be made safer; and that Bryco did not investigate what other manufacturers were doing to make their firearms safer."[16] Can you imagine an auto manufacturer that did not review its products "to see if they can be made safer"? Product-liability lawsuits eventually drove Bryco into well-deserved bankruptcy, but many thousands of its handguns remain in circulation.

The gun industry concocts a host of arguments to avoid legal responsibility for failing to make its products safer.

First, the industry argues that guns are different from other products because their entire purpose is to be dangerous; indeed, they are desired by consumers because they are dangerous. This is an entirely legitimate distinction that, as I have argued, justifies a degree and kind of regulation—for example, criminal background checks on gun buyers—that we would not impose on other potentially dangerous products. It is a distinction, however, that furnishes no excuse for gun makers to design products that are unnecessarily unsafe. Although guns are designed to be lethal, presumably neither the manufacturer nor the consumer intends that they be used to accidentally kill or injure anyone. To the extent that guns can be designed to reduce the risk of accidental discharge, but still serve their lethal purpose, gun makers should be legally accountable if they make design choices that expose gun consumers and the public to unnecessary risks. As the New Mexico Court of Appeals in the Bryco case cogently argued, "The fact that handguns are meant to fire projectiles which can cause great harm is to our view all the more reason to allow the tort system to assess whether the product is reasonably designed to prevent or help avoid unintended—albeit careless—firings such as occurred here."[17]

Second, gun makers go to elaborate lengths to imagine shooting scenarios in which safety devices will impede the use of the gun. "What if you're in a firefight with a criminal," they argue, "and the magazine drops out of your pistol? With a magazine-disconnect safety, you can't fire the round left in the chamber." Product-liability law, however, requires courts to assess both the risks and benefits of alternative product designs versus the current design.[18] Most safety features on products are not risk free. There are cases in which seat belts and air bags have caused injury or death, instead of preventing them. The issue is whether the risks of the safety feature are outweighed by the benefits. It is difficult to believe that magazine-disconnect safeties, load indicators, and internal locks would cost nearly as many lives as they would save.

Third, the industry argues that gun makers should not be liable for the negligent acts of others. Here the industry's favorite tactic is to blame its customers. If a gun owner is stupid enough to leave a gun accessible to a child, and to fail to keep the child away from the gun, the industry asserts, the gun owner should be legally responsible, not the manufacturer. As we have seen, though, it is well established in the law that manufacturers are held to a duty to design their products to reduce the risk of injury from product misuse that is reasonably foreseeable. Most auto accidents involve some kind of driver negligence, often involving illegal conduct like speeding or running stop signs. Yet we don't insulate car makers from liability because their customers make mistakes, often egregious ones. Moreover, imposing liability on gun makers for injuries involving the tragic mistakes of gun owners does not "make the manufacturer liable for the negligence of others." The gun manufacturer is not liable for the gun owner's conduct but for the manufacturer's own unreasonable choices. The manufacturer has choices in the design of its guns. It can install a magazine-disconnect safety, or a load indicator, or an internal lock—or it can omit those features. In the cases I have discussed, courts have recognized that a gun maker can be liable not for the gun owner's misconduct, but for the manufacturer's own choices that expose people to an unreasonable risk of harm. Nor does the manufacturer's liability insulate the negligent gun owner from liability. Under well-accepted law, their liability is shared.

The gun industry's efforts to shift all responsibility for tragic accidents to gun owners is supremely ironic because the industry's marketing of its products—particularly handguns—actually has encouraged its customers to engage in dangerous conduct. In court, the industry decries gun owners who leave loaded handguns in the nightstand and claims it had no way of anticipating such reckless behavior by its customers. But for years, this same industry has tried to sell more handguns by exploiting the fear of being defenseless against a violent home intruder—precisely the fear that leads gun owners to store loaded guns unlocked in the nightstand. In one notorious ad by Colt's Manufacturing Company, which appeared in a 1992 Southeast regional edition of *Ladies Home Journal*, a mother was seen tucking her young daughter into bed at night, a darkened window in the background. The headline read "Self-Protection Is More Than Your Right . . . It's Your Responsibility." The ad recommended the purchase of a Colt semiautomatic pistol "for protecting yourself and your loved ones" and compared a firearm to a home fire extinguisher, stating, "It may be better to have it and not need it, than to need it and not have it." The message to young mothers? That danger lurks in the night outside your home; that if you care about protecting your child's safety, buying a gun is practically a moral obligation, and that failing to have a gun may expose your child to great harm. Of course, the ad failed to disclose that, according to the best available scientific evidence, bringing a gun into the home will expose that young family to far more danger than not having a gun. Apart from the deceptiveness of the message conveyed, there is surely no doubt that consumers convinced by such fear-based advertising to buy handguns are more likely to store their guns at the ready for immediate self-defensive use, loaded and unlocked.

Another fear-mongering ad by Beretta went even further by actually depicting irresponsible gun storage. The ad showed a Beretta .380 semiautomatic pistol and a bullet for the gun sitting unsecured on what appeared to be a nightstand table. Next to the gun were a photo of a woman with two young children and an alarm clock showing the time as 11:26 p.m. The headline read "Tip the Odds in Your Favor." The text addressed those who are "considering a handgun for personal protection." Here the message was plainly addressed to single mothers: the night holds great danger for you and your children, and you need every advantage to repel a home invader. Incredibly, a pistol was shown unsecured on a nightstand next to its equally unsecured ammunition, in a home with two young kids, thus depicting a consumer who has disregarded Beretta's warnings, and every sensible rule of safe gun storage. It is as if General Motors ran an ad showing one of its cars with the driver and young children unsecured by seat belts, after warning in its owner's manual that seat belts should always be buckled. Yet Beretta has argued in product-liability lawsuits that it should escape all liability for accidental shootings caused by parents who leave guns accessible to children.

Finally, the industry argues that those who want to require safety features on guns should take their case to legislative bodies, not courts. If this argument justifies exempting gun makers from legal liability, then it should justify a similar exemption from makers of other dangerous products. Yet the courts did not dismiss the liability lawsuits against Ford on the ground that the only remedy for victims of exploding Pintos was to seek greater safety regulation of autos from Congress. With other industries, it is recognized that the incentives for safer products originate from two sources: regulatory bodies created by legislatures and the threat of damages awarded by courts. Thus, cars are subject to both the regulatory requirements of the National Highway Traffic Safety Administration and the civil liability system. Other consumer products are subject to safety standards and recalls under the Consumer Product Safety Act, but they are certainly not exempt from product-liability lawsuits. As discussed previously, courts have held that disposable-lighter manufacturers can be liable for failing to child-proof their lighters. The Consumer Product Safety Commission also has issued safety standards requiring cigarette lighters to be child-resistant. For products other than guns, the regulatory system and the civil liability system work in tandem to create incentives for safer products. The gun industry's argument amounts to pleading for special, favored treatment for makers and sellers of the most dangerous consumer product of all.

For any product, not just guns, safety standards set by legislators and regulators are no substitute for accountability in court for selling unsafe products. When a legislature gives a regulatory body the power to set safety standards, those standards operate only prospectively. If working properly, they make products safer, but they compensate no victims who have been injured by the manufacture and sale of unsafe products in the first place. Nor do safety standards hold companies accountable for their decision to sell unsafe products; they require them only to change those products. If product manufacturers and sellers are exempt from civil liability for unsafe products, they have to fear only that someday a regulatory agency will order them to change their products. They will nevertheless be able to retain the profits from the past sale of unsafe products with no accountability for the damage those products caused. Obviously the threat of civil damages to injured persons is a powerful incentive to make safer products. The prospect of future safety standards set by a regulatory body, although important, is a far weaker incentive.

Of course, it is particularly disingenuous for the gun industry to argue that product safety should be a matter for legislatures and regulators, instead of courts, since, as we have seen, *the gun industry is already exempt from federal product-safety regulation.* Having achieved an exemption from safety regulation that applies to other consumer products, the gun industry now has an exemption from the civil liability system as well. The result is that gun makers have little reason to fear being held accountable for the deaths of children that could have been prevented with feasible, inexpensive safety features. Gun manufacturers are now protected from liability when kids unintentionally kill their friends because they took the magazine out of a pistol, thinking the gun was unloaded, even though a simple device could have prevented it from firing.[19]

With the NRA at your back, the gun industry has shown that anything is possible. Gun makers must be the envy of every other industry.

BLAME THE CRIMINALS, NOT THE GUN INDUSTRY

Setting aside the issue of unsafe guns, the gun industry will argue that it at least deserves protection from lawsuits seeking to blame it for the use of guns in crime. How could the company that made the gun, or sold the gun, be legally responsible when the gun is used in a criminal act? At least a gun's design is the product of a gun-maker's decisions. How could the decisions of a gun maker or seller have anything to do with the harm inflicted by criminals using guns?

In fact, gun manufacturers and sellers repeatedly make irresponsible business decisions that increase the risk of criminal gun violence. And well-established legal principles support their liability to the victims of those decisions. Consider, for example, one of the worst mass shootings in American history and the supplier of the gun used in the shooting.

Gian Luigi Ferri was a gunman with a grudge. A failed businessman, he blamed his misfortunes on lawyers, particularly those at the prestigious law firm that once represented him, San Francisco's now-defunct Pettit & Martin. On July 1, 1993, Ferri stepped onto an elevator at the sleek high-rise office building at 101 California Street in San Francisco's financial district. He was toting a briefcase containing enough firepower for a small army. He pushed the button to take him to the Pettit & Martin offices on the 34th floor and then proceeded to quickly and efficiently unpack the briefcase and prepare for his mission: to kill as many lawyers as possible.[20] By the time he stepped onto the 34th floor, he had two TEC-DC9 assault pistols strapped across his chest, equipped with high-capacity ammunition magazines containing from forty to fifty rounds of 9mm ammunition, along with a .45 caliber handgun.

He quickly came upon a conference room where a deposition was being conducted. Raking it with gunfire through its curtained windows and then entering the room and continuing to fire, Ferri killed lawyer Jack Berman and witness Jody Sposato, while wounding lawyer Deana Eaves and court reporter Sharon O'Roke. Berman and Sposato were shot five or six times each. Ferri calmly walked out of the conference room and proceeded down a hallway, methodically shooting down anyone who looked like a lawyer. In a matter of minutes, on three floors of the building, Ferri killed eight people and wounded six others. With the firepower of the TEC-DC9s allowing him to fire scores of rounds without pausing to reload, Ferri was able to, in the words of a police investigator, "walk through the building as if invulnerable." On the 33rd floor, Ferri found John Scully, a young lawyer, and his wife, Michelle, hiding in the corner of John's office. John covered Michelle with his body, suffering several fatal wounds as he saved the life of his young bride. On the 32nd floor, where Ferri mistakenly entered the offices of Trust Company of the West, he spray-fired Mike Merrill's office, killing him with four shots, shot Victoria Smith five times in her office (she survived), and shot Shirley Mooser four times and Deborah Fogel nine times. Finally, retreating to a stairwell as the police approached, Ferri committed suicide.

In planning his deadly mission, Ferri chose, as his primary weapon, the TEC-DC9, a gun especially well adapted to a military-style assault on multiple targets. In a lawsuit brought by some of the 101 California victims and their families against Navegar, Inc., the gun's manufacturer, police experts described the TEC-DC9 gun as a "military-patterned weapon" of the type "typically issued to specialized forces such as security personnel, special operations forces, or border guards." The gun's standard 32-round ammunition magazine could be emptied in seconds, and the gun could be equipped with even larger capacity magazines, as Ferri did. This was firepower of the kind "associated with military or police, not civilian shooting requirements," as one expert testified. A police firearms expert testified that the TEC-DC9 was designed especially for "spray-fire" from the hip and was "completely useless for hunting," with "no legitimate sporting use." Government crime-gun statistics confirmed the popularity of the gun with criminals. One study found it "disproportionately associated with criminal activity." As the Bureau of Alcohol, Tobacco, and Firearms said about assault weapons like the TEC-DC9: "You will not find these guns in a duck blind or at the Olympics. They are mass-produced mayhem." Navegar's executives were acutely aware of the mayhem and seemed to revel in it. Michael Solodovnick, the company's marketing director, when asked about reports of TEC-DC9's popularity among criminals, told the *New York Times* that he was "kind of flattered" by such talk. "Hey, it's talked about, it's read about, the media write about it," he added. "That generates more sales for me. It might sound cold and cruel, but I'm sales oriented." Referring to the use of an AK-47 type assault rifle to murder school children in Stockton, California, Mike "Solo," as he was nicknamed, commented that "whenever anything negative has happened, sales have gone tremendously high."

Navegar's own advertising made it clear that the company did not have sportsmen in mind as its "target market." Its ads, in magazines like *Soldier of Fortune, SWAT,* and *Combat Handguns,* referred to the gun as an "assault-type" pistol, with "excellent resistance to fingerprints." In a sworn deposition, Solo acknowledged that this representation could be interpreted to mean that "fingerprints would not be left on this weapon," a feature uniquely interesting to those intending to use the gun in a criminal act. During his tenure as Navegar's marketing director, Solo was indicted for conspiracy to violate federal gun laws by distributing manuals and videotapes on how to illegally convert semiautomatic assault weapons to fully automatic fire.

When confronted with these facts about Navegar's TEC-DC9 and the company's conduct in marketing it, the California Court of Appeal ruled, in September of 1999, that the victims of the 101 California Street massacre had a valid legal claim against Navegar for negligence in the design and sale of the gun. The court acknowledged that because "the risk of harm from the criminal misuse of firearms is always present" in a society in which the presence of firearms is widespread, a gun maker may not be found negligent merely because it manufactures and sells guns. However, the court found that gun makers have a "duty to use due care not to increase the risk beyond that inherent in the presence of firearms in our society."[21] The court ruled the evidence sufficient to allow the victims to go to trial, not because Navegar had acted illegally but rather because "the manner in which Navegar manufactured and marketed the TEC DC-9 and made it available to the general public created risks above and beyond those citizens may reasonably be expected to bear."[22]

As with cases involving unintentional shootings, the foreseeability of the harm is key to legal liability for those whose negligence contributed to a criminal act. As the court made clear in the *Navegar* case, a negligent actor can be liable even where the injury was inflicted by the *criminal* act of another, if the criminal act was the foreseeable result of the negligence. For example, courts have held that the owner of a vehicle who left the keys in the ignition in a high-crime area may be liable for injuries inflicted by a thief who recklessly caused an accident.[23] The court wrote in *Navegar*: "Here, the likelihood that a third person would make use of the TEC DC-9 in the kind of criminal rampage Ferri perpetrated is *precisely* the hazard that would support a determination that Navegar's conduct was negligent." "It is immaterial," the court concluded, "whether the hazardous conduct . . . is negligent or criminal."[24] In *Navegar*, it borders on the frivolous to suggest that the company that advertised its gun as an "assault-type pistol" with "excellent resistance to fingerprints" had no reason to foresee that its gun would be used in a criminal assault.

The appeals court ruling in the *Navegar* case was later reversed by the California Supreme Court, but not because the victims' legal claim lacked merit under general principles of liability law.[25] Rather, the State Supreme Court held that, regardless of its validity under those principles, the case was barred by a statute passed by the California legislature in 1982 to limit the liability of the gun industry. Because Justice Kathryn Mickle Werdegar, the dissenting judge and the appointee of a Republican governor, found the 1982 statute inapplicable, she was the only California Supreme Court justice to address the validity of the claims under general legal principles. She found that the victims should have been allowed to go to trial. "The evidence . . . in this case demonstrated that Navegar's management not only should have known, but actually did know, that the technical and aesthetic characteristics of the TEC-9/DC9, together with its price, the manner of its promotion, and Navegar's instructions for its use, attracted criminal and mentally ill segments of the civilian gun market, foreseeably leading to the kind of mayhem that has produced this lawsuit."[26]

The *Navegar* case, then, furnishes a powerful response to the idea that gun manufacturers and sellers should never be liable for injuries inflicted by their products. But, it may be argued, Navegar's conduct certainly was not typical of the gun industry. It manufactured an extreme product and promoted it in an extreme manner. Should makers and sellers of conventional firearms, marketed in conventional ways, be legally responsible when their guns are used in crime?

Internal industry documents uncovered in other liability cases, along with the testimony of industry insiders, show that "conventional" gun makers and sellers also increase the risk of gun violence by violating the duty of using due care in their business activities. Although their negligence may seem less sensational than Navegar's, it is arguably far more damaging to public health and safety.

A FEW BAD APPLES

We have seen that massive numbers of guns move rapidly from licensed gun dealers into the illegal market. In the words of the former chief of ATF's Crime Gun Analysis Branch, "The most important single source of firearms for the illegal market is still illegal traffickers who are acquiring firearms from retail outlets."[27] We know that gun traffickers buy large numbers of guns from gun shops, often using "straw buyers." As we have seen, because of this close connection between licensed dealers and the criminal market, strong regulation of licensed dealers can help dry up the supply of illegal guns. But this connection between gun dealers and illegal guns also raises a different issue: to what extent should gun dealers be held legally accountable for criminal gun violence?

Crime-gun trace data reveals an astonishing fact: *almost 60 percent of crime guns originate with only 1 percent of licensed gun dealers.*[28] This strongly suggests that the conduct of a relatively small number of gun dealers is feeding the supply of illegal guns. Especially when you consider that, *in a typical year, 85 percent of gun dealers sell no guns traced to crime.*[29]

Take Traders Sports of San Leandro, California, outside Oakland. In 2005 alone, 447 crime guns were traced to Traders Sports, making it the second largest supplier of crime guns of any retailer in the country.[30] Traders Sports supplied 46 percent of the crime guns recovered in Oakland;[31] in 2005, law enforcement recovered crime guns sold by Traders at an average rate of more than one every day.[32]

The gun industry typically claims that a large number of crime-gun traces doesn't necessary suggest a dealer is "doing anything wrong," but may simply be due to the dealer's large sales volume. According to the industry, dealers who sell lots of guns necessarily will have more guns end up being used in crime than smaller-volume dealers. A nice theory, but it doesn't reflect reality. In the case of Traders Sports, for example, the shop's crime-gun traces during the period 2003–2005 amounted to approximately 12 percent of its sales volume, a startling average of one of every eight guns sold traced to crime.[33] During the same period, two other large-volume California dealers had crime-gun traces constituting only 4 percent and 1 percent of their sales, respectively.[34] An internal study by the ATF reported the results of intensive government inspections of the

1 percent of dealers across the nation that had ten or more crime-gun traces in 1999. Although these high-trace dealers accounted for more than 50 percent of crime guns in 1999, they accounted for less than 20 percent of guns sold in that year. The ATF report concluded, "Sales volume alone does not account for the disproportionately large number of traces associated with these firearms dealers."[35] A later study of California gun dealers also found that a dealer's sales volume could not account for differences in the number of handguns traced to crime.[36]

What are these "high-risk" gun dealers doing that makes them such a dependable source of guns for traffickers?

First, far too many gun dealers are willing to facilitate "straw purchases" for gun traffickers because they don't think they'll be caught. In chapter 2, I related the case of two New Jersey police officers who were grievously wounded with a gun sold by a West Virginia dealer to an obvious straw buyer for an out-of-state gun trafficker. Chicago and Wayne County, Michigan, filed suit against local gun dealers after conducting videotaped sting operations in which undercover officers posed as straw purchasing teams. In Chicago, undercover officers were able to purchase hundreds of firearms from suburban dealers, even though the person picking out the weapons and paying for them was not the person filling out the federal paperwork, in violation of federal law. Officers even went so far as to indicate to the dealers they wanted the guns to settle scores or engage in other illegal activity, but they were still not turned away.[37] Wayne County conducted similar stings of ten suburban dealers, and nine were willing to make an obvious straw sale. During one transaction, after being informed that the gun buyer had a felony record, a store clerk at a Sports Authority coached the undercover officer posing as a straw buyer:

> "When the manager comes over to check this, it's your gun."
> "You're not purchasing it for him."
> "This is called a straw purchase."
> "It's highly illegal."

"I don't know why . . . it's just . . ."

"They consider it highly illegal."

After openly acknowledging its illegality, the clerk nevertheless completed the sale and handed a gun and two boxes of ammunition to the officer posing as a convicted felon.[38] A study that tracked illegal gun-trafficking indicators over time found that the Chicago and Wayne County lawsuits were associated with significant reductions in the flow of new handguns to criminals.[39] More recently, New York City used undercover investigators to conduct similar stings on dealers in five states that accounted for large numbers of New York crime guns. Twenty-seven dealers were videotaped completing obvious straw sales.[40] The offending dealers were then sued by New York City, and nearly all the defendant dealers settled the cases by agreeing to sweeping changes in their business practices to prevent illegal sales. A subsequent study showed a post-lawsuit reduction in the odds that guns sold by those same gun shops would be recovered as a crime gun in New York City.[41] Clearly, gun dealers are far too willing to engage in illegal sales. When those practices are challenged in court, it diminishes the flow of guns into the illegal market. Also, even if straw buyers are not involved, dealers often sell such large quantities of guns to single buyers that the dealers must know the guns will be sold into the underground market. In chapter 1, I recounted the serial racial shootings committed by white supremacist Benjamin Nathaniel Smith. Since Smith was under a domestic-violence restraining order, a background check had blocked him from buying a gun from a licensed dealer.[42] Instead, he turned to the classified section of the Peoria, Illinois, newspaper, which featured ads placed by a gun trafficker named Donald Fiessinger.[43] Fiessinger, in turn, was supplied by a licensed dealer, Old Prairie Trading Post of Pekin, Illinois. Fiessinger routinely purchased the same make and model of Bryco handguns from Old Prairie, reselling them for a substantial profit. Over a two-year period, the dealer sold Fiessinger seventy-two Bryco handguns. The sales were staggered in an obvious effort to avoid the federal notice requirement for sales of two or more handguns in a five-day period. During a six-month stretch in 1998, Fiessinger received one gun from Old Prairie every Monday for twenty-five consecutive weeks.[44]

Or take the case of Sauers Trading, a licensed dealer in South Williamsport, Pennsylvania, that sold eleven guns to drug-addicted gun trafficker Perry Bruce, all cheap, easily concealable handguns with the exception of one assault pistol, a TEC-9.[45] Bruce used his welfare card for identification and gave his occupation as "unemployed," yet he paid for his guns with thousands of dollars in cash.[46] On at least one occasion, a Sauers sales clerk waited until all other customers had left the store before selling to Bruce.[47] Bruce testified that when he bought guns from Sauers, he often was high on drugs.[48] He also testified that Sauers "had to know what I was doing."[49] One of the guns Sauers sold to Bruce was used to shoot and kill seven-year-old Nafis Jefferson on a street in South Philadelphia.[50]

Should these dealers be liable in damages for the harm inflicted in these shootings? Certainly where their conduct is illegal—like knowingly engaging in straw sales—they should be liable, just as a tavern should be liable for knowingly selling alcohol to a minor. But gun dealers can engage in very dangerous conduct that violates no laws, or at least exposes them to little danger of prosecution, because our gun laws are so weak and because the gun lobby has succeeded in making them so difficult to enforce. As we have seen, under federal law a dealer can legally sell a hundred assault weapons to a single buyer, even though there is little doubt that those guns will end up in the underground market. However, as we saw with the *Navegar* case, a defendant's conduct can be entirely legal, yet still be so irresponsible, and create such a foreseeable risk of harm, that it can be the basis for civil liability to its victims.

For example, in a landmark ruling, the Florida Supreme Court unanimously held that Kmart could be liable for the sale of a rifle to Thomas Knapp, who had consumed a fifth of whiskey and a case of beer up until he left a local bar to travel to the Kmart to buy a gun.[51] Although there was no direct evidence that the clerk knew Knapp was drunk, he required help with filling out the required paperwork because his handwriting was so illegible. Shortly after the purchase, Knapp returned to the bar, waited until his estranged girlfriend, Deborah Kitchen, left the bar, followed her car, forced it off the road, and shot her in the neck. She was rendered a permanent quadriplegic by the wound. While recognizing that Kmart violated no statute in selling a gun to an obviously intoxicated buyer, the court nevertheless upheld a jury's award of damages to Deborah Kitchen. It was not enough, said the Florida Supreme Court, for Kmart to act legally; rather, because firearms are "dangerous instrumentalities," the "highest degree of care is necessary . . . to avoid injuries to others."[52] Other courts also have held gun dealers can be liable for a wide range of negligent conduct, even though it violated no law, including selling to a buyer showing signs of mental illness,[53] failing to take reasonable precautions to guard against theft of firearms,[54] or failing to institute sufficient controls to account for the firearms taken into inventory.[55]

Given the general principle that gun dealers owe the "highest degree of care" to avoid injury, a strong case can be made for civil liability for dealer conduct that funnels guns into the criminal market, even if the conduct is not illegal or cannot be proven to violate a statute. Dealers like Donald Fiessinger or Sauers Trading, who have every reason to believe they are supplying gun traffickers, create a foreseeable risk of harm at least as great as the Kmart clerk who sold to an intoxicated Thomas Knapp. Such dealers should be held accountable, not because their guns were used in violent crimes but because their own irresponsible conduct *enabled* those guns to be used in violent crimes.

SEE NO EVIL, HEAR NO EVIL, SPEAK NO EVIL

But, the industry will argue, even if it may be appropriate to hold a few gun dealers accountable for selling guns to traffickers, why should gun manufacturers be liable? The manufacturers did not sell guns to straw buyers or gun traffickers. Nor were they even aware of these transactions. Returning to our alcohol analogy, the industry will argue that even if a tavern can be liable for selling beer to a minor, or for continuing to supply a customer long after he has become intoxicated, surely Budweiser cannot be liable for the tavern's irresponsibility.

This sounds like a reasonable position, until we imagine a different set of facts about Budweiser. What if Budweiser knew that almost 60 percent of drunk drivers were served by about 1 percent of the nation's taverns? What if Budweiser had the means to know the identities of those taverns and thus the means to know whether those taverns were serving Budweiser? What if the government actually offered to give Budweiser the information by which it could identify that 1 percent of taverns? What if Budweiser had made a conscious decision to remain ignorant of the identities of those taverns and, indeed, had refused the government's offer for help? What if Budweiser could enforce a code of conduct on those taverns to prevent irresponsible sales of beer and had refused to do so, even after being urged to take action by people within the beer industry and by the government? If these facts were true, then Budweiser's conduct would be far more similar to the conduct of gun makers. The dirty little secret of the gun industry is that manufacturers have maintained a conscious policy of "hear no evil, see no evil, speak no evil" when it comes to the stark reality of corrupt gun dealers.

How is it that gun makers can know so much about which gun dealers are funneling the most guns into the criminal market? The story starts with crime-gun tracing.

As we have seen, ATF has, for many years, traced guns recovered by law-enforcement authorities in connection with criminal investigations. A trace involves using the serial number of the recovered gun to document the sales history of the gun down to the first retail buyer from a licensed dealer. By its nature, a crime-gun trace begins with the manufacturer, whose name, after all, appears on the gun itself. The manufacturer then discloses to ATF the identity of the distributor, who discloses the dealer, who discloses the first purchaser. Each ATF trace request, therefore, notifies the manufacturer that one of its guns has been associated with a crime.[56] There is, of course, no doubt that the manufacturer could find out, from its own distributors, the identity of the dealer that sold each of those crime guns. Every gun manufacturer is capable of collecting information, from its own distributors and dealers, about how many of its dealers' guns have been traced to crime. It also could find out how many of those guns were traced a short time after they were sold, an indicator of gun trafficking. In short, each manufacturer could know, if it wanted to, whether its guns are being sold by the small minority of dealers who are the primary source of the crime-gun problem. But no gun manufacturer wants to know. Apparently, they prefer to be willfully ignorant. This makes it easier for them to avoid all responsibility for the problem, while they profit from each dealer sale to a straw purchaser or a gun trafficker.

Incredibly, gun makers even refused such information when the government offered to give it to them. In February 2000, ATF offered to provide gun manufacturers and importers with a list, by serial number, of their guns that had been traced as crime guns during the previous year.[57] ATF made this offer of data to "enable the manufacturers and importers to police the distribution of the firearms they sell." ATF reiterated this offer in correspondence with specific manufacturers. For example, Special Agent Forrest Webb wrote to gun maker Taurus suggesting that it should use tracing data to determine whether "there is an unusually high number of Taurus firearms being traced to certain Federal firearms licensees" and advising that in such a case Taurus "look at [the licensees'] business practices more carefully."[58] This obviously was ATF's modest effort to enlist manufacturers like Taurus to help the bureau combat trafficking from licensed dealers. In response, Taurus did nothing. Likewise, gun maker Sturm, Ruger responded to ATF's offer of data with a letter making it clear that the company wanted no part of the tracing information, adding that it would rather rely on ATF itself to address problems with Ruger's dealers funneling guns to crime.[59]

The ATF trace data, by clarifying and quantifying the connection between the industry's distribution system and the illegal market, was profoundly threatening to the industry. It also was threatening to the NRA because it suggested that regulation of the legal gun market could reduce the flow of guns to the illegal market. For the gun lobby, the solution was to suppress the data itself, through what became known as the Tiahrt Amendments to appropriations legislation funding ATF's activities. The Tiahrt Amendments, named after then congressman Todd Tiahrt, since 2003 have barred the use of federal funds to disclose trace data to the public.[60] When he introduced the amendment, Representative Tiahrt explained, "I wanted to make sure I was fulfilling the needs of my friends who are firearms dealers."[61] It also has given the manufacturers a ready excuse for not using the trace data to identify problem dealers. The Tiahrt Amendments, like the restrictions on CDC-funded research into gun violence, exemplify the "ignorance is bliss" approach of the NRA and gun industry: when the inconvenient truths about guns start to emerge, make sure the public knows as little as possible. Data is a strong antidote to mythology.

The manufacturers' willful ignorance of ATF crime-gun trace data is only part of a broader strategy of ignoring any suggestion that they are knowingly doing business through reckless and corrupt gun dealers. For years, the manufacturers have been warned about the "bad apple" dealer problem, often by those within the industry itself.

Until he passed away in 1996, Bill Bridgewater was a gun dealer in a small town in North Carolina and a passionate believer in gun rights. He was also a sharp thorn in the side of the gun industry. As the head of the leading gun-dealer trade association, Bridgewater was angry that responsible dealer were forced to compete with the dealers who would rather cut corners and violate the law. It became difficult for the manufacturers to pretend they knew nothing of the "bad dealer" problem when Bridgewater insisted on reminding them of it. In his newsletter to the industry, Bill Bridgewater pulled no punches:

> No U.S. made firearm ever leaves the plant marked "For delivery to Felon—To be used only in criminal activities!" Yet for us to pretend that none of our firearms achieves that status or that the

flow of firearms into the hands of criminals is not our concern requires a level of stupidity that can seldom be achieved without major brain surgery.[62]

Bridgewater scoffed at the manufacturers and distributors who disavowed all responsibility because they sold only through dealers licensed under federal law:

> If we don't separate ourselves from those who do divert firearms into the black market, we will be shut down in their name.
>
> These "licensees" who engage in the black market are perceived as no different than you and me by the general public, and certainly by law enforcement and the media. That is our fault for sitting quietly and saying nothing, knowing full well that there are felons hidden among us.
>
> You may continue to help shield these folks who operate this firearms black market among us and you will surely go down the drain with them whenever the public gets tired of every snot-nosed 13-year-old poking a gun in its face and demands draconian action.[63]

Bridgewater posed the issue to the gun industry in stark terms. "It is really your choice—do something about the felons among you who disguise themselves as legitimate businesses or die with them because their excesses are intolerable to our society."[64] Less than a year after he wrote those words, he was pressured to step down from the board of a trade association that included the major manufacturers and distributors, all of which had received his newsletter.[65] Bridgewater was not alone among gun dealers in pleading with his industry to take action. Robert Lockett owned and operated the Second Amendment Gun Shop in Overland Park, Kansas. A columnist for *Shooting Sports Retailer* magazine, Lockett filed a column in 1999 calling on manufacturers and distributors to "wake-up" and control their distribution systems by requiring that dealers "adhere to some strict guidelines." Like Bridgewater, Lockett could not abide the manufacturers' "ignorance is bliss" posture toward corrupt dealers. He wrote in his column,

> I've been told INNUMERABLE times by various manufactur-
> ers that they "have no control" over their channels of distribu-
> tion. . . . IF YOU DO NOT KNOW WHERE AND HOW
> YOUR PRODUCTS ARE ULTIMATELY BEING SOLD—
> YOU SHOULD HAVE KNOWN OR ANTICIPATED
> THAT THEY WOULD BE ILLEGALY SOLD AND
> SUBSEQUENTLY MISUSED. Let's just get down and dirty.
> We manufacture, distribute, and retail items of deadly force.[66]

The column sparked controversy even before it was published. A draft circulated within the top ranks of the industry, and the *Wall Street Journal* ran a story on the draft version and its implications.[67] When the column finally appeared in *Shooting Sports Retailer*, Lockett's text had been significantly changed. Whereas Lockett's version had addressed "Mr. Manufacturer," the edited version now addressed "Mr. Firearms Businessman" in a transparent effort to shift blame away from the manufacturers.[68]

Just as Bill Bridgewater had, Lockett discovered that the gun industry does not respond kindly to criticism from within its ranks. After his column appeared (even in its edited form), several distrib-utors retaliated by refusing to supply his gun shop. The publisher of *Shooting Sports Retailer* told Lockett that gun manufacturer Glock pulled its advertising from the magazine because of the column.[69] The magazine never printed another Bob Lockett column.[70]

The explosive testimony of whistleblower Robert Ricker shows that the industry received the message dealers like Bridgewater and Lockett were sending—and decided to do nothing about it. In many ways, Ricker was the consummate industry insider. For eigh-teen years he worked tirelessly for the gun lobby, starting as a lawyer at the NRA and eventually rising to lead a large trade association. Ricker participated in formulating and advocating gun-industry policy on every important issue—from the Brady Bill to child-safety locks to lawsuits, among others.

In a sworn affidavit submitted in support of the lawsuits against the industry filed by California cities,[71] Ricker confirmed what industry executives still try to deny: the "firearm industry . . . has long known" of "the diversion of firearms from legal channels of commerce to the illegal black market," in which "firearms pass quickly from licensed dealers to juveniles and criminals . . . by corrupt dealers or distributors who go to great lengths to avoid detection by law enforcement authorities." "Leaders in the industry," said Ricker, "have long known that greater industry action to prevent illegal transactions is possible and would curb the supply of firearms to the illegal market." Nevertheless, industry leaders "have consistently resisted taking constructive voluntary action to prevent firearms from ending up in the illegal gun market and have sought to silence others within the industry who have advocated reform." Ricker reported on regular meetings of industry lawyers in which some discussed whether the industry should take greater voluntary action to curb illegal guns. "The prevailing view," he reported, "was that if the industry took action voluntarily it would be an admission of responsibility for the problem." Eventually, the lawyer meetings were ended because, in the words of one industry lawyer, the open discussion of such issues was becoming too "dangerous." As Ricker described it, the industry adopted a "see no evil, hear no evil, speak no evil approach" that encourages "a culture of evasion of firearms laws."

Internal industry documents uncovered in litigation confirm the industry's knowledge of the corrupt-dealer problem. But whenever an industry official suggested the need for action to address it, the idea was quickly squelched. The industry's leading trade association, the National Shooting Sports Foundation (NSSF), was a graveyard for reform ideas. For example, a memo from NSSF official Doug Painter in 1993 reported on a random sampling of dealers by ATF showing that an astonishing 34 percent had committed federal firearms violations. Painter suggested a "proactive industry strategy" to address the serious "potential for illegal firearms trans-actions through ostensibly 'legal' FFL [federal firearms licensees] channels."[72] He proposed in the memo that the industry act "as an important step in better regulating the distribution of its products and as a means of minimizing the possibility of illegal transactions through unscrupulous FFL holders." Without even reviewing the ATF report, NSSF's executive director Robert Delfay rejected Painter's idea, instructing him to file the memo "for future reference," because the chair of NSSF's board, Arlen Chaney, was "not keen on doing anything right now." Having learned his lesson not to rock the boat, Painter eventually rose through the ranks to become NSSF's executive director.

The industry's public position is to insist that, even if it could identify the problem dealers, the manufacturers can do nothing about them. Manufacturers have no control over the conduct of retail dealers, the argument goes. Indeed, they generally sell their products to distributors, who in turn sell to retail dealers. Once guns leave their loading docks, they cannot control who sells them or who buys them, or so they claim.

The gun makers, however, seem to be powerless to deal with problem dealers only when the problem involves diversion of guns to criminals. When it comes to protecting the bottom line, manufacturers are able to find multiple ways of making sure dealers adhere to company policies.

My favorite example is Beretta. Gun makers like Beretta, who sell through distributors, typically have written contracts with their distributors imposing a variety of requirements designed to ensure the effective promotion of the manufacturer's products. Beretta was apparently concerned that its American retailers were selling Beretta guns outside the United States in competition with its foreign sales representatives. It therefore inserted a provision in its standard distributor agreement requiring the distributor to actively discourage dealers from selling its products overseas. The agreement makes it clear that any such foreign sales that "our distributors know or should have known are occurring" constitute violations of the agreement that could be grounds for termination of the distributor.[73]

Litigation against the industry revealed a letter Beretta had written to one of its distributors explaining the indicators that should put a distributor on notice that a dealer likely was engaged in unauthorized international sales. These included "the size of the order, past history of the particular dealer, the size and nature of the order relative to normal buying practices of the dealer et cetera."[74] According to Donald Campbell, Beretta's national sales manager, Beretta was trying to "control the distribution process."[75]

As vigilant as Beretta was in preventing diversion of its guns to foreign markets, it showed no such determination to prevent diversion of its guns to the illegal market. Beretta imposed no requirements on its distributors to monitor the number of crime guns a dealer sold, the number of suspect multiple sales it had made, or whether it had been cited by ATF for legal violations. Campbell testified that he never thought it was part of his job to try to curb the flow of guns into the illegal market, that he never tried to think about ways to prevent it, and that he knew of no measures Beretta instituted to prevent it during his entire tenure with the company.[76] See no evil. Hear no evil. Speak no evil. And do nothing.

This industry attitude showed contempt for the pleas of federal law-enforcement authorities who repeatedly urged the industry to take action. ATF wrote that its "enforcement efforts would benefit if the firearms industry takes affirmative steps to track weapons and encourage proper operation of Federal Firearms Licensees to ensure compliance with all applicable laws."[77] The Justice Department urged gun manufacturers to "self-police" their distribution systems, urging them to "develop a code of conduct for dealers and distributors, requiring them to implement inventory, story security, policy and record keeping measures to keep guns out of the wrong hands."[78]

The gun industry's plea of powerlessness required, of course, that the industry march in lockstep. Once one company showed action is possible to curb corrupt dealers, then the argument collapses for all of them.

During the 1990s, Smith & Wesson repeatedly threatened to spoil the party for the entire industry. It implemented a code of ethics for its dealers and informed them it might terminate sales to those who did not agree to refrain from making sales to straw purchasers.[79] It was the only gun maker to instruct its distributors to terminate sales to Chicago-area dealers who had been indicted for having made sales to undercover police officers posing as straw buyers for criminals.[80]

Then, on St. Patrick's Day 2000, the company committed an unforgiveable sin. It entered into an agreement with many of the cities that had filed suit against the industry and with the Clinton administration (which had threatened a lawsuit). In that agreement, Smith & Wesson committed itself to imposing a far-reaching code of conduct on its distributors and dealers to help prevent sales into the illegal market.[81] In order to be authorized to sell Smith & Wesson products, a dealer had to implement safe sales practices that went far beyond the minimum legal requirements. The dealer had to do the following:

- refrain from selling any gun until the Brady background check was completed (thus solving the "default proceed" problem)
- refuse to sell at a gun show unless every seller at the show, including unlicensed sellers, conducts background checks on all sales (thus closing the "gun-show loophole")
- have its employees attend annual training and pass an exam on how to recognize the signs of a suspicious sale and on how to promote safe handling of guns
- sell guns only to persons who have passed a certified firearms-safety course or exam
- implement specific security measures to prevent gun theft
- maintain an electronic record of every time one of its guns was traced to crime and submit those records to Smith & Wesson on a monthly basis

Smith & Wesson CEO Ed Schultz said, in announcing the agreement, "A decision to enter this agreement, we realized, would not be popular with everyone. But we believe . . . it is the right thing to do."[82]

The agreement was a grave threat to the rest of the industry. It amounted to an admission by a major gun manufacturer that it was in a position to require its dealers to engage in safer sales practices, in the same way it would require them to effectively promote its products. This was a direct challenge to the industry's longtime strategy of avoiding responsibility for dealer misconduct by pretending there was nothing manufacturers could do to curb it. Hard-liners in the industry also knew that if one or two other manufacturers entered into similar agreements, it could fundamentally change the way guns are sold for many years to come.

The NRA and its industry allies were not about to let that happen. The NRA denounced Smith & Wesson as a foreign-owned business (its corporate parent was a British company) that had "run up the white flag of surrender" to the Clinton administration. The NRA's rage, and the inevitable calls for a boycott of Smith & Wesson products, was enough to terrify the other companies into submission. Industry hard-liners, in turn, went into overdrive to make sure no one else agreed to the Smith & Wesson reforms. NRA loyalist Robert Delfay, head of the industry's leading trade association, issued a statement that he was "deeply disturbed" that Smith & Wesson allowed the Clinton administration to "manipulate the company in this manner," but added, "We are confident that no other major manufacturers will desert."[83]

Andrew Cuomo, then secretary of housing and urban development, who had played a key role in negotiating the deal with Ed Schultz, said, "It seems like the industry is doing everything it can to make an example out of Smith & Wesson."[84] Richard Blumenthal, then Connecticut attorney general, who had actively supported the agreement, described Smith & Wesson as "under an absolutely unprecedented pressure, both financial and personal within the gun industry, with threats that are almost violent in nature, and I have heard the fear that it could be put out of business."[85] It almost was. Major distributors stopped selling the company's products. Its sales slowed to a trickle. Ed Schultz left the company. The agreement was never implemented. An example had been made.

At the same time the NRA and the gun industry were vilifying Smith & Wesson, Delfay's trade association commissioned a nationwide poll to find out public attitudes about the settlement. The survey found that 79 percent of those polled favored the settlement, with only 15 percent opposed. Even a majority of NRA members supported the agreement.[86] For obvious reasons, the survey was never released to the public; it was uncovered in pretrial discovery in the municipal lawsuits against the industry. What could be more damning than a survey, commissioned by the industry itself, showing how far the industry was out of step with the American people?

As inexcusable as the industry's conduct has been, is it the basis for legal liability? In other contexts, courts have held manufacturers of dangerous products legally accountable for using irresponsible intermediaries to distribute and sell their products. These courts recognize that since manufacturers choose how to distribute their products and who to do business with, they cannot hide from responsibility by having other companies and individuals do their dirty work. For example, courts have held that a waste-disposal company can be liable for using irresponsible companies to dispose of toxic waste,[87] a bulk manufacturer of paint thinner can be liable for danger to children when it did nothing to prevent retailers from packaging the product in used milk containers,[88] and a chemical company can be liable for selling chemicals to a company making illegal and dangerous fireworks.[89] In none of these cases was the manufacturer able to avoid liability simply because it did not directly engage in the wrongful conduct, but instead used others to do so.

Appeals courts in Ohio,[90] New Jersey,[91] and Indiana[92] have all held that gun makers may be liable for distributing their products through irresponsible dealers, while showing willful blindness to their conduct. In a case brought by the NAACP in which the industry's conduct was scrutinized in a lengthy trial, a federal judge in

New York issued a searing indictment of the industry, finding that its irresponsible distribution of guns so substantially contributes to the illegal gun market as to constitute a public nuisance.[93] Judge Jack Weinstein found that "careless practices and lack of appropriate precautions on the part of some retailers lead to the diversion of a large number of handguns from the legal primary market into a substantial illegal secondary market." "The flow of guns into criminal hands in New York," he wrote, "would substantially decrease if manufacturers and distributors insisted that retail dealers who sell their guns be responsible." Instead, "members of the industry continue to fail to take many obvious easily implemented steps" that "would substantially reduce the stream of illegally possessed handguns flowing into New York."

Judge Weinstein also found evidence of the gun industry's motive in continuing to sell guns through irresponsible dealers: a huge percentage of the industry's production serves the illegal market, generating significant profits. A study introduced into evidence showed that 18 percent of handguns sold in 1990 were in the hands of violent criminals or used in violent crimes by the year 2000. Every gun sold to a straw buyer or a gun trafficker adds to the sales and profits of the dealer, the distributor, and the manufacturer. No one in the supply chain has an incentive to curb those sales, unless, that is, they are held liable for the damage they inflict on individuals and communities.

It should be obvious, then, that the lawsuits against the gun industry sought to hold manufacturers and sellers liable, not simply because guns are misused by dangerous people but because the industry's own irresponsible choices, in the design and distribution of its products, enable and facilitate that misuse. The industry knew its choices lead to death and injury, knew it could make different choices, and refused to do so because it would hurt the bottom line. And the rest of us continue to pay a terrible price.

Yet the gun industry has had striking success misrepresenting the legal claims against it and portraying itself as the victim of greedy trial lawyers and rabid gun haters bent on holding it responsible for every shooting by a gangbanger. In enacting the Protection of Lawful Commerce in Arms Act in 2005, Congress thought it was barring lawsuits that would be comparable to "holding Budweiser responsible for drunk drivers" because that's how the gun lobby's friends in Congress framed the issue. Here's how the lawsuits were characterized by one of the bill's key supporters, Senator Jeff Sessions (R-Alabama): "The anti-gun activists . . . want to blame . . . violent, illegal acts by criminals—on manufacturers of guns, *because they manufactured the gun, and they want to be able to sue the seller who sold the gun simply for selling them* [emphasis added]. This does not make sense."[94] Of course, that's not what the lawsuits against the industry tried to do.

The sponsors of the bill repeatedly assured their colleagues that the legislation would not protect companies who engaged in objectionable conduct. Senator Larry Craig (R-Idaho), the bill's primary Senate sponsor and an NRA board member, put the matter this way: "[This bill] does not protect members of the gun industry from every lawsuit or legal action that could be filed against them. It does not prevent them from being sued for their own misconduct. This bill only stops one extremely narrow category of lawsuits, lawsuits that attempt to force the gun industry to pay for the crimes of third parties over whom they have no control."[95] Senator Lindsay Graham (R-South Carolina), another supporter, explained that the legislation "doesn't relieve you of duties that the law imposes upon you to safely manufacture and to carefully sell," but Congress was "not going to extend it to a concept where you are responsible, *after you have done everything right*, for what somebody else may do who bought your product."[96] Senator Max Baucus (D-Montana) offered similar assurances: "This bill . . . will not shield the industry from its own wrongdoing or from its negligence."[97]

Of course, after the bill was enacted into law, these assurances by the gun industry's defenders in Congress did not deter the industry from immediately using the new statute to seek dismissal of the suits against it for engaging in negligence and wrongdoing. Suits brought by municipalities and gun violence victims alleging industry negligence in the distribution of guns were dismissed as barred by the new law.[98] The legislation brought to a halt the court-ordered discovery of internal industry documents that had begun to reveal the knowing complicity of gun companies in fueling the illegal market. The gun lobby won in Congress by portraying gun makers as the victims of frivolous lawsuits that were never brought, while diverting attention from the gun industry's own knowing, callous, and highly profitable system of ensuring a ready supply of guns to criminals—a system that functions efficiently to this day. We all know who the real victims are.

CHAPTER EIGHT

THE SECOND AMENDMENT
IS THE FIRST FREEDOM

Charlton Heston was nearing the end of his rousing speech to the 2000 NRA convention in Charlotte, North Carolina, where he accepted a third term as the group's president. After decrying "the divisive forces that would take freedom away," with square-jawed resolve he hoisted in one hand, high above his head, a colonial-era musket, symbol of rebellion against the powerful to ensure American liberty. Then, in his booming baritone that was close to a lion's roar, Heston issued his trademark challenge to the faithful gathered to heed the call: "*From my cold, dead hands* . . ." The moment was electric, the audience ecstatic, the response deafening. Heston kept the musket aloft for several seconds, soaking in the adulation, basking in the shared blood oath everyone in the room had implicitly taken. His message: I am willing to die for my guns. Their response: So are we.

Heston's musket drew a direct, visible link between the fight against tyranny that gave birth to our nation and the NRA's fight against the perceived tyranny of gun control. Patriots then and patriots now. For the committed NRA activist, moreover, Heston was symbolically drawing a connection to the Founding Fathers that is real and eternal because they wrote it indelibly into the charter of our freedoms—the Bill of Rights.

The second of the first ten amendments to the Constitution speaks of "the right of the people to keep and bear Arms" and commands that this right "shall not be infringed." For the "gun rights" partisan, the Second Amendment is the trump card in the gun debate, the argument of last resort. The gun control advocate can talk about the dangers of guns, their toll on society, and the need to regulate them at least as much as other dangerous products such as cars. But these arguments invariably draw the response that guns aren't like other dangerous products because the right to possess guns is uniquely protected by the Constitution. The NRA characterizes the Second Amendment as America's "first freedom" because, to its devoted following, the amendment is the foundation for all our other freedoms.

There has, however, always been a problem with the NRA's use of the Second Amendment. Its words don't quite fit the NRA's narrative. If its intent was to guarantee a right to possess guns for private purposes like self-defense and hunting, its words seem oddly chosen:

> A well regulated Militia, being necessary to the security of a free State, the right of the people to keep and bear Arms, shall not be infringed.

The gun-rights community has always been somewhat vexed by the language about the "well regulated Militia" and its necessity "to the security of a free State." What are such words doing in a provision that guarantees the right to have guns to defend one's home and family? What is their function? Even the phrase "keep and bear Arms" seems strange. The framers could have written something like, "The right of the people to possess and use guns shall not be infringed." Why didn't they?

The NRA's primary strategy for dealing with the troublesome language about the "well regulated Militia" has been to pretend it isn't there. For many years, the NRA headquarters building, on Thomas Circle in Washington, DC, featured a heavily edited version of the Second Amendment on its facade. The first thirteen words were omitted.

Until its decision in *District of Columbia v. Heller*, the Supreme Court had been unwilling to interpret the Second Amendment by ignoring half of its text. In fact, in *United States v. Miller*, in 1939, the Supreme Court's only extensive discussion of the amendment prior to *Heller*, the Court assigned decisive importance to the militia language. In *Miller*, a unanimous Court held that the "obvious purpose" of the guarantee of the people's right to "keep and bear Arms" was "to assure the continuation and render possible the effectiveness" of state militia forces and that the amendment "must be interpreted and applied with that end in view."[1] Indeed, in *Miller*, the High Court upheld the defendants' indictment for transporting a sawed-off shotgun across state lines without complying with the National Firearms Act because there was no evidence that such a gun could have a "reasonable relationship to the preservation or efficiency of a well regulated militia," noting that it could not simply assume "that this weapon is any part of the ordinary military equipment or that its use could contribute to the common defense."[2] The *Miller* Court found no reason to even address the question of whether such a gun could have utility for self-defense or some other non-militia activity.

Prodigious historical research into the origins of the Second Amendment confirms that it was intended to address the distribution of military power in society, not the need to have guns for self-defense or other private purposes. The Anti-Federalists, who opposed the Constitution as written and sought the addition of a Bill of Rights, were deeply worried that the Constitution had given Congress the power to raise a standing army (i.e., a professional military force), which many feared would become a tool of federal tyranny, as well as excessive power over the state militias. The state militias were nonprofessional military forces composed of ordinary citizens and were regarded as a strong check on the power of a federal standing army.

Leading Anti-Federalists argued that the Constitution's grant of power to Congress to organize and arm the militia amounted to an exclusive power to do so, thus rendering the state militias vulnerable to federal hostility or neglect. For example, Anti-Federalist George Mason argued during the Virginia ratification debates that Congress's new power would allow Congress to destroy the militia by "rendering them useless—by disarming them. . . . Congress may neglect to provide for arming and disciplining the militia; and the state governments cannot do it, for Congress has an exclusive power to arm them."[3]

Historians tell us that the Second Amendment was an effort by the Federalist defenders of the Constitution to allay these concerns by making the keeping and bearing of arms in a state militia a "right of the people," not dependent on federal action.[4] The Second Amendment was passed as a "fail safe" provision, ensuring that the state militias would be armed, even if Congress abandoned them.

For decades after *Miller* the lower courts consistently held that the Second Amendment guarantees the people the right to be armed only in connection with service in an organized state militia. Since the state militia of the founding era—a system of compulsory military service imposed on much of the adult male population—had long ago disappeared into the mists of time, the courts routinely upheld gun control laws of every conceivable variety against Second Amendment challenges. Indeed, the judicial consensus on the meaning of the amendment had grown so strong that, in 1991, former chief justice Warren Burger—a conservative jurist who also was a gun owner—accused the NRA of perpetrating a "fraud on the American public" by insisting that the right to be armed existed apart from service in an organized militia.[5]

Historian Paul Finkelman has written that "while the justices in the majority in [*Heller* and *McDonald*] profess to believe in a jurisprudence of original intent, the Court's historical analysis could not get a passing grade in any serious college history course."[6] It is revealing that of the sixteen professional historians who joined briefs amicus curiae in *Heller*, only one supported the view that the Second Amendment guarantees an individual right to be armed for self-defense. In *McDonald*, twenty-four historians joined a brief attacking *Heller*'s historical analysis, but the same 5–4 majority nevertheless extended the Second Amendment to the states through the Fourteenth Amendment's Due Process Clause. The academic consensus that the High Court had gotten the history wrong in *Heller* led Justice Steven Breyer to pose this question in *McDonald:* "If history, and history alone, is what matters, why would the Court not now reconsider *Heller* in light of these more recently published historical views?" Justice Breyer's obviously tongue-in-cheek question supplies its own answer. Justice Scalia's version of originalism in *Heller* is not really about history. It's about ideology and nothing else.

In addition to the scathing analyses of *Heller* from historians, some of the sharpest criticism has come from conservative legal theorists with a long history of opposition to judicial activism.[7] In an extraordinary article disclosing his own family's gun violence tragedy some years ago, Pepperdine University law professor Douglas Kmiec, who once shared an office with Samuel Alito in the Reagan Justice Department, praised Justice Scalia's career of "reminding his fellow judges how important it is not to read their own personal experiences or desires into the law." But Kmiec found that principle dishonored in Scalia's *Heller* opinion. "From their high bench on that morning," he wrote, "it would not be the democratic choice that mattered, but theirs. Constitutional text, history, and precedent all set aside."[8]

Judge Richard Posner of the US Court of Appeals for the Seventh Circuit, who is also a law professor at the University of Chicago and undoubtedly the leading conservative legal thinker of our time, found the *Heller* decision to be "evidence that the Supreme Court, in deciding constitutional cases, exercises a freewheeling discretion strongly flavored with ideology."[9] Commenting on the sheer length of Scalia's majority opinion (almost twenty thousand words), Posner found it "evidence of the ability of well-staffed courts to produce snow jobs."

A third broadside has come from Judge J. Harvie Wilkinson III of the US Court of Appeals in Richmond, Virginia, who was on the short list for the Supreme Court throughout the George W. Bush administration (and was, incidentally, my constitutional law professor at the University of Virginia Law School long before he was appointed to the bench). Judge Wilkinson is somewhat more charitable than Kmiec and Posner about the evidence presented by the *Heller* majority supporting the "personal rights" view of the Second Amendment. Nevertheless, he sees *Heller* as improper "judicial lawmaking" in defiance of conservative legal principles counseling restraint and deference to the judgments of popularly elected legislatures.[10] "In fact, *Heller* encourages Americans to do what conservative jurists warned for years they should not do: bypass the ballot and seek to press their political agenda in the courts," he writes.[11] Wilkinson especially singles out Justice Scalia for committing the same sins of judicial activism in *Heller* that Scalia has spent a career denouncing in *Roe v. Wade*.[12]

Given that Justice Scalia's *Heller* opinion is so transparently based on ideology masquerading as history, that its historical account is so profoundly flawed, and that *Heller* itself is a radical departure from Supreme Court precedent, it is quite conceivable that neither *Heller* nor *McDonald* will survive a reexamination of the historical evidence by a future Supreme Court, a prospect that surely has become less speculative following Justice Scalia's death. Paul Finkelman has compared *Heller* to other now-disgraced Supreme Court decisions of the past: *Dred Scott v. Sandford*, which perpetuated slavery, and *Plessy v. Ferguson*, which found "separate but equal" racial segregation consistent with the Constitution. "Just as *Dred Scott* and *Plessy* have been relegated to the dust bin of history, so too can we expect that a different Court will overturn *Heller* and *McDonald*," writes Finkelman. Although this would be a triumph for principled constitutional interpretation, as the following discussion suggests, it is not at all clear that *Heller*'s demise would, in the long run, be a triumph for gun control.

IS *HELLER* A LETHAL WEAPON AGAINST GUN CONTROL?

As we have seen, the Supreme Court's unprecedented recognition of an individual right to be armed for private purposes may, in the long run, help gun control advocates respond more effectively to the slippery-slope argument and thereby counter the NRA's strategy of making the debate about banning guns. But as helpful as *Heller* may eventually be in this regard, there is another side to the ledger: won't the new right recognized in *Heller* pose a direct threat to the constitutionality of other gun laws?

For those involved in the gun control debate, there is an odd "good news, bad news" quality to the *Heller* opinion. (What part is good news and what part is bad, of course, depends on your point of view.) For the gun lobby, the good news is that there is now an established right to have guns in the home that is entirely divorced from militia service. However, the bad news is that *Heller* contains some extraordinary language suggesting that a wide range of gun control laws do not violate this new right. "Like most rights, the right secured by the Second Amendment is not unlimited," wrote the *Heller* majority. According to the Court, "the right was not a right to keep and carry any weapon whatsoever in any manner whatsoever and for whatever purpose."[13]

It is highly unusual for a court, in interpreting the Constitution, to comment on the constitutionality of laws not before it, particularly when it is not citing prior court rulings on the issue. The *Heller* majority, however, went out of its way to offer the assurance that "nothing in our opinion should be taken to cast doubt" on a wide range of gun control laws, which the Court said remain "presumptively lawful" under the Court's ruling.[14] These include

- laws imposing "conditions and qualifications" on the commercial sale of arms (a category that could be read as broad enough to include background checks, waiting periods, licensing, registration, safety training, limits on large-volume sales, etc.);
- prohibitions on gun possession by felons and the mentally ill;
- prohibitions on carrying concealed weapons;
- laws forbidding firearms in "sensitive places" such as schools and government buildings; and
- bans on "dangerous and unusual weapons" (which could include machine guns and assault weapons).

As if this list were not enough to make the NRA squirm, the Court added that these "presumptively lawful regulatory measures" are given "only as examples" and that the list "does not purport to be exhaustive."[15]

Later in the opinion, the Court stated that its analysis also does not "suggest the invalidity of laws regulating the storage of fire-arms to prevent accidents,"[16] which presumably would include laws against leaving loaded guns accessible to kids. It is equally significant that the Court, in commenting on the many cases in which gun laws have been upheld against Second Amendment challenge under the "militia purpose" view, cautioned that "it should not be thought that the cases decided by these judges would necessarily have come out differently under a proper interpretation of the right."[17]

Why did the *Heller* majority so gratuitously suggest that its historic ruling recognizing a constitutional right to be armed for self-defense may have little practical impact on gun control laws? It is not unreasonable to speculate that much of this reassuring language was inserted as the price of getting four other justices to join Scalia's opinion. Intuitively, it seems unlikely that such language originated with Justice Scalia, an avid gun enthusiast who, in February 2016, passed away at an exclusive hunting reserve in Texas, rather than being a concession by him to other justices.

It also is unclear how the majority derived its categories of "presumptively lawful" gun control measures. Although the majority seems to attach great importance to whether the gun restrictions at issue are "long-standing," the opinion leaves unclear how long-standing they must be. It also is unclear whether a specific restriction (such as a waiting period) must be long-standing, or whether the specific restriction must be part of a category of restrictions (e.g., "laws imposing conditions and qualifications on the sale of arms") that is long-standing.

However the language came about, and recognizing its uncertain scope, the commentary on other gun control laws in *Heller* is nonetheless significant because it is a signal to the lower federal courts that the Supreme Court has drawn a sharp distinction between laws that function to ban guns commonly possessed in the home for self-defense (like the DC law) and other laws that impose regulation on guns, even tight regulation, but yet allow individuals, not governments, to make the ultimate decision about gun ownership.

It also is significant that the *Heller* majority did not adopt a stringent legal standard for future judicial review of gun control laws, though the lawyers for Mr. Heller vigorously urged the Court to do so. The strict scrutiny test, urged by Mr. Heller and used in certain First Amendment cases, would require courts reviewing gun laws to determine whether the law being challenged is "narrowly tailored to achieve a compelling government interest."[18] Though the prevention of death and injury from gunfire would seem to qualify as a "compelling government interest," the requirement that the law be "narrowly tailored" would invite right-wing activist judges to decide that gun control laws they don't like are insufficiently narrow in their impact on gun rights. As Justice Breyer's separate dissenting opinion notes, the *Heller* majority implicitly rejected a strict scrutiny test.[19] Indeed, the majority adopted no test at all. Whereas strict scrutiny would have erected a strong presumption against the constitutionality of gun control laws, requiring narrow tailoring to overcome the presumption, the *Heller* majority described a lengthy list of gun control measures as "presumptively lawful."

Although the *Heller* majority makes some comparison of its new Second Amendment right to our First Amendment rights,[20] its surprising commentary on gun control laws and failure to endorse strict scrutiny of those laws suggest that at least some justices in the majority understand that the right to possess handguns in the home is dramatically different in nature from our First Amendment rights. It should be obvious, but bears saying anyway, that the right to possess lethal weapons affects the public's interest in safety and security more directly than the right to express oneself. Pro-gun advocates will continue to make analogies to the First Amendment, like David Kopel of the libertarian Independence Institute, who says, "Guns are like books or churches."[21] But it is hard to maintain that the *Heller* decision treats guns "like books or churches."

As one federal appeals court put it, "The risk inherent in firearms and other weapons distinguishes the Second Amendment right from other fundamental rights that . . . can be exercised without creating a direct risk to others."[22] Perhaps Judge Wilkinson put it most eloquently in urging judicial caution before extending Second Amendment rights beyond the right to have a handgun in the home:

> This is serious business. We do not wish to be even minutely responsible for some unspeakably tragic act of mayhem because in the peace of our judicial chambers we miscalculated as to Second Amendment rights. . . . If ever there was an occasion for restraint, this would seem to be it.[23]

To date, *Heller* has not proven to be a grave threat to existing gun laws, as the lower federal courts, at least implicitly, have recognized the unique and inherent dangerousness of the Second Amendment right. As law professor Allen Rostron has written, although a small minority of lower court judges has read *Heller* to require strict judicial scrutiny of gun laws, "Judges have generally continued to apply a form of intermediate scrutiny that is very deferential to reasonable legislative determinations about what restrictions on guns address legitimate public safety concerns."[24] As a result, a wide range of gun laws have been upheld, even though some are (arguably) not included in the "presumptively lawful" categories of gun laws mentioned in *Heller*. Thus, in recent years, courts have upheld the federal law barring licensed dealers from selling handguns to persons under the age of twenty-one (against an NRA lawsuit asserting the constitutional right of eighteen-year-olds to buy handguns), registration of both handguns and long guns (including a fingerprint and photograph requirement), bans on semiautomatic assault weapons and high-capacity magazines, and a state law prohibiting gun possession in places of worship.[25]

Heller found a Second Amendment right to have a handgun in the home for self-defense; it did not, however, recognize such a right outside the home. Whether the Second Amendment right extends beyond the home and, if it does, what limitations on that right are permissible, is of enormous consequence. As discussed previously, gun carrying in public places introduces risk to the community at large. In the words of one federal appeals court judge,

> It is common sense . . . that a gun is dangerous to more people when carried outside the home. [Citation omitted] When firearms are carried outside of the home, the safety of a broader range of citizen is at issue. The risk of being injured or killed now extends to strangers, law enforcement personnel, and other private citizens who happen to be in the area.[26]

We have seen that many state legislatures, under intense NRA pressure, have made concealed carry far easier. However, there remain very populous and urbanized states, including California, Illinois, New Jersey, Maryland, and Massachusetts, that still have restrictive laws that would be jeopardized by a new constitutional right to carry guns in public.

Justice Scalia's opinion in *Heller*, in explaining that the right "was not a right to keep and carry any weapon whatsoever in any manner whatsoever and for whatever purpose," gives the example of the general consensus of nineteenth-century courts "that prohibitions on carrying concealed weapons were lawful under the Second Amendment or state analogues."[27] Indeed, even the cattle towns of the so-called Wild West featured strict regulation of public gun carrying. Law professor Adam Winkler uncovered a photo of the main street of Dodge City, Kansas, in 1879 featuring a large sign with this message: "The Carrying of Fire Arms Strictly Prohibited."[28] Thus, federal appeals courts have upheld strict concealed-carry laws after *Heller* and *McDonald*, including New York's law requiring "proper cause," such as a special need for protection, for a license to carry concealed; New Jersey's law requiring a showing of "justifiable need" for a carry permit; and Maryland's requirement of a "good and substantial reason" for concealed carry.[29] However, the US Court of

Appeals for the Seventh Circuit struck down the only state law to completely ban the carrying of guns in public in an opinion written by Judge Richard Posner,[30] who, as discussed above, had previously expressed his contempt for the *Heller* decision itself. After again reviewing the historical consensus at odds with Justice Scalia's analysis, Judge Posner nevertheless concluded (with notable irony) that the implication of that analysis is that the right to possess and carry weapons "in case of confrontation" must extend beyond the home to public places where such confrontations could occur. Public carrying of guns could be prohibited by Dodge City in 1879, but not by the State of Illinois in 2016.

Although there remains some uncertainty about the scope and meaning of the *Heller* right, particularly what it may eventually mean for the regulation of guns in public places, *Heller* has no doubt been a disappointment to pro-gun partisans who viewed it as the beginning of the end of gun control. Indeed, the disappointment has been keenly felt within the Supreme Court itself. Two months before his death, Justice Scalia joined an opinion, written by Justice Clarence Thomas, dissenting from the Court's decision not to review an appeals court ruling upholding the Illinois ban on semiautomatic assault weapons and high-capacity magazines.[31] Their frustration with the lower courts' application of *Heller*, and with their own Court's consistent refusal to review those rulings, is palpable. After noting that several courts of appeal had upheld similar bans, Justice Thomas wrote that "noncompliance with our Second Amendment precedents warrants this Court's attention as much as any of our precedents." Supreme Court review is necessary, he wrote, to prevent the lower court "from relegating the Second Amendment to a second-class right." In light of this dissent by Justices Thomas and Scalia, it now seems clear that the language in *Heller* affirming the presumptive constitutionality of broad categories of gun restrictions was a concession Justice Scalia was forced to make to achieve a narrow majority. It may well be a concession that nullified much of what Justice Scalia was trying to achieve in that landmark case.

THE SECOND AMENDMENT AS AN ARGUMENT AGAINST GUN CONTROL

We have seen that *Heller* may not pose a lethal threat to the future constitutionality of gun laws less restrictive than a broad gun ban, although uncertainty remains about laws regulating gun carrying outside the home. Although the legal risk to gun laws may well be low, there is yet another possible impact of *Heller* to consider. *Heller* gives guns a protected constitutional status enjoyed by no other product. Doesn't that special status help the gun lobby argue forcefully against analogies between guns and other dangerous products for which government regulation is commonplace and widely accepted?

We have noted that pro-gun advocates typically respond to the cars/guns analogy by noting that there is no constitutional right to have a car. Before *Heller* it was possible for gun control advocates to respond that there is no constitutional right to have a gun either. We have seen that, from a strictly legal standpoint, *Heller* does not seem to create a strong presumption against gun control laws generally, since the vast majority of post-*Heller* challenges to gun laws have failed. But does it create a new presumption against gun control in the public's mind, placing a greater burden on gun control advocates to justify their proposals as sound policy?

Heller would appear to have this impact on the gun control debate only if support for gun control before *Heller* were dependent, to a substantial extent, on the public's belief that the Second Amendment does not guarantee a broad, non-militia right. We have seen, from public-opinion polls, that supermajorities of the public have long supported a broad gun control agenda, the only exception being a ban on handguns. If this support were somehow premised on the public's conviction that the Constitution does not protect a right to gun ownership for private purposes, then *Heller*, by destroying that premise, could be expected to shake the foundation of the public's support for gun control.

But, in fact, public-opinion surveys have long shown that the public believes that the Second Amendment is concerned with individual rights, not militias. A 1995 *U.S. News & World Report* poll reported that 75 percent of Americans believe that "the

Constitution guarantees you the right to own a gun."[32] On the day *Heller* was argued in the Supreme Court, the *Washington Post* released a nationwide poll showing that 72 percent of those surveyed believe the Second Amendment "guarantees the right of individuals to own guns," while only 20 percent said it guarantees "only the right of the states to maintain militias."[33] While one could quarrel with the wording of these poll questions, they do suggest that the "militia purpose" view—long dominant in the courts—did not seriously penetrate the public's consciousness in the modern era. This is hardly surprising, given the strangeness, to modern ears, of the phrase "well regulated Militia."

This means that a large majority of Americans has long believed, and continues to believe, *simultaneously* in a broad gun control agenda and in a broad interpretation of the Second Amendment. For the general public, the *Heller* ruling is consistent with what it had long understood to be true: the Second Amendment guarantees a right to have guns, but that right is not absolute and is subject to sensible restrictions.

Given the public's long-standing view of how the Second Amendment affects gun control, *Heller* may actually weaken the argument that gun control proposals should be rejected because the Constitution guarantees a right to possess guns.

Before *Heller*, gun control advocates typically would respond to the Second Amendment argument in two ways. First, they would argue that the courts already had determined that the Second Amendment relates only to the militia and thus was no barrier to gun control laws. Although this argument was true, it did not conform to the public's beliefs about the Amendment's meaning—beliefs that were difficult to alter given the constant din of gun lobby propaganda on the constitutional issue and the fact that courts don't issue press releases. Second, gun control advocates would assert that even if the Second Amendment were broader than militia service, no rights are absolute, and the right to be armed surely should be subject to reasonable restrictions. This argument had substantial persuasive appeal before *Heller* because it was consistent with public attitudes. It has even greater appeal after *Heller*, given the *Heller* Court's reassuring language about the presumptive constitutionality of gun regulation. When pro-gun partisans trot out the Second Amendment, they can now be met with the response that the *Heller* opinion itself—written by one of most conservative and gun-loving justices in recent history—found no inconsistency between the Second Amendment and a host of gun regulations. The record of the lower courts in upholding gun laws after *Heller* reinforces the conclusion that gun control is entirely consistent with an individual right to be armed.

As we have seen, the public's support for gun control has never been premised on a belief that the Second Amendment guarantees only a militia-related right. The polling data suggests that, for most Americans, their views about gun control are not dependent on their beliefs about the Second Amendment; indeed, it is more accurate to say that most Americans adjust their views about the Second Amendment to accommodate them to their views about gun control. If they think gun control is sound public policy, they will conclude that it is not prohibited by the Constitution.

Thus, seven years after the *Heller* decision, the public still supports specific policies to strengthen gun laws. In one 2015 survey, support for requiring background checks for all gun sales remained high, with 85 percent of gun owners and 83 percent of non-owners favoring such a law.[34] Overall, support for an assault weapon ban was at 63 percent and support for banning large-capacity magazines was at 60 percent. Although these figures vary over time, and between polls, it seems clear that the American public continues to be able to reconcile specific gun control proposals with a broad view of the Second Amendment right.

The reality is that, of all the gun lobby's arguments, the constitutional argument has been the least effective in resisting gun control. For all its symbolic and emotional importance to the NRA, the gun lobby has never convinced the public that gun control violates our constitutional values. By recognizing gun rights and, at the same time, confirming the public's long-held belief that gun regulation is entirely compatible with those rights, *Heller* may well, over the long term, further diminish the importance of the Second Amendment argument as a barrier to the enactment of strong gun laws.

So we return to the paradox of the *Heller* ruling. In *Heller* the "gun rights" advocates achieved vindication for their view of the meaning of the Second Amendment, though the Supreme Court had to abandon every pretense of devotion to neutral, principled constitutional interpretation to give them that victory. There is, however, good reason to believe that *Heller*, if it survives future Supreme Court consideration of the Second Amendment, will continue to prove sharply disappointing to the gun lobby as a weapon against gun control laws short of a handgun ban, while weakening both the slippery-slope argument and the constitutional argument itself as reasons to oppose gun regulation. Viewing *Heller* from the perch of the NRA's leadership, an old expression comes to mind: "Be careful what you wish for. It could come true."

BEYOND MYTHOLOGY TO LIFE-SAVING LAWS

On the snowy morning of April 16, 2007, the bucolic, sprawling Blacksburg, Virginia, campus of Virginia Polytechnic Institute and State University—better known as Virginia Tech—became the scene of the bloodiest mass shooting in American history. A mentally disturbed student, senior Seung-Hui Cho, murdered thirty-two and wounded seventeen students and faculty.[1] The horror began around 7:15 in the morning, when Cho entered West Ambler Johnson dormitory and fatally wounded student Emily Hilscher. Moments earlier, Emily had been dropped off at the dorm by her boyfriend, who was a student at Radford University but who lived in Blacksburg. Why Cho singled out Emily Hilscher is still unknown.

Hearing noises from Emily's room, Ryan Clark, a resident adviser who lived next door, checked to see what was happening. He, too, was shot and killed. Cho was able to leave the building without being stopped. He did not claim his next victim until over two hours later, when he carried two handguns and almost four hundred rounds of ammunition packed in high-capacity magazines into Norris Hall, a building of classrooms, and chained shut the pair of doors at each of the building's three main entrances used by students. He walked into an Advanced Hydrology engineering class in room 206, shot and killed the instructor, and methodically fired on the students, killing nine and injuring two others. He crossed the hall and entered room 207, shot the professor teaching a German class, and then killed four students while wounding six others. He attacked two other classrooms, returning to most of the classrooms more than once to continue shooting.

It took Cho only about ten to twelve minutes to murder twenty-five students and five teachers in Norris Hall. Another seventeen were shot, but they survived. He fired at least 174 rounds from his two semiautomatic pistols. The police found seventeen empty ammunition magazines, each capable of holding ten to fifteen rounds. The rampage ended with Cho taking his own life as the police closed in.

As we remember the tragedy at Virginia Tech, I invite the reader to join me in a flight of imagination. Picture, for a moment, a world in which the mythology of the gun lobby no longer dictates our nation's gun policies. Picture, rather, a world where reason and common sense have prevailed over ideology and bumper-sticker slogans on the gun issue. Would the thirty-two innocent students and teachers slain at Virginia Tech still be alive? Could the seventeen others who were wounded have escaped the excruciating pain and lifelong trauma of those gunshots?

We know that no gun law would have cured Cho of the mental illness that fed his violence. But could a gun law have denied him the weapon that enabled him to become a mass murderer? The answer is yes.

The Brady Act should have stopped Cho from buying his guns. Cho was able to walk into two gun shops, undergo the mandatory Brady background checks, and within minutes, walk out with the guns *even though he was legally prohibited from buying guns.* How did this happen? Because, as we have noted, the record disqualifying Cho from buying guns was not in the database checked by the Virginia authorities.

In December 2005 Cho was found by a Virginia judge to be both mentally ill and a danger to himself. That court order disqualified him from future gun purchases by virtue of the provision of the 1968 Gun Control Act barring gun sales to persons "adjudicated as a mental defective." (The use of the term "mental defective" provides a glimpse into the unenlightened view of the mentally ill prevailing in the late '60s.) Federal regulations define the term "adjudicated as a mental defective" as a "determination by a court . . . or other lawful authority that a person, as a result of . . . mental illness . . . is a danger to himself or to others." Cho clearly was prohibited.[2]

The court order disqualifying Cho, however, never made it into the federal database checked by the Virginia State Police. Why? Because the Virginia authorities were entirely focused on reporting mental-health records that they believed disqualified Virginia gun buyers under *Virginia* law but appeared to recognize no need to report mental-health records that disqualified gun buyers under *federal* law. Because Cho was ordered by the Virginia court to undergo only outpatient treatment, the Virginia authorities apparently thought he was not disqualified under state law and thus his court order need not be reported.[3] But his disqualification under federal law cannot be disputed.

The failure of Virginia authorities to report Cho's disqualifying court order to the federal background-check system turned out to be the tip of a gigantic and deadly iceberg. Ironically, Virginia, at the time of Cho's gun purchase, actually led the nation in reporting mental-health records to the Brady system. Overall, the performance of the states in this regard had been nothing short of miserable. As of 2006, less than 10 percent of an estimated 2.6 million disqualifying mental-health records had been transmitted to the federal database.[4] It's easy to dismiss this as a paperwork problem, until you realize that every one of those millions of missing records represents a person *who already has been found too dangerous to have a gun*. Fortunately, the Virginia Tech shooting galvanized Congress to take action, and it responded by passing legislation that created new incentives for states to submit prohibiting mental-health records to the NICS background-check system.[5] The number of such records reported to NICS tripled between 2011 and 2014, although twelve states still have reported fewer than a hundred records.[6]

Although some committed gun control opponents might use Cho's crime as an illustration of the futility of gun laws ("When guns are outlawed, only outlaws will have guns"), such an argument would be transparently specious. The Virginia Tech shooting was not a failure of the Brady Act but a failure of the Brady Act to be properly administered.

Does the Virginia Tech shooting support the NRA's argument that we don't need new laws but simply need to enforce existing laws? No, because the NRA's argument is that we should have strong enforcement as a *substitute* for strong laws. Following the NRA's logic, we should never have enacted the requirement of Brady background checks in the first place; we should have just better enforced the laws against gun sales to felons and the dangerously mentally ill. The Virginia Tech shooting is compelling proof that we need strong laws *and* strong enforcement of those laws.

What if Cho had been turned away from the gun store empty-handed? What then? Cho was the kind of gun buyer least likely to be able to find an alternative source of guns. He was not a member of a violent street gang with ready access to black-market gun sources. Indeed, he was an incommunicative loner, with no social network at all, much less a network that would lead him to a supplier of illegal guns. He could, of course, have searched the Internet for a legal private seller not required to do background checks, or perhaps have attended a local gun show where such private sellers abound. But in our imaginary world, background checks would be required on all gun purchases, not just those from licensed dealers. Even if Cho found a private seller, he would be stopped by a background check.

Although theft would have been another possible avenue for Cho to have acquired a gun, it does not seem to be a realistic alternative in his case. He would have needed to find a vulnerable gun owner and then execute a crime against that owner for which he was not caught, even though Cho likely had never committed a crime of any kind in his life. A gun theft is a far different matter than planning a shooting destined to end with the shooter's own death. And in our imaginary world, all guns would be required to have an internal lock or other personalization system to block use by unauthorized owners. And all gun owners would be legally obligated to store their guns locked. Thus, it is unlikely that Cho would have been able to use a gun that he acquired by theft.

Can we say that Cho would definitely have been denied a gun in our imaginary world? Perhaps not. But we don't demand absolute certainty of success from other laws. In Cho's case, there is every reason to believe that he would have been denied a gun had the right laws been enacted and properly enforced. With no gun, it is still possible that he would have initiated a violent attack with a knife or other similar weapon. But there is no way that thirty-two people would have died.

Still, in our imaginary world, let's assume that somehow Cho was able to get his guns from a licensed dealer despite the legal barriers. Would his rampage still have occurred? Maybe not.

Remember that over two hours elapsed between Cho's murder of Emily Hilscher and Ryan Clark in the dormitory and his mass shooting of students and teachers in the classroom building. During that time, police were called to the dorm and began their investigation. They were on the scene by 7:30 a.m. They began interviewing students in the dorm and learned that Emily had been visiting her boyfriend. They also learned his name and that he owned a gun. The boyfriend immediately became a "person of interest" in the investigation. The police sent out an alert for his pickup truck and searched for it in the campus parking lots. At 9:30, just as Cho was preparing his assault on Norris Hall, the police stopped the boyfriend's pickup on the road. He passed a field test for gunpowder residue. They knew then that the boyfriend was a false lead.

For the first two hours after the dormitory shootings, the police were pursuing the reasonable, but incorrect, theory that they were dealing with a double murder that was most likely the result of a domestic argument and that the shooter was no longer on campus. The police initially reported the incident to university officials as a possible murder-suicide and then as a domestic dispute, and then they said that the suspect probably had left the campus. The police did not urge the administration to take further action to protect against additional violence.

In our imaginary world, how would this course of events have been altered?

First, in a world where the NRA's mythology has been exposed and discredited, federal law would require every semiautomatic pistol to be equipped with microstamping technology that imprints the gun's serial number on each ejected shell casing. Those shell casings littered Emily Hilscher's dorm room after the shootings.

Second, in our imaginary world, the gun lobby's opposition to handgun registration would have been overcome, the restrictions in federal law on computerization of handgun records would have been repealed, and the police would be able to use a gun's serial number to access information about every legal seller and purchaser of the gun with the click of a computer mouse. Given this capability, it is reasonable to assume that police investigating reports of a shooting would have a laptop at the ready, with easy access to computerized gun records. Since reading serial numbers from ejected shell casings would have become standard operating procedure in any shooting investigation, the police also would be equipped with magnifying equipment for accomplishing that task. The detectives in Emily's dorm room, therefore, would quickly trace the gun used in the shooting to find its last lawful owner. With microstamping, they would be able to trace the gun from the casings left behind, with no need for the gun itself.

What would the gun trace have revealed? That the last legal purchaser of the gun was Seung-Hui Cho, not Emily Hilscher's boyfriend. Literally within minutes of their arrival on the scene, and hours before the Norris Hall massacre, investigators would have known Cho's name. A phone call to the Virginia Tech registrar's office would have established that Cho was a current student and indicated where he was living. It is hardly much of a stretch to think that Cho could have been stopped for questioning before he entered the classroom building with his arsenal. Cho returned to his dorm room after the first shootings, where he stayed until at least 7:25 and perhaps as late as 8:00. Thereafter, he was observed in several public places, including near the Virginia Tech Duck Pond and the off-campus post office in Blacksburg, where he mailed a package to NBC News in New York containing a CD with a group of about twenty videos of himself presenting his largely incoherent complaints against the world, as well as pictures of himself wielding weapons.

Even if Cho had not been apprehended, the immediate identification of Cho as the last owner of the gun used in the dorm shooting, ending suspicion of the off-campus boyfriend, likely would have changed the university's reaction to the event. As described by the Virginia Tech Review Panel, appointed by then governor Tim Kaine, as a result of the premature assumption that the shooting was a single, violent event that had come to an end, with no danger of a gunman on the loose on campus, "the university body was not put on high alert by the actions of the university administration and was largely taken by surprise by the events that followed."[7] The panel continued, "Warning the students, faculty, and staff might have made a difference. Putting more people on guard could have resulted in quicker recognition of a problem or suspicious activity, quicker reporting to police, and quicker response of police. Nearly everyone at Virginia Tech is adult and capable of making decisions about potentially dangerous situations to safeguard themselves. So the earlier and clearer the warning, the more chance an individual had of surviving."[8]

In our imaginary world of strong, sound gun laws, once Cho fired those semiautomatic pistols, everything would have been different. Of course, no one can predict with certainty that the shootings at Norris Hall would not have occurred. But the Virginia Tech Review Panel concluded that "all things considered," if the university had canceled classes and announced it was closed after the first shooting, "the toll could have been reduced."[9] These actions would have been far more likely if Cho had been linked to the murder weapon shortly after the dormitory shootings. He may well have arrived at Norris Hall with his arsenal, only to find no one inside.

The gun lobby responds to every mass shooting by asserting that no gun law could have prevented the carnage. The issue, however, is not whether a single gun law could have prevented any particular shooting, but whether adopting a broad range of strong gun laws will end the recurring American nightmare of mass shootings, as well as reducing the daily toll of gun violence on our streets and in our homes. It's impossible to be certain about how many lives would have been saved if Cho had found himself in our imaginary world. But can anyone seriously argue that the toll of death and injury would have been the same had Cho been confronted with the reality of strong, sensible gun laws? Can anyone seriously assert that our national toll of gun death and injury would be the same if the gun lobby's mythology were no longer triumphant in the American gun debate?

Innocent people died that day at Virginia Tech because our nation has allowed myths to replace reason and evidence in making gun policy. Innocent people die every day for the same reason. They die on inner-city streets, in suburban shopping malls, in schools of every description, and in homes in every neighborhood. If the students attending their classes at Virginia Tech that snowy April day were not safe, then none of us is safe. If the first graders at Sandy Hook Elementary School were not safe, then none of us is safe.

Ideas have consequences. The gun lobby's mythology has lethal consequences. But it has those consequences only because the American people have yet to demand a different national discussion of guns and violence. They have yet to insist on more from their elected officials than rote repetition of empty slogans.

Ultimately, if we continue to allow bumper-sticker mythology to dictate gun policy to deadly effect, we have ourselves to blame. We know that guns do kill people, and they do it more effectively, and more often, than any other weapons. We know that the issue is not "outlawing" guns but preventing them from falling into dangerous hands. We know that irrational fear of the "slippery slope" is an empty excuse for inaction. We know we already have an armed society that is anything but polite. We know that strong gun laws can prevent "bad guys" from getting guns, and that guns, on balance, make "good guys" less safe. We know that strong law enforcement is not a substitute for strong laws. We know that gun makers and sellers should be accountable not for the violence of others but for their own conduct that enables the violence of others. We know that our Constitution does not condemn us to a future of perpetual gun tragedies, and that the "cold, dead hands" that should move us are those of the innocent victims of gun violence, not the fantasy of self-styled patriots who risk little in promoting their extreme and dangerous agenda.

Now we must act on what we know. There are lives to save.

Acknowledgments

I want to express my appreciation to Helene Atwan, Amanda Beiner, and the team at Beacon Press for seeing the value of a new look at the mythology at the core of our nation's failure to address the American gun violence epidemic. They made this a better book than I would have written alone. Special thanks also to Becca Knox, who has made her own lasting contributions to the struggle for sensible gun policies and who provided key editorial contributions. Dr. David Hemenway of the Harvard School of Public Health, a pioneer in gun violence research, also guided me to important new research that informed my treatment of the issues.

Finally, and of greatest value, I am grateful for the understanding support of my wife, Tara, and my daughter, Kylie, and particularly for Tara's indispensable editorial assistance.

Appendices

1. Firearm Violence (Total Fatal and Nonfatal) 1993–2011

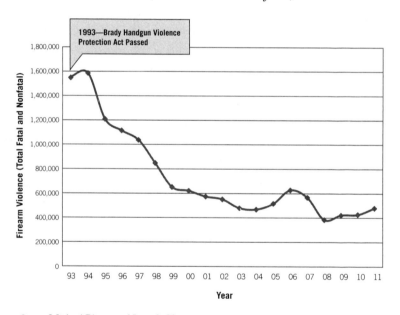

Source: Michael Planty and Jennifer Truman, *Firearm Violence, 1993–2011*, Bureau of Justice Statistics, NCJ 241730, Table 1, May 2013.

2. State Firearm Deaths and Death Rates per 100,000 (2014)

State	Firearm Death Rate	Deaths
Louisiana	18.9	890
Alaska	18.8	142
Mississippi	18.0	539
Alabama	16.7	808
Arkansas	16.4	491
Wyoming	16.0	92
New Mexico	15.8	336
Montana	15.8	170
Oklahoma	15.6	608
South Carolina	15.5	764
Missouri	15.2	939
Tennessee	14.7	986
Nevada	14.7	426
West Virginia	14.5	284
Kentucky	13.8	627
Georgia	13.7	1,388
Arizona	13.4	917
Idaho	13.1	212
Indiana	12.3	812
Utah	12.3	337
Colorado	12.1	658
North Dakota	12.1	94
North Carolina	11.7	1,201
Oregon	11.7	497
Florida	11.5	2,408
Kansas	11.3	328
Michigan	11.1	1,093

(continued)

State	Firearm Death Rate	Deaths
Delaware	11.1	102
Texas	10.6	2,823
Pennsylvania	10.5	1,389
Ohio	10.3	1,203
Virginia	10.3	885
South Dakota	10.3	89
Vermont	10.3	69
Washington	9.6	698
Nebraska	9.4	178
Maine	9.3	132
Illinois	9.0	1,167
Maryland	9.0	544
New Hampshire	8.6	121
Wisconsin	8.2	486
California	7.4	2,935
Iowa	7.4	239
Minnesota	6.6	374
New Jersey	5.3	468
Connecticut	4.9	186
New York	4.2	869
Massachusetts	3.2	227
Rhode Island	2.9	33
Hawaii	2.6	40

Source: Centers for Disease Control and Prevention, "Firearm Mortality by State: 2014," http://www.cdc.gov/nchs/pressroom/sosmap/firearm/htm.

3. Homicide by Firearm Rates in High-Income Nations (2007)

Country	Homicide Rate by Firearm per 100,000
United States	2.97
Switzerland	0.77
Italy	0.71
Belgium	0.68
Luxembourg	0.62
Canada	0.51
Ireland	0.48
Finland	0.45
Sweden	0.41
Netherlands	0.33
Denmark	0.27
Austria	0.22
Spain	0.20
Germany	0.19
New Zealand	0.16
Australia	0.14
Israel	0.09
United Kingdom (England and Wales)	0.07
France	0.06
Norway	0.05
Singapore	0.02

Source: United Nations Office on Drugs and Crime (UNODC) Small Arms Survey, via the *Guardian*: "Gun Homicides and Gun Ownership Listed by Country," 2012, http://www.theguardian.com/news/datablog/2012/jul/22/gun-homicides-ownership-world-list.

4. Homicide Rates in High-Income Nations (2013)

Country	Homicide Rate per 100,000
United States	3.8
Belgium	1.9
Finland	1.7
Israel	1.7 (in 2012—no data available in 2013)
Canada	1.4
France	1.2
Ireland	1.1
Australia	1.1
New Zealand	1.0
United Kingdom	1.0
Sweden	0.9
Norway	0.9
Italy	0.8
Denmark	0.7
Netherlands	0.7
Austria	0.7
Germany	0.7
Switzerland	0.7
Spain	0.6
Singapore	0.3
Luxembourg	0.2

Source: UNODC *Global Study of Homicide 2013*, https://www.unodc.org/gsh/

Notes

PROLOGUE: A TORTURED MYTHOLOGY

1. Erin Grinshteyn and David Hemenway, "Violent Death Rates: The US Compared with Other High-Income OECD Countries, 2010," *American Journal of Medicine* (2015), http://dx.doi.org/10.1016/j.amjmed.2015.10.025.
2. Ibid.
3. "Remarks by the President on Project Safe Neighborhoods," White House press release, May 14, 2001, http://georgewbush-whitehouse.archives.gov /news/releases/2001/05/20010514-1.html.
4. In the gun violence context, Handgun Control, Inc. (later named the Brady Campaign to Prevent Gun Violence) first used this phrase in an award-winning poster contrasting the number of handgun murders in the United States with the number in other industrialized countries.
5. Joel Achenbach, Scott Higham, and Sari Horwitz, "How NRA's True Believers Converted a Marksmanship Group into a Mighty Gun Lobby," *Washington Post*, January 12, 2013.
6. *National Journal*, March 5, 2005, 645.
7. Harris Interactive, "The American Red Cross, AARP, the Nature Conservancy and the U.S. Chamber of Commerce Are Among the Most Trusted Beltway Groups," Harris Poll #88, December 13, 2006, http://www.harrisinteractive .com/harris_poll/printerfriend/index.asp?PID=715.
8. NBC News/Wall Street Journal poll (by Peter Hart and Robert Teeter), Study 6038, November 2003.
9. Emma McGinty et al., "Public Opinion on Gun Policy Following the Newtown Mass Shooting and Disconnect with Political Action," in *Updated Evidence and Policy Developments on Reducing Gun Violence in America*, ed. Daniel Webster and Jon Vernick (Baltimore: Johns Hopkins University Press, 2014).
10. David Hemenway, *Private Guns, Public Health* (Ann Arbor: University of Michigan Press, 2004), 163.
11. Edith Honan, "Poll Finds Gun Owners, Even NRA Members, Back Some Restrictions," Reuters, July 24, 2012.
12. Douglas S. Weil and David Hemenway, "'I Am the NRA': An Analysis of a National Random Sample of Gun Owners," *Violence and Victims* 8 (1993): 353–65, 377–85.

13. Robert Spitzer, *The Politics of Gun Control*, 3rd ed. (Washington, DC: CQ Press, 2004).
14. Bill Clinton, *My Life* (New York: Knopf, 2004), 630.
15. Bob Cusack and Elizabeth Fulk, "The Last Nail in Gun Control," *Hill*, February 20, 2005.
16. James Bovard, "What's Happened to John McCain?," *America's First Freedom* (July 2001): 29.
17. National Rifle Association, *Gun Ban Obama*, http://www.gunbanobama.com.
18. Chris Cillizza, "What President Obama Said About Gun Control in the 2012 Campaign," *Washington Post*, December 16, 2012.
19. Mike DeBonis, "Garland's Gun Record Has Been Distorted by NRA, Second Amendment Experts Say," *Washington Post*, March 31, 2016.
20. Law Center to Prevent Gun Violence, www.smartgunlaws.org.
21. Philip J. Cook and Kristin A. Goss, *The Gun Debate: What Everyone Needs to Know* (Oxford, UK: Oxford University Press, 2014), 199.
22. Brady Campaign to Prevent Gun Violence, "Child Access Prevention (CAP) Laws," www.bradycampaign.org/facts/issues.
23. Cook and Goss, *The Gun Debate*, 197.
24. Justin McCarthy, "Quarter of U.S. Voters Say Candidate Must Share View on Guns," Gallup, October 19, 2015, http://www.gallup.com/poll/186248/quarter-voters-say-candidate-share-view-guns.aspx.
25. Peter M. Aronow and Benjamin T. Miller, "Policy Misperceptions and Support for Gun Control Legislation," *Lancet* 387 (January 16, 2016): 223, http://dx.doi.org/10.1016/S0140-6736(16)00042-8.
26. Art Swift, "Americans' Desire for Stricter Gun Laws Up Sharply," Gallup, October 19, 2015, http://www.gallup.com/poll/186236/americans-desire-stricter-gun-laws-sharply.aspx.
27. Evan Halper and Mark Z. Barabak, "Democrats Campaigning Aggressively on Gun Control, Dropping Longtime Reticence," *Los Angeles Times*, December 10, 2015.
28. Barack Obama, "Guns Are Our Shared Responsibility," op-ed, *New York Times*, January 7, 2016.
29. Spitzer, *Politics of Gun Control*, 102.
30. Gary Langer, "Mental Health Measures Broadly Backed, but Culture Gets More Blame Than Guns," ABCNews.com, April 23, 2007, http://abcnews.go.com/Politics/print?id=3068449.
31. Jennifer Agiesta, "CNN/ORC Poll: Guns, Immigration, Abortion Increasingly Important to Voters," CNN.com, September 14, 2015, http://www.cnn.com/2015/09/14/politics/cnn-poll-guns-immigration-abortion-2016/.
32. Joseph Dolman, "Mayor's Promise on Guns Is Noble," *Newsday*, February 15, 2006.
33. James Carville and Paul Begala, *Take It Back: Our Party, Our Country, Our Future* (New York: Simon & Schuster, 2006), 50.
34. Ibid., 49.

35. Ibid.

36. The name of the agency was changed in 2003, when it was moved from the Department of the Treasury to the Department of Justice, and is now the Bureau of Alcohol, Tobacco, Firearms, and Explosives. ATF will be used to refer to the agency as it functioned before and after the name change.

37. ATF, *Gun Shows: Brady Checks and Crime Gun Traces* (Washington, DC: Dept. of the Treasury/Dept. of Justice/ATF, January 1999), 7.

38. District of Columbia v. Heller, 554 U.S. 570 (2008), https://www.oyez.org /cases/2007/07-290.

39. McDonald v. Chicago, 561 U.S. 742 (2010), https://www.oyez.org/cases /2009/08-1521.

CHAPTER ONE: GUNS DON'T KILL PEOPLE, PEOPLE KILL PEOPLE

1. Quote from gun dealer Max Bosworth to KPVI-NBC, Newschannel 6, October 10, 2003, www.kpvi.com.

2. Tom Clancy, foreword to Wayne LaPierre, *Guns, Crime, and Freedom* (Washington DC: Regnery, 1994), xiv.

3. *Whose Right to Keep and Bear Arms? The Second Amendment as a Source of Individual Rights: Hearing before the Subcommittee on the Constitution, Federalism and Property Rights of the Senate Committee on the Judiciary*, 105th Cong. (1998) 33 (Testimony of Charlton Heston).

4. Kevin M. Cunningham, "When Gun Control Meets the Constitution," *St. John's Journal of Legal Commentary* 10 (1994): 59, 61.

5. Allen Beck et al., *Survey of Adult Inmates 1991*, NCJ-136949 (Washington, DC: Dept. of Justice, Bureau of Justice Statistics, 1993).

6. Joseph M. Durso et al., *Background Checks for Firearm Transfers, 2012—Statistical Tables*, NCJ 247815 (Washington, DC: Dept. of Justice, Bureau of Justice Statistics, December 9, 2014).

7. National Rifle Association, "Firearms Safety in America 2007," NRA-ILA fact sheet, October 19, 2007.

8. Robert J. Spitzer, *The Politics of Gun Control* (Chatham, NJ: Chatham House, 1995), 59.

9. Arthur L. Kellermann et al., "Injuries and Deaths Due to Firearms in the Home," *Journal of Trauma* 45 (1998): 263.

10. Arthur L. Kellermann et al., "Suicide in the Home in Relation to Gun Ownership," *New England Journal of Medicine* 327 (1992): 467.

11. David A. Brent et al., "Firearms and Adolescent Suicide: A Community Case Control Study," *American Journal of Diseases of Children* 147 (1993): 1066.

12. Consumer Product Safety Commission, "CPSC Bans Lawn Darts," CPSC Document #5053, http://www.cpsc.gov/cpscpub/pubs/5053.html.

13. Data derived from National Center for Health Statistics Vital Statistics System, 1996–1998, United States, Unintentional Firearm Deaths and Rates per 100,000 in 1999–2000, United States, http://www.cdc.gov/ncipc/wisqars.

14. Elizabeth C. Powell, Edward Jovtis, and Robert Tanz, "Incidence and Circumstances of Nonfatal Firearm-Related Injuries Among Children and Adolescents," *Archives of Pediatrics and Adolescent Medicine* 55 (December 2001): 1364–68.

15. News release #79–007, US Consumer Product Safety Commission (February 5, 1979).

16. News release #79–031, US Consumer Product Safety Commission (June 29, 1979).

17. News release #95–009, US Consumer Product Safety Commission (October 17, 1994).

18. Philip J. Cook, *Guns in America: Results of a Comprehensive National Survey on Firearms Ownership and Use* (Washington, DC: Police Foundation, 1996), 39.

19. Michael Planty and Jennifer Truman, *Firearm Violence, 1993–2011*, NCJ 241730 (Washington, DC: Dept. of Justice, Bureau of Justice Statistics, May 2013).

20. Craig Perkins, *Weapon Use and Violent Crime*, NCJ 194820 (Washington, DC: Dept. of Justice, Bureau of Justice Statistics, September 2003).

21. Jane Leavy, *Sandy Koufax: A Lefty's Legacy* (New York: Harper Perennial, 2002), 162.

22. 18 U.S.C. § 922(x)(1); 18 U.S.C. § 922(b)(1).

23. Gary Kleck, *Targeting Guns: Firearms and Their Control* (Edison, NJ: Aldine Transaction, 1997), 221.

24. Henri E. Cauvin and Patricia Davis, "Sniper Suspect Lee Boyd Malvo Shot from Afar, He Says, but He Stalked from Up Close," *Washington Post*, November 22, 2003.

25. Ibid.

26. Garen Wintemute, "Guns and Gun Violence," in *The Crime Drop in America*, ed. A. Blumstein and J. Wallman (New York: Cambridge University Press, 2000), 56–57.

27. Kim A. MacInnis, "Mass Murder (Shootings)," in *Guns in American Society: An Encyclopedia of History, Politics, Culture, and the Law*, vol. 2, ed. Gregg Lee Carter (Santa Barbara, CA: ABC-CLIO, 2002).

28. Stephen Halbrook, "Does the United States Need a National Database for Ballistic Fingerprints?," *Insight*, November 26, 2002.

29. Franklin Zimring, "Is Gun Control Likely to Reduce Violent Killings?," *University of Chicago Law Review* 35 (1968): 721, 728. See also Franklin Zimring and Gordon Hawkins, *Crime Is Not the Problem: Lethal Violence in America* (New York: Oxford University Press, 1997), 114.

30. Linda Saltzman et al. "Weapon Involvement and Injury Outcomes in Family and Intimate Assaults," *Journal of the American Medical Association* 267 (June 10, 1992): 3043.

31. Zimring and Hawkins, *Crime Is Not the Problem*, 108.

32. Josefina Card, "Lethality of Suicidal Methods and Suicide Risk: 2 Distinct Concepts," *Omega Journal of Death and Dying* 5 (1974): 37.

33. Zimring and Hawkins, *Crime Is Not the Problem*, 728.
34. Jeremy Olson, "Outside Metro Areas, Access to Guns Is Easy," *Omaha World-Herald*, May 16, 2005.
35. Ibid.
36. Ibid.
37. Zimring and Hawkins, *Crime Is Not the Problem*, 35–39.
38. Matthew Miller, Deborah Azrael, and David Hemenway, "Firearms and Violent Death in the United States," in *Reducing Gun Violence in America: Informing Policy with Evidence and Analysis*, ed. Daniel W. Webster and Jon S. Vernick (Baltimore: Johns Hopkins University Press, 2013), 1–2.
39. Zimring and Hawkins, *Crime Is Not the Problem*, 109.
40. Ibid., quoting Ronald Clarke and Pat Mayhew, "The British Gas Suicide Story and Its Criminological Implications," in *Crime and Justice: A Review of Research*, vol. 10, ed. Michael Tonry and Norval Morris (Chicago: University of Chicago Press, 1988), 107.
41. E. Grinshteyn and D. Hemenway, "Violent Death Rate: The US Compared with Other High-income OECD Countries, 2010," *American Journal of Medicine*, published online November 6, 2015, doi:10.1016/j.amjmed.2015 .10.025.
42. Ibid.
43. David Hemenway, *Private Guns, Public Health* (Ann Arbor: University of Michigan Press, 2006), 199, and studies cited therein.
44. Molly Ivins, "Taking a Stab at Our Infatuation with Guns," *Seattle Times*, March 15, 1993, http://community.seattletimes.nwsource.com/archive/?date =19930315&slug=1690536.
45. Eloisa Ruano Gonzalez, "NRA Gun Instructor Shoots Student by Accident," *Orlando Sentinel*, February 21, 2010.
46. Kleck, *Targeting Guns*, 296.
47. Ibid.
48. Ibid.
49. Gail Sullivan, "Firing-Range Instructor Hands 9-Year-Old an Uzi. Now He's Dead," *Washington Post*, August 27, 2014.
50. David Abel, "Boy's Death Spurs Hard Look at Laws for Guns, Children," *Boston Globe*, October 28, 2008.
51. Mark Obmascik and David Olinger, "Two Killers Rampaged as 6 Officers Awaited Aid," *Denver Post*, May 16, 2000.
52. Howard Kurtz, "Let the Blame Begin," *Washington Post*, April 26, 1999.
53. Chuck Raasch, "Gingrich: Liberalism Led to Colo. Massacre," *USA Today*, May 13, 1999.
54. Fred Hiatt, "A Littleton Massacre Every Day," *Washington Post*, April 25, 1999.
55. Ibid.
56. Michael Janofsky, "Columbine Victims Were Killed Minutes into Siege at Colorado School, Report Reveals," *New York Times*, May 17, 2000.

57. Philip Cook et al., "Regulating Gun Markets," *Journal of Criminal Law and Criminology* 86 (1995).

58. Lynn Bartels, "Gun Dealers Rejected Columbine Killers," *Rocky Mountain News,* January 27, 2000.

59. David Olinger, "Following the Guns," *Denver Post,* August 1, 1999.

60. Tom W. Smith, *1999 National Gun Policy Survey of the National Opinion Research Center: Research Findings* (Chicago: National Opinion Research Center, July 2000), 12.

61. Marttila Communications Group, *National Gun Control Survey* (Boston, July 11–14, 2003), 6.

62. Spitzer, *The Politics of Gun Control,* 133. The reaction of the US Congress to the school shootings stands in marked contrast to the legislative reaction in other developed countries to mass shootings. The murder of sixteen schoolchildren and a teacher in Dunblane, Scotland, in March 1996 led to a nearly total prohibition of handguns, with a compulsory buy-back of handguns already legally owned. In April of that year, the Port Arthur massacre, in which a lone gunman killed thirty-five persons with a semiautomatic rifle, led Australia to prohibit certain categories of weapons with a buy-back of those weapons, along with new licensing, registration, safe storage, and firearm-training requirements. See Peter Reuter and Jenny Mouzos, "A Massive Buyback of Low-Risk Guns," in *Evaluating Gun Policy: Effects on Crime and Violence,* ed. Jens Ludwig and Philip J. Cook (New York: Oxford University Press, 2003), 121–56.

63. 145 Cong. Rec. H4582, June 17, 1999 (statement of Rep. Smith).

64. 145 Cong. Rec. H4581, June 17, 1999 (statement of Rep. Everett).

65. 145 Cong. Rec. H4582, June 17, 1999 (statement of Rep. Peterson).

66. 145 Cong. Rec. H4578, June 17, 1999 (statement of Rep. Rothman).

67. 145 Cong. Rec. H4605, June 17, 1999 (statement of Rep. McCarthy).

CHAPTER TWO: WHEN GUNS ARE OUTLAWED, ONLY OUTLAWS WILL HAVE GUNS

1. "Excerpts: Charlie Gibson Interviews GOP Vice President Candidate Sarah Palin," ABC News, September 12, 2008, http://abcnews.go.com /print?id=5789483.

2. See "Guns: Gallup Historical Trends," showing polling 2010–2015, http:// www.gallup.com/poll/1645/guns.aspx.

3. Josh Sugarmann, *Every Handgun Is Pointed at You: The Case for Banning Handguns* (New York: New Press, 2001). Two prominent gun control organizations, the Coalition to Stop Gun Violence and the Violence Policy Center, have advocated a ban on the manufacture and sale of handguns as part of their policy agendas.

4. For an interesting discussion of the use of red-herring arguments in the gun control debate (and of the origin of the term "red herring"), see Andrew Jay McClurg, "The Rhetoric of Gun Control," *American University Law Review* 42 (1992): 53.

5. Americans for Gun Safety, *No Questions Asked: Background Checks, Gun Shows, and Crime* (Washington, DC: Americans for Gun Safety Foundation, April 2001), 10.

6. Richard Gardiner, director of state and local affairs, Institute for Legislative Action, National Rifle Association, quoted in Osha Gray Davidson, *Under Fire: The NRA and the Battle for Gun Control* (New York: H. Holt, 1993), 45.

7. The "change the subject" strategy often involves simply misrepresenting the gun control proposal at issue to make it appear to be equivalent to a gun ban. For example, any proposal to require guns to have specified safety mechanisms is labeled a "gun ban" by the NRA because it would "ban" any gun that doesn't have the mechanism. The issue, of course, is whether it is feasible to install the mechanism. If it is, then the choice of whether to sell the gun with the safety mechanism is the manufacturer's. The government has not "banned" the gun; the manufacturer has simply chosen not to make its guns safer. If a manufacturer decided to take its cars off the market rather than install seat belts and air bags to comply with government regulations, we would not say the government had "banned cars."

8. Marttila Communications Group, National Gun Control Survey, conducted July 11–14, 2003.

9. District of Columbia v. Heller, 554 U.S. 570 (2008), https://www.oyez.org/cases/2007/07-290.

10. Sandra Froman, President's Column, *America's 1st Freedom*, National Rifle Association (December 2006): 10.

11. Daniel D. Polsby and Dennis Brennen, *Taking Aim at Gun Control* (Chicago: Heartland Institute, 1995), 9–10.

12. Although the NRA says it supports laws barring felons from possessing guns, it worked hard to defend a ridiculous federal program to use taxpayers' money to restore gun rights to felons who somehow were able to convince ATF that they can be trusted with a gun. See Michael Isikoff, "BATF Allows Some Felons to Own Guns," *Washington Post*, September 24, 1991. Congress shut the program down in 1992 by barring appropriated monies from being spent by ATF for this purpose. See Public Law 102–393 (October 6, 1992).

13. Garen J. Wintemute et al., "Prior Misdemeanor Convictions as a Risk Factor for Later Violent and Firearm-Related Criminal Activity Among Authorized Purchasers of Handguns," *Journal of the American Medical Association* 341 (1998): 2083–87.

14. J. D. Wright and P. H. Rossi, *Armed and Considered Dangerous: A Survey of Felons and Their Firearms* (Piscataway, NJ: Aldine de Gruyter Transaction, 1986).

15. Bradley A. Buckles, foreword, in Bureau of Alcohol, Tobacco and Firearms (hereafter ATF), *Following the Gun: Enforcing Federal Laws Against Firearms Traffickers* (Washington, DC: Dept. of the Treasury, ATF, June 2000), iii.

16. Mike Seate, "Gun Pros Say House Has Wrong Target," *Pittsburgh Tribune-Review*, September 12, 2006.

17. The incorrect assumption that criminals are both smart and rational appears to underlie the oversimplified view of the Brady Act by "rogue economist" Steven Levitt in his runaway best seller *Freakonomics*. Levitt and his coauthor, Stephen Dubner, observe that the Brady Act "may have seemed appealing to politicians, but to an economist it doesn't make much sense. Why? Because regulation of a legal market is bound to fail when a healthy black market exists for the same product. With guns so cheap and so easy to get, the standard criminal has no incentive fill out a firearm application at his local gun shop and then wait a week. The Brady Act, accordingly, has proven to be practically impotent in lowering crime." Stephen D. Levitt and Stephen J. Dubner, *Freakonomics: A Rogue Economist Explores the Hidden Side of Everything* (New York: William Morrow, 2005), 132. This analysis suffers from several problems. First, it does not recognize that, for guns, the legal market is the primary source for the illegal market. Second, it makes the mistake of basing public policy conclusions on the assumption that everyone behaves rationally. The assumption of rationality is unjustified for the public at large; it is even more so for the criminally inclined. It may make no sense to an economist that after Brady, criminals would try to buy guns from gun dealers, but we know they have continued to do so. Finally, whatever effect the Brady Act has on the "standard criminal" (whatever that is), it may well have substantial public-safety benefits if it interferes with access to guns by only a subset of the criminal population. Needless to say, *Freakonomics* makes no attempt to explain why the dramatic decline in violent gun crime coincided almost exactly with the implementation of the Brady Act.

18. M. A. Wright, G. J. Wintemute, and F. Rivera, "Effectiveness of a Program to Deny Legal Handgun Purchase to Persons Believed to Be at High Risk for Firearm Violence," *American Journal of Public Health* 89 (1999): 88.

19. Kleck, *Targeting Guns*, 377.

20. Bureau of Justice Statistics, US Dept. of Justice, "Crimes Committed with Firearms, 1973–2006," in *Key Facts at a Glance* (Washington, DC: Dept. of Justice, Bureau of Justice Statistics, January 5, 2008), www.ojp.usdoj.gov/bjs/glance/tables/guncrimetab.htm.

21. Planty and Truman, *Firearm Violence, 1993–2011*, table 1.

22. Bureau of Justice Statistics, "Crimes Committed with Firearms, 1973–2006."

23. Jennifer Karberg, Ronald Frandsen, Joseph Durso, and Allina Lee, "Background Checks for Firearm Transfers, 2012: Statistical Tables (Washington, DC: US Dept. of Justice, Bureau of Justice Statistics, NCJ 247815, December 2014), table 1.

24. Planty and Truman, *Firearm Violence, 1993–2011.*.

25. Douglas Weil and Rebecca Knox, "Effects of Limiting Handgun Purchases On Interstate Transfer of Firearms," *Journal of the American Medical Association* 275 (June 12, 1996): 1759.

26. Because federal law requires gun dealers to obtain from purchasers proof of residence in the gun dealer's state, a gun trafficker from New York City could not walk into a Virginia gun store and buy a handgun. See 18 U.S.C. § 922(b) (3). She must recruit a Virginia resident to act as an intermediary or straw buyer.

27. Quotation of Agent Patrick Hynes in Philip Cook, Stephanie Molliconi, and Thomas Cole, "Regulating Gun Markets," *Journal of Criminal Law and Criminology* (1995): 59, 72n56.

28. 18 U.S.C. § (g)(3)(A).

29. Weil and Knox, "Effects of Limiting Handgun Purchases," 1760.

30. Ibid.

31. Peter Baker, "Va. Gun Sale Law Curbs Traffic to North, Study Says," *Washington Post*, August 3, 1995.

32. Toby Coleman, "The Trading Game," *Charleston Daily Mail*, February 26, 2004.

33. See Complaint, Lemongello v. Will Company, Inc. et al., Civil Action No. 02-C-2952 (November 14, 2002), 6–7.

34. ATF, Youth Crime Gun Interdiction Initiative, *Crime Gun Trace Analysis Reports: The Illegal Youth Firearms Market in 27 Communities* (Washington, DC: Dept. of the Treasury, ATF, October 1998), 12.

35. Ibid.

36. Ibid., part II.

37. Ibid.

38. Hemenway, *Private Guns, Public Health*, 231.

39. US Census Bureau, *Statistical Abstract of the United States: 2012*, Table 309, "Crime Rates by Type—Selected Large Cities: 2009."

40. ATF, "Top 15 Source States for Firearms with a District of Columbia Recovery, January 1, 2014–December 31, 2014," in *ATF District of Columbia* (Washington, DC: ATF, 2014).

41. Joseph Tartaro, "When Is a Gunowner Database Not a Registry?," *Gun Week*, November 10, 2004, 15.

42. 18 U.S.C.§923(g)(6).

43. William J. Vizzard, *Shots in the Dark: The Policy, Politics and Symbolism of Gun Control* (Lanham, MD: Rowman & Littlefield, 2000), 162.

44. California Attorney General, "Attorney General Lockyer Announces Arrest Warrants Issued for Two Los Angeles Men on Gun Possession and Trafficking Charges," press release, May 4, 2005.

45. Aaron Diamant, "I-Team: Trail of a Gun," TMJ4 Milwaukee, February 15, 2007, http://www.todaystmj4.com/features/iteam/5808641.html.

46. D. W. Webster, J. S. Vernick, and L. M. Hepburn, "Relationship Between Licensing, Registration, and Other Gun Sales Laws and the Source State of Crime Guns," *Injury Prevention* 7 (2001): 184–89.

47. Ibid., 189.

48. Daniel W. Webster et al., "Preventing the Diversion of Guns to Criminals Through Effective Firearm Sales Laws," in Webster and Vernick, *Reducing Gun Violence in America*.

49. Ibid., 21.

50. Jens Ludwig and Philip Cook, "Homicide and Suicide Rates Associated with Implementation of the Brady Handgun Violence Prevention Act," *Journal of the American Medical Association* 284 (2000): 585–91.

51. Douglas Weil, *Traffic Stop: How the Brady Act Disrupts Interstate Gun Trafficking* (Washington, DC: Center to Prevent Handgun Violence, 1997).

52. Ludwig and Cook, "Homicide and Suicide Rates," 590.

53. Jens Ludwig and Philip Cook, "Impact of the Brady Act on Homicide and Suicide Rates," letter, *Journal of the American Medical Association* 284 (2000): 2721.

54. See, generally, Spitzer, *The Politics of Gun Control*, 111.

55. The NRA has described the machine gun regulatory system as follows: "Under the NFA, persons wishing to purchase an automatic firearm had to be at least 21 years old, submit to an extensive criminal background check by the FBI, pay a $200 transfer tax, make formal application for such transfer by duplicate copies including photographs and fingerprints and have a local law enforcement official certify that they had no felony record and met the requirements for purchase. The applicant would have to wait three to six months between purchase and delivery of the machine gun." National Rifle Association, *Monitor* 13, no. 13 (August 15, 1986).

56. The bureau's name has since been changed to the Bureau of Alcohol, Tobacco, Firearms, and Explosives. I will refer to it throughout as ATF.

57. Kleck, *Targeting Guns*, 109.

58. National Center for Policy Analysis, "Will Banning Assault Weapons Reduce Crime?," Brief Analysis No. 102 (Dallas: National Center for Policy Analysis, February 7, 1994), www.ncpa.org/ba/ba102.html.

59. Kleck, *Targeting Guns*, 109.

60. Philip J. Cook and Kristin A. Goss, *The Gun Debate: What Everyone Needs to Know* (Oxford, UK: Oxford University Press, 2014), 136.

61. Federal Bureau of Investigation, *NICS Operations Reports, 2010–2014*. See also Government Accounting Office, *Potential Effects of Next-Day Destruction of NICS Background Check Records* 13, no. 17 (July 2002).

62. Spitzer, *The Politics of Gun Control*, 111.

63. National Center for Health Statistics, *National Vital Statistics Report* 50, no. 15 (September 16, 2002).

64. Cook and Goss, *The Gun Debate*, 34.

65. Hemenway, *Private Guns, Public Health*, 36.

66. Ibid., 38.

67. Ibid., 39.

68. Brent et al. "Firearms and Adolescent Suicide," 1066.

69. Colin Loftin et al., "Effects of Restrictive Licensing of Handguns on Homicide and Suicide in the District of Columbia," *New England Journal of Medicine* 325 (1991): 1615–20.

70. David Lester and Mary E. Murrell, "The Influence of Gun Control Laws on Suicidal Behavior," *American Journal of Psychiatry* 137 (January 1980): 121–22; Bijou Yang and David Lester, "The Effect of Gun Availability on Suicide Rates," *Atlantic Economic Review* 19 (1991): 74. See generally Hemenway, *Private Guns, Public Health*, 44.

71. Myron Boor and Jeffrey H. Bair, "Suicide Rates, Handgun Control Laws, and Sociodemographic Variables," *Psychological Reports* 66 (1990): 923.

72. David C. Grossman et al., "Gun Storage Practices and Risk of Youth Suicide and Unintentional Firearm Injuries," *Journal of the American Medical Association* 293 (February 9, 2005): 707.

73. Daniel Webster et al., "Association Between Youth-Focused Firearm Laws and Youth Suicides," *Journal of the American Medical Association* 292 (August 4, 2004): 594.

74. Garen Wintemute et al., "Mortality Among Recent Purchasers of Handguns," *New England Journal of Medicine* 341 (1999): 1583.

75. General Accounting Office, *Gun Control: Implementation of the National Instant Criminal Background Check System* (Washington, DC: GAO, February 2000), 10.

76. National Center for Injury Prevention & Control, US Centers for Disease Control and Prevention, *Web-Based Injury Statistics Query & Reporting System (WISQARS) Injury Mortality Reports, 1999–2010, for National, Regional, and States* (Washington, DC: National Center for Injury Prevention & Control, December 2012).

77. David Hemenway, "Gun Accidents," in *Guns in American Society: An Encyclopedia of History, Politics, Culture, and the Law*, vol. 1, ed. Gregg Lee Carter (Santa Barbara, CA: ABC-CLIO, 2002).

78. Daniel Webster and Marc Starnes, "Reexamining the Association Between Child Access Prevention Gun Laws and Unintentional Shootings Deaths of Children," *Pediatrics* 106 (December 2000): 1466, 1468.

79. Centers for Disease Control and Prevention, "Fatal Injury Reports, National and Regional, 1999–2014," http://webappa.cdc.gov/sasweb/ncipc/mortrate10_us.html.

80. Michael Luo and Mike McIntire, "Children and Guns: The Hidden Toll," *New York Times*, September 28, 2013.

81. David Hemenway and Sara Solnick, "Children and Unintentional Firearm Death," *Injury Epidemiology* 2 (2015): 26.

82. Grinshteyn and Hemenway, "Violent Death Rate."

83. National Rifle Association, "Firearms Safety in America 2007."

84. Hemenway, "Gun Accidents," 3.

85. Tom W. Smith, *National Gun Policy Survey of the National Opinion Research Center: Research Findings* (Chicago: National Opinion Research Center, December 2001). See also Renee Johnson et al., "Firearm Ownership and Storage Practices, US Households, 1992–2002: A Systematic Review," *American Journal of Preventive Medicine* 27 (2004): 173, 181 (reviewing studies finding

between 30 percent to 35 percent of US households contain guns); and Tom W. Smith and Jaesok Son, *General Social Survey: Trends in Gun Ownership in the United States, 1972–2014* (Chicago: NORC, March 2015), http://www.norc.org/PDFs/GSS%20Reports/GSS_Trends%20in%20Gun %20Ownership_US_1972-2014.pdf.

86. Grossman et al, "Gun Storage Practices," 707.

87. Webster and Starnes, "Reexamining the Association Between Child Access Prevention Gun Laws and Unintentional Shootings Deaths of Children," 1467.

88. Ibid., 1468.

89. Christopher Ingraham, "Guns Are Now Killing as Many People as Cars in the U.S.," *Washington Post*, December 17, 2015. (Citing data from the Centers for Disease Control.)

90. See the excellent summary of the history of auto safety in Hemenway, *Private Guns, Public Health*, 10–19.

91. Jon S. Vernick et al., "Unintentional and Undetermined Firearm Related Deaths: A Preventable Death Analysis for Three Safety Devices," *Injury Prevention* 9 (2003): 307.

92. Davidson, *Under Fire*, 44.

93. Centers for Disease Control and Prevention, NCHS, "Firearm Mortality by State: 2014."

94. Fox Butterfield, "Social Isolation, Guns and a 'Culture of Suicide,'" *New York Times*, February 13, 2005.

95. Ibid.

96. CDC, "Firearm Mortality by State: 2014."

97. Children's Defense Fund, *Protect Children, Not Guns 2013* (Washington, DC: Children's Defense Fund, July 24, 2013), table 4. Data from Centers for Disease Control, NCHS.

98. Dorothy Samuels, "Congress 101: If You Want Success, Don't Mess With the Gun Lobby," *New York Times*, October 3, 2004.

99. Gary Kleck and Don B. Kates, *Armed: New Perspectives on Gun Control* (Amherst, NY: Prometheus Books, 2001), 21.

100. National Institute of Justice, *Felony Defendants in Large Urban Counties* (Washington, DC: US Dept. of Justice, Office of Justice Programs, Bureau of Justice Statistics, 1998).

101. Philip J. Cook, Jens Ludwig, and Anthony A. Braga, "Criminal Records of Homicide Offenders," *Journal of the American Medical Association* 294 (August 3, 2005): 598.

102. "'Who Were These Boys?' Pair Carried an Arsenal—and a Grudge, Witnesses Say," *South Florida Sun-Sentinel*, March 26, 1998; and John Kifner et al., "From Wild Talk and Friendship to Five Deaths in a Schoolyard," *New York Times*, March 29, 1998.

103. Anne Rochell, "Arkansas School Shooting Grandfather of Suspect Says Boys Stole Guns; 'Everybody's Lives Are Ruined,'" *Atlanta Journal and Constitution*, March 25, 1998.

CHAPTER THREE: GUN CONTROL IS A SLIPPERY SLOPE TO CONFISCATION

1. LaPierre, *Guns, Crime, and Freedom*, 48.
2. NRA, Institute for Legislative Affairs, "Firearms Registration: New York City's Lesson," January 27, 2000, https://www.nraila.org/articles/20000127/firearms-registration-new-york-city-s.
3. National Rifle Association, Institute for Legislative Affairs, "One Gun a Month: Rationing a Constitutionally-Protected Right," March 9, 2000, https://www.nraila.org/articles/20000309/one-gun-a-month-rationing-a-constituti.
4. Warren Cassidy quoted in Osha Gray Davidson, *Under Fire: The NRA & the Battle for Gun Control* (New York: H. Holt, 1993), 44.
5. Charlton Heston, "Winning the Cultural War," Harvard Law School Forum, February 16, 1999, available at http://alumnus.caltech.edu/~marcsulf/heston.html.
6. Ibid., 44.
7. This slippery-slope fallacy is discussed outside the gun context in Eric Lode, "Slippery Slope Arguments and Legal Reasoning," *California Law Review* 87 (1999): 1469, 1499–1500. See also Frederick Schauer, "Slippery Slopes," *Harvard Law Review* 99 (1985): 361, 379 ("Such arguments illustrate the fallacy of assuming that the lack of an obvious stopping point along a continuum renders imprecise the point that is ultimately chosen.").
8. The version of the Brady Bill signed into law provided that, during the first five years the law was in effect, law enforcement would have five business days to complete the background checks. The five-day period was a recognition that time would be required to manually review criminal-history records that had not been computerized in many states. The Brady Bill also authorized funds to assist the states in computerizing their criminal records. After this five-year "interim" period, the National Instant Criminal Background Check System (NICS) became operational, with the checks to be completed by federal authorities within three business days. The computerization of records under NICS was inadequate years after the system was established. If the NICS system had gone into effect in 1994, as the NRA proposed, it would have been completely ineffective in blocking over-the-counter gun purchases by criminals.
9. See, e.g., Joseph E. Olson and David B. Kopel, "All the Way Down the Slippery Slope: Gun Prohibition in England and Some Lessons for Civil Liberties in America," *Hamline Law Review* 22 (1999): 399; and Eugene Volokh, "The Mechanisms of the Slippery Slope," *Harvard Law Review* 116 (2003): 1026.
10. "The *post hoc* fallacy is said to occur when it is concluded that *A* causes *B* simply because one or more occurrences of *A* are correlated with one or more occurrences of *B*. The full Latin name for this traditional fallacy is *post hoc, ergo propter hoc*, meaning 'after this, therefore, because of this.'" Douglas N. Walton, *Informal Logic: A Handbook for Critical Argumentation* (New York: Oxford University Press, 1989), 213.
11. See, e.g., Olson and Kopel, "All the Way Down the Slippery Slope," 399.

12. NRA, Institute for Legislative Affairs, "Firearms Registration: New York City's Lesson."
13. Ibid.
14. See Allegheny County Sportmen's League v. Edward G. Rendell, 860 A.2d 10 (Pa. 2004).
15. See D. Webster et al., "Relationship Between Licensing, Registration, and Other Gun Sales Laws and the Source State of Crime Guns," *Injury Prevention* 7, no. 3 (September 2001): 186.
16. See 18 U.S.C. 922(o).
17. Volokh, "The Mechanisms of the Slippery Slope."
18. Interview with Chuck Michel, transcript of *To the Point*, hosted by Warren Olney, Public Radio International, July 1, 2008.

CHAPTER FOUR: AN ARMED SOCIETY IS A POLITE SOCIETY

1. LaPierre, *Guns, Crime, and Freedom*, 23.
2. The Kennesaw law was enacted in 1982 to "send a message" in response to local gun bans in places like Morton Grove, Illinois. The ordinance included no penalties for its violation and was never enforced as a serious attempt to require private gun ownership. This did not prevent Kennesaw city officials from boasting of dramatic decreases in burglaries from 1981 to 1985, a claim of success that was echoed by pro-gun writers like Don Kates and Gary Kleck. It turns out that this claimed decrease in burglaries was a statistical mirage, the result of an atypical spike in burglaries in the first six months of 1981, followed by a return to more typical levels in the years after. Scholars who compared burglaries in Kennesaw during a more meaningful time period (1976–1986) found that "burglaries were relatively stable through the entire period" with "no visible change following introduction of the ordinance." David McDowall, Brian Wiersema, and Colin Loftin, "Did Mandatory Firearm Ownership in Kennesaw Really Prevent Burglaries?," *Sociology and Social Research* 74 (October 1989): 48, 49.
3. Zimring and Hawkins, *Crime Is Not the Problem*, 37–39.
4. Grinshteyn and Hemenway, "Violent Death Rate."
5. Cook and Goss, *The Gun Debate*, 2; Small Arms Survey, "Estimated Civilian Owned Firearms," *Research Notes, Armed Actors*, no. 9 (September 2011).
6. Don Kates, "Proposition H: Mythology Instead of Criminology," (Oakland, CA: Independent Institute, November 23, 2005), http://independent.org /news/room/article.asp?id=1621.
7. Ibid.
8. LaPierre, *Guns, Crime, and Freedom*, 170–71.
9. Ibid., 171.
10. Small Arms Survey, "Estimated Civilian Owned Firearms," table 1. See also Hemenway, *Private Guns, Public Health*, 197; David Hemenway and Matthew Miller, "Firearm Availability and Homicide Rates Across 26 High-Income Countries," *Journal of Trauma* 49 (December 2000): 985–88.

11. Cook and Goss, *The Gun Debate*, 61.
12. Embassy of Switzerland, Canberra, Australia, Information Service 2004, "Swiss Gun Legislation," http://www.ssaa.or.au/un/swiss.html. See also Wendy Cukier and Victor W. Sidel, *The Global Gun Epidemic: From Saturday Night Specials to AK-47s* (Westport, CT: Praeger Security International, 2006), 191.
13. LaPierre, *Guns, Crime, and Freedom*, 171.
14. Embassy of Switzerland, "Swiss Gun Legislation."
15. Ibid.
16. LaPierre, *Guns, Crime, and Freedom*, 174.
17. Ibid.
18. Hemenway, *Private Guns, Public Health*, 46, 200; Hemenway and Miller, "Firearm Availability," 986.
19. Walter Rodgers, "Strict Israeli Gun Control Laws Aim for Security Balance," CNN.com, September 17, 1999, http://www.cnn.com/WORLD/meast /9909/17/israel.gun.control/.
20. Ibid.
21. Dan Williams, "Under the Gun," *Jerusalem Post*, November 17, 2000.
22. Froman, "President's Column," 10.
23. Matthew Miller, Deborah Azrael, and David Hemenway, "Rates of Household Firearm Ownership and Homicide Across US Regions and States, 1988–1997," *American Journal of Public Health* 92 (December 2002): 1988, 1989. This study used the percentage of suicides committed with guns as a "proxy" for firearms ownership, which, as noted above, is a widely accepted technique for measuring relative firearm availability. A later study by the same Harvard team reached a similar conclusion, using survey-based estimates of household firearm ownership. See Matthew Miller, David Hemenway, and Deborah Azrael, "State-Level Homicide Victimization Rates in the US in Relation to Survey Measures of Household Firearm Ownership, 2001–2003," *Social Science & Medicine* 64 (2006): 656.
24. Miller, Azrael, and Hemenway, "Rates of Household Firearm Ownership," 1990.
25. Ibid., 1990–91.
26. Ibid., 1992.
27. Miller et al., "State-Level Homicide Victimization Rates," 656.
28. Philip J. Cook and Jens Ludwig, "Guns and Burglary," in Ludwig and Cook, *Evaluating Gun Policy*, 74.
29. Ibid., 88.
30. Ibid., 98.
31. See Kleck, *Targeting Guns*, 183; David B. Kopel, "Lawyers, Guns, and Burglars," *Arizona Law Review* (Summer 2001): 345–67.
32. Cook and Ludwig, "Guns and Burglary," 81.
33. Ibid.
34. Ibid., 104.

35. Kleck, *Targeting Guns*, 244.

36. Ibid.

37. James D. Wright and Peter H. Rossi, *Armed and Considered Dangerous: A Survey of Felons and Their Firearms*, expanded edition (New York: Aldine de Gruyter, 1994), 150.

38. David Hemenway, Sara Solnick, and Deborah Azrael, "Firearms and Community Feelings of Safety," *Journal of Criminal Law and Criminology* 86 (1995): 121, 124.

39. Ibid.

40. The photo is in Dennis Henigan, *Lethal Logic: Exploding the Myths That Paralyze American Gun Policy* (Washington, DC: Potomac Books, 2009), 115.

41. See www.shotshow.com (accessed March 10, 2016).

CHAPTER FIVE: THE ONLY THING THAT STOPS A BAD GUY WITH A GUN IS A GOOD GUY WITH A GUN

1. See, e.g., National Rifle Association, "U.S. Conference of Mayors: Strong on Dislike of Guns, Weak on Facts," October 6, 1999 ("Guns are used for self-protection approximately 2.5 million times annually [citing Kleck] . . . , up to five times the number of firearm-related violent crimes" [citing the FBI!].

2. Gary Kleck and Marc Gertz, "Armed Resistance to Crime: The Prevalence and Nature of Self-Defense with a Gun," *Journal of Criminal Law and Criminology* 86 (1995): 150, 184, table 2.

3. Hemenway, *Private Guns, Public Health*, 240.

4. David McDowall and Brian Wiersema, "The Incidence of Defensive Firearm Use by US Crime Victims, 1987 Through 1990," *American Journal of Public Health* 84 (December 1994): 1982.

5. Hemenway, *Private Guns, Public Health*, 69.

6. McDowall and Wiersema, "The Incidence of Defensive Firearm Use," 1984.

7. Ibid.

8. Jacquielynn Floyd, "Under the Gun, She Was in Control," *Dallas Morning News*, November 10, 2000.

9. Ibid.

10. Cam Edwards, "Granny Deserves Self-Defense," *Town Hall*, November 16, 2005, http://townhall.com/columnists/CamEdwards/2005/11/16/granny_deserves_self-defense.

11. Hemenway, *Private Guns, Public Health*, 239.

12. Kleck, *Targeting Guns*, 153.

13. Hemenway, *Private Guns, Public Health*, 241.

14. Ibid., 242.

15. Douglas Weil, "Gun Control Laws Can Reduce Crime," *The World & I* (February 1997): 300, 303.

16. Ibid.

17. Dept. of Justice, Federal Bureau of Investigation, *Uniform Crime Reports, Crime in the United States, 2007*, Expanded Homicide Data Table 14

("Justifiable Homicide by Weapon, Private Citizen, 2003–2007") (Washington, DC, September 2008).

18. Kleck and Gertz, *Targeting Guns*, 163.

19. D. Hemenway, D. Azrael, M. Miller, "Gun Use in the United States: Results from Two National Surveys," *Injury Prevention* 6 (2000): 263, 265.

20. Ibid., 266.

21. Ibid.

22. Gary Kleck, "Struggling Against 'Common Sense': The Pluses and Minuses of Gun Control," *The World & I* (February 1997): 287, 295.

23. Bureau of Justice Statistics, *Criminal Victimization, 2004* 10 (September 2005) (showing 1,054,820 incidents of non-fatal violent gun crime in 1993).

24. ABC News transcripts, *20/20*, December 30, 2005.

25. I owe this insight to my former colleague, Doug Weil.

26. Arthur L. Kellermann et al., "Weapon Involvement in Home Invasion Crimes," *Journal of the American Medical Association* 273 (June 14, 1995): 1759, 1761.

27. Ibid.

28. Kellermann et al., "Injuries and Deaths," 263, 265.

29. Arthur L. Kellermann and Donald T. Reay, "Protection or Peril? An Analysis of Firearm-Related Deaths in the Home," *New England Journal of Medicine* 314 (June 12, 1986): 1557, 1558.

30. Arthur L. Kellermann et al., "Gun Ownership as a Risk Factor for Homicide in the Home," *New England Journal of Medicine* 329 (October 7, 1993): 1084.

31. Kleck, *Targeting Guns*, 244.

32. James E. Bailey et al., "Risk Factors for Violent Death of Women in the Home," *Archives of Internal Medicine* 157 (April 14, 1997): 777.

33. Peter Cummings et al., "The Association Between the Purchase of a Handgun and Homicide or Suicide," *American Journal of Public Health* 87 (June 1997): 974.

34. Charles C. Branas et al., "Investigating the Link Between Gun Possession and Gun Assault," *American Journal of Public Health* (November 2009): 2034–40.

35. Mike Stobbe, "Would-Be Gun Violence Researchers Face Many Challenges in Career Path," Associated Press, October 25, 2015.

36. Everytown for Gun Safety, *Analysis of Recent Mass Shootings* (July 2014), 6.

37. "Accidental Gunshot Hurts 2 at Restaurant," *Indianapolis Star-News*, November 11, 1997.

38. Scott Croteau, "Police Chiefs Blast Healey on Gun Permits," *Worcester (MA) Telegram & Gazette*, October 19, 2006. Quoting Worcester police chief Gary J. Gemme.

39. Mason-Dixon poll conducted May 6–8, 1995, cited in Marcus Nieto, *Concealed Handgun Laws and Public Safety* (Sacramento: California Research Bureau, California State Library, November 1997).

40. Mason-Dixon poll conducted January 13–15, 1995, cited in ibid.

41. David McHugh, "Bill Would Let More Carry Guns," *Detroit Free Press*, November 23, 1994.

42. Paul Sloca, "State Senator Leaves Cuba to Cast Critical Vote on Guns," Associated Press, September 12, 2003, at http://www.semissourian.com/story /print/119491.html.

43. Pauline Vu, "Lawmakers Go AWOL When Military Calls," Stateline.org, November 1, 2006, http://www.stateline.org/live/printable/story?contentId =153573.

44. David Hemenway, Deborah Azrael, and Matthew Miller, "U.S. National Attitudes Concerning Gun Carrying," *Injury Prevention* 7 (2001): 282–85.

45. Hemenway, *Private Guns, Public Health*, 99.

46. Hemenway, Azrael, and Miller, "U.S. National Attitudes Concerning Gun Carrying."

47. Laurence Hammack et al., "Fort Hood Shooting Suspect Hasan Left Few Impressions in Schools He Attended," *Roanoke (VA) Times*, November 7, 2009.

48. Lillian Thomas, "LA Fitness Shooter Had Lethal Plan," *Pittsburgh Post-Gazette*, August 6, 2009.

49. Ramit Plushnick-Masti and Dan Nephin, "Gun Man 'Lying in Wait' Killed 3 Pittsburgh Officers," Associated Press, April 5, 2009.

50. Shaila Dewan and A. G. Sulzberger, "Officers Identify Alabama Gunman," *New York Times*, March 12, 2009.

51. "Charges Approved for Concealed Gun Licensee; Man Faces Manslaughter Count in School Shooting," *Tulsa World*, February 12, 1997.

52. "Black Oak Man Is Killed Following Argument at Café," *Jonesboro Sun*, February 25, 1999.

53. "Mother 'Played by the Rules,' and She and Daughter Died," Associated Press, December 21, 1998.

54. "Police Link Grudge to Doctor's Slaying; Handyman with Disability Arrested in Surgeon's Death," *Sun Sentinel* (Fort Lauderdale, FL), January 19, 1999.

55. "Once Inside He Immediately Started Firing," *Seattle Times*, July 29, 2006.

56. Adam Liptak, "15 States Expand Right to Shoot in Self-Defense," *New York Times*, August 7, 2006.

57. William C. Rempel and Richard A. Serrano, "Felons Get Concealed Gun Licenses Under Bush's 'Tough' Gun Law," *Los Angeles Times*, October 3, 2000.

58. Megan O'Matz and John Maines, "License to Carry: A Sun-Sentinel Investigation," *Sun Sentinel*, January 29, 2007.

59. John R. Lott Jr. and David B. Mustard, "Crime, Deterrence, and Right-To-Carry Concealed Handguns," *Journal of Legal Studies* 26 (January 1997): 1.

60. The scholarly response to Lott is concisely summarized in Hemenway, *Private Guns, Public Health*, 101.

61. Center to Prevent Handgun Violence, *Concealed Truth: Concealed Weapons Laws and Trends in Violent Crime in the United States* (Washington, DC: Center to Prevent Handgun Violence, 1999).

62. John J. Donahue, "The Impact of Concealed Carry Laws" in Ludwig and Cook, *Evaluating Gun Policy.*

63. John Donahue and Ian Ayres, "More Guns, Less Crime Fails Again: The Latest Evidence from 1977–2006," *Econ Journal Watch* 6 (May 2009): 218–38.

CHAPTER SIX: WE DON'T NEED NEW GUN LAWS. WE NEED TO ENFORCE THE LAWS WE HAVE.

1. Quoted in Megan O'Matz and John Maines, "Investigation Reveals Criminal Pasts of Those Toting Guns," *Sun-Sentinel,* January 29, 2007.

2. Wayne LaPierre, *Guns, Crime, and Freedom,* 178, quoting Congressman John Dingell (D-Mich.).

3. "Cult Had Illegal Arms, Expert Says," *New York Times,* January 15, 1994.

4. LaPierre, *Guns, Crime, and Freedom,* 191.

5. Ibid.

6. Ibid.

7. NRA, "Time for Congress to Rein in BATF," *American Rifleman,* April 1995, 39.

8. Ibid.

9. Wayne LaPierre, "Standing Guard," *American Rifleman,* January/February 1995, 7.

10. Wayne LaPierre, "Standing Guard," *American Rifleman,* April 1995, 7.

11. Peter H. Stone, "NRA Under New Fire for Rhetoric on Assault Weapons Ban, U.S. Authorities," *Baltimore Sun,* May 8, 1995.

12. Guy Gugliotta, "NRA, Backers Have Focused Ire on ATF," *Washington Post,* April 26, 1995.

13. Stone, "NRA Under New Fire."

14. Wayne LaPierre, NRA fund-raising letter, April 13, 1995. See Fox Butterfield, "Long Before Bombing, Gun Lobby Was Lashing Out at Federal Agents," *New York Times,* May 8, 1995.

15. Lou Michael and Dan Herbeck, *American Terrorist: Timothy McVeigh and the Oklahoma City Bombing* (New York: Harper, 2001), 228.

16. Paul Stephens, "'Detached' Letter from McVeigh," *USA Today,* May 3, 1995.

17. Michael and Herbeck, *American Terrorist,* 120.

18. Ibid., 137.

19. For a more extensive discussion of the "insurrectionist theory" of the Second Amendment, see Dennis A. Henigan, "Arms, Anarchy and the Second Amendment," *Valparaiso University Law Review* 26 (1991): 107. See also, Carl T. Bogus, "The Hidden History of the Second Amendment," *UC Davis Law Review* 31 (1998): 309, 386–405; Garry Wills, *A Necessary Evil: A History of American Distrust of Government* (New York: Simon & Schuster, 1999), 189–223.

20. Seth Mydans, "California Gun Control Law Runs into Rebellion," *New York Times,* December 24, 1990.

21. Associated Press, "Bush Quits NRA After Assailing 'Slander' Against Federal Agents," *Atlanta Journal-Constitution,* May 11, 1995.

22. Wayne LaPierre, "Standing Guard," *American Rifleman,* May 1997, 10.

23. Ibid.

24. Ibid.

25. National Rifle Association, "Line Up and Shut Up. Face Forward. Stay In Line. Last Name First," *American Rifleman*, January 1994, 32.

26. Brief *Amicus Curiae* of the National Rifle Association of America in Support of Petitioners, *Printz v. United States* (Nos. 95–1478, 95–1503). The Supreme Court ultimately struck down only the provision in the Brady Act requiring local police to do background checks, as a violation of the Tenth Amendment to the Constitution. Printz v. United States, 521 U.S. 898 (1997). It rejected the NRA's plea that the entire law be struck down, finding the mandatory background-check provision severable from the rest of the statute. The Supreme Court's ruling kept in place the five-day period during which law-enforcement authorities could *voluntarily* perform background checks on gun purchasers. Local police were, of course, quite willing to do so. The core of the Brady Act thus remained in effect despite the NRA-supported lawsuits, and Brady background checks have stopped over two million prohibited purchasers from buying guns from licensed dealers.

27. National Rifle Association, *America's 1st Freedom*, February 2001, 29.

28. Ibid.

29. Americans for Gun Safety Foundation, *The Enforcement Gap: Federal Strategy Neglects Sources of Crime Guns* (Washington, DC: Americans for Gun Safety Foundation, October 2004), 26.

30. Office of the Inspector General, US Dept. of Justice, *Review of the Bureau of Alcohol, Tobacco, Firearms and Explosives' Enforcement of Brady Act Violations Identified Through the National Instant Criminal Background Check System*, Report Number I-2004–06 (Washington, DC: US Dept. of Justice, July 2004), viii.

31. Bryan v. United States, 524 U.S. 184, 190 (1998).

32. See, e.g., United States v. One Assortment of 89 Firearms, 465 U.S. 354, 355–56 (1984).

33. ATF, *Following the Gun*, 43.

34. Any other inspection can only be conducted with a search warrant. To obtain a warrant, ATF is in the catch-22 of being required to already have information that a dealer is violating record-keeping laws, when ATF generally can uncover those violations in the first place only by conducting an inspection.

35. *Federal Firearms Licensing: Hearing Before the Subcommittee on Crime and Criminal Justice of the House Committee on the Judiciary*, 103rd Cong., 1st Sess., 1993 (statement of Steven Higgins).

36. Inspector General, US Dept. of Justice, *Inspections of Firearms Dealers by the Bureau of Alcohol, Tobacco, Firearms and Explosives* (Washington, DC: US Dept. of Justice, 2004), 20.

37. See Pub.L. 95–429, 92 Stat. 1002 (Oct. 10, 1978).

38. See 18 U.S.C. §926(a).

39. ATF, *Gun Shows*, 1.
40. See 18 U.S.C. § 921(a)(21)(C), (a)(22).
41. ATF, *Gun Shows*, 2.
42. ATF, *Following the Gun*, 13.
43. National Rifle Association, "Fight Begins to Repeal Machine Gun Ban," *American Rifleman*, August 1988.
44. Ronald Reagan, "Why I'm for the Brady Bill," *New York Times*, March 29, 1991.
45. See 18 U.S.C. § 922 (t)(2)(C).
46. Petition for a Writ of Certiorari, *National Rifle Association et al. v. John Ashcroft* (US Supreme Court), 13–15.
47. *National Rifle Association v. Reno*, 216 F.3d 122 (D.C. Cir. 2000), *cert. denied*, 533 U.S. 928 (2001).
48. US Dept. of Justice, *National Instant Criminal Background Check Regulation*, 66 Fed. Reg. 6471 (January 22, 2001).
49. US Dept. of Justice, *National Instant Criminal Background Check System*, 66 Fed. Reg. 35,567 (July 6, 2001).
50. US General Accounting Office, "Potential Effects of Next-Day Destruction of NICS Background Check Records," (GAO-02–653, July 2002), 4.
51. Ibid.
52. Inspector General, US Dept. of Justice, *Inspections of Firearms Dealers*, 53.
53. Christopher Ingraham, "From 2004 to 2014, over 2,000 Terror Suspects Legally Purchased Guns in the United States," *Washington Post*, November 16, 2015.
54. *ABC World News Tonight*, March 8, 2005.
55. See "Gallup Historical Trends—Guns," http://www.gallup.com/poll/1645/guns.aspx.
56. Smith, *National Gun Policy Survey* (2001).
57. Peter M. Aronow and Benjamin T. Miller, "Policy Misperceptions and Support for Gun Control Legislation," *Lancet* 387 (January 16, 2016): 223.
58. Judy Rumerman, "Aviation Security," US Centennial of Flight Commission, www.centennialofflight.net/essay/Government_Role/security/POL18.htm, accessed April 4, 2016.
59. Brian Michael Jenkins, "Safeguarding the Skies," *San Diego Union Tribune*, September 30, 2001.
60. Martha T. Moore, "Mayors Unite to Get Guns off the Street," *USA Today*, October 25, 2006.
61. Another game the pro-gun partisans play on the enforcement issue could be called the "How many gun laws do we have?" game. Often the "just enforce existing laws" argument will be presented this way: "We already have twenty thousand gun laws. We don't need another gun law; we need to enforce the laws we have." If there really were twenty thousand gun laws on the books restricting access to firearms, it would at least superficially seem to strengthen the argument that another law would make little difference. The "twenty

thousand gun laws" figure has achieved a status in the pro-gun community similar to the "2.5 million defensive gun uses" figure. Yet how was it derived and what does it include? Johns Hopkins University researchers Jon Vernick and Lisa Hepburn investigated the history, and accuracy, of the figure. Jon S. Vernick and Lisa M. Hepburn, "State and Federal Gun Laws: Trends for 1970–99," in Ludwig and Cook, *Evaluating Gun Policy.* Vernick and Hepburn found that it originated in 1965 testimony by Rep. John Dingell (D-Mich.), the same John Dingell who first called ATF agents "a jack-booted group of fascists." Dingell gave no source or basis for the figure, nor apparently has anyone else. The Hopkins researchers actually did attempt a count of existing laws. They identified approximately three hundred different state gun laws and about ninety local laws in cities of at least 250,000 in population that apply to the manufacture, design, sale, purchase, and possession of guns, to add to the handful of federal gun laws. Of course, if you add laws relating to the use of guns—like the Texas law prohibiting the shooting of a gun across Lake Texarkana (I'm not kidding)—you would get a higher count. But it is fanciful to think the number would be anything close to twenty thousand. In any event, the number of gun laws on the books is immaterial. The issue is whether the laws are sufficient to protect the public. As should be readily apparent from the discussion in this text, the answer is clearly no.

62. Wayne LaPierre, *America's 1st Freedom*, December 2002, 34.

63. Chris Cox, *Chris Cox's Political Report*, July 2005, https://www.nraila.org /articles/20050701/chris-w-coxs-political-report-july-2.

CHAPTER SEVEN: IS BUDWEISER RESPONSIBLE FOR DRUNK DRIVERS?

1. Ruby L. Bailey, "Showdown over Guns Drags on in Courts," *Detroit Free Press*, January 3, 2003, at http://freep.com/news/metro/guns3_20030103.htm.

2. Michelle Ye He Lee, "Bernie Sanders's Misleading Characterization of a Controversial Gun Law," *Washington Post*, July 10, 2015.

3. Gallup News Service, "New Gun Control Efforts Draw Mixed Support from Americans," July 13, 1999.

4. Cathey v. Bernard, 467 So.2d 9, 11 (La. Ct. App. 1985).

5. Perkins v. Wilkinson Sword, Inc., 700 N.E.2d 1247, 1250 (1998).

6. Ibid., 1252.

7. Philip J. Cook and Jens Ludwig, "Guns in America: National Survey on Private Ownership and Use of Firearms," *National Institute of Justice, Research in Brief*, May 1997, 7.

8. Mark A. Schuster et al., "Firearm Storage Patterns in U.S. Homes with Children," *American Journal of Public Health* 90 (April 2000): 588, 590.

9. Garen J. Wintemute et al., "When Children Shoot Children, 88 Unintended Deaths in California," *Journal of the American Medical Association* 257 (June 12, 1987): 3107, 3108.

10. City of Cincinnati v. Beretta U.S.A. Corp. et al., 768 N.E.2d 1136, 1147 (Ohio 2002).

11. Hurst v. Glock, 684 A.2d 970 (NJ App. Div. 1996).
12. Ibid., 972.
13. Ibid., 973.
14. Smith v. Bryco Arms, 33 P.3d 638 (Ct. App. N.M. 2001).
15. Ibid., 645.
16. Ibid., 649.
17. Ibid., 645.
18. See, e.g., Barker v. Lull Engineering Co., 573 P.2d 443, 453 (Cal. 1978).
19. See Adames v. Sheahan, 233 Ill.2d 276, 909 NE.2d 742 (Ill. Sup. Ct. 2009).
20. The factual discussion that follows is taken from the opinion of the Califor-
    nia Court of Appeal in Merrill v. Navegar, Inc., 89 Cal.Rptr. 2d 146 (1999),
    a lawsuit in which the author represented victims of the shootings at 101
    California Street.
21. Merrill v. Navegar, Inc., 89 Cal.Rptr.2d 146, 163 (1999), *rev'd on other grounds,*
    28 P.3d 116 (2001).
22. Ibid.
23. Palma v. U.S. Industrial Fasteners, Inc., 36 Cal. 3d 171 (1984).
24. Merrill v. Navegar, Inc., 89 Cal. Rept.2d at 169.
25. Merrill v. Navegar, Inc., 28 P.3d 116 (2001).
26. Merrill v. Navegar, Inc., 28 P.3d at 135 (J. Werdegar dissenting).
27. Expert Report of Joseph J. Vince Jr., City of New York v. Beretta, No.
    CV-3641 (E.D.N.Y. 2005).
28. ATF, *Commerce in Firearms in the United States* (Washington, DC: Dept. of
    the Treasury, February 2000), 2.
29. Ibid., 23.
30. US Dept. of Justice, Memorandum of Points and Authorities in Opposition
    to Motion for Preliminary Injunction filed in Trader Sports v. Gonzales, No.
    C 06–001136 VRW (N.D. Cal.), at 1.
31. ATF, *Crime Gun Trace Reports 2000: Oakland, CA* (Washington, DC: Dept.
    of the Treasury, July 2002), 6.
32. Declaration of Sania Franken in Opposition to Motion for Preliminary
    Injunction filed in Trader Sports, Inc. v. Gonzales, No. C 06–001136 VRW
    (N.D. Cal.), Exhibit B.
33. Ibid.
34. Ibid.
35. ATF, *Report to the Secretary on Firearms Initiatives* (Washington, DC: Dept.
    of the Treasury, November 2000), iii, https://assets.documentcloud.org
    /documents/11255/atf-regulatory-actions-report-to-secretary-on-firearms
    -initiatives.pdf.
36. Garen Wintemute et al., "Risk Factors Among Handgun Retailers for Fre-
    quent and Disproportionate Sales of Guns Used in Crime," *Injury Preven-
    tion* 11 (2005): 357.
37. See Second Amended Complaint, Chicago v. Beretta U.S.A. Corp., No.
    98-CH-015596 (Cook County Circuit Court, Nov. 12 1998).

38. See Complaint, McNamara v. Arms Technology, No. 99–912662 NZ (Wayne County Circuit Court, April 26, 1999).
39. Daniel W. Webster and Jon S. Vernick, "Spurring Responsible Sales Practices through Litigation," in Webster and Vernick, *Reducing Gun Violence in America*.
40. See Complaint, City of New York v. A-1 Jewelry & Pawn, Inc., et. al., No. CV 06–2233 (E.D.N.Y. May 15, 2006); City of New York v. Bob Moates' Sport Shop, Inc., et. al., No. CV-6504 (E.D.N.Y. December 7, 2006).
41. Webster and Vernick, "Spurring Responsible Sales Practices," 128.
42. Amended Complaint, Anderson v. Bryco Arms, No. 00-L-7476 (Circuit Court, Cook County, April 10, 2002), at ¶ 151.
43. Ibid., 53–58.
44. Plaintiffs' Memorandum in Opposition to Defendant Old Prairie Trading Post's Motion to Dismiss, Anderson v. Bryco Arms, No. 00-L-7476 (Circuit Court, Cook County, Illinois, April 10, 2002), 5–7, 8–11.
45. Expert Report of Joseph J. Vince, Jr., Jefferson v. Rossi, No. 02218 (Pa. Common Pleas, May 3, 2002), 23–24, 31.
46. Deposition of Perry Bruce, *Jefferson v. Rossi*, at 32, 39.
47. Ibid., 35–37, 40.
48. Ibid., 25, 51.
49. Ibid., 38.
50. Complaint, Jefferson v. Rossi, No. 02218 (Pa. Common Pleas, May 3, 2002).
51. Kitchen v. K-Mart Corporation, 697 So.2d 1200 (1997).
52. Ibid., 1206. Quoting Skinner v. Ochiltree, 5 So.2d 605 (1941).
53. See, e.g., Phillips v. Roy, 431 So.2d 849 (La. Ct. App. 1983).
54. See, e.g., Pavlides v. Niles Gun Show, Inc., 679 N.E.2d 728 (Ohio Ct. App. 1996).
55. See, e.g., Johnson v. Bull's Eye Shooter Supply, WL 21639244 (June 27, 2003).
56. According to ATF, traced "crime guns" include "any firearm that is illegally possessed, used in a crime, or suspected by enforcement officials of being used in a crime." ATF, *The Illegal Youth Firearms Market in 17 Communities* (Washington, DC: ATF, 1997), 3.
57. ATF, "Treasury, ATF Release Firearms Report, Gun Trafficking Actions," news release, February 4, 2000, 2.
58. Documents produced by plaintiffs in the Judicial Council Coordination Proceeding No. 4095 (Cal. Super Ct.) (PLTF 101149–53).
59. Documents produced by Sturm, Ruger in the Judicial Council Coordination Proceeding No. 4095 Cal. Super. Ct. (SR 21972).
60. See, generally, "Curtailing Dangerous Sales Practices by Licensed Firearm Dealers," in Webster and Vernick, *Reducing Gun Violence in America*, 137.
61. James V. Grimaldi and Sari Horwitz, "Industry Pressure Hides Gun Traces, Protects Dealers from Public Scrutiny," *Washington Post*, October 24, 2010.
62. National Alliance of Stocking Gun Dealers, *Alliance Voice*, February 1994.

63. Ibid.
64. Ibid.
65. Declaration of Robert A. Ricker, *People v. Arcadia Machine & Tool, Inc. et al.*, (January 31, 2003), at 7–8.
66. Documents produced by plaintiffs in the *Judicial Council Coordination Proceeding No. 495* (Cal. Super. Ct.) (PLTF 100007–10).
67. Paul M. Barrett, "Loaded Words: A Dealer Breaks Rank; Blaming Gun Makers," *Wall Street Journal*, June 22, 1999.
68. Documents produced by plaintiffs in the *Judicial Council Coordination Proceeding No. 4095* (Cal. Super. Ct.) (PLTF 101388–89).
69. Deposition of Robert Lockett on August 9, 2002, in ibid.
70. Ibid., 41:21–42:12.
71. The quotations from Bob Ricker are taken from his "Declaration" in *People v. Arcadia.*
72. Document produced by NSSF in the Judicial Council Coordination Proceeding No. 4095 (Cal. Super. Ct.) (NSSF 13898–13900).
73. Document produced by Beretta in the Judicial Council Coordination Proceeding No. 4095 (Cal. Super. Ct.) (NUSA 16843).
74. Ibid.
75. Deposition of Donald Campbell, *Judicial Council Coordination Proceeding No. 4095* (Cal. Super. Ct.), 89.
76. Ibid., 155.
77. ATF, *Strategic Plan 2000–2005* (Washington, DC: Dept. of the Treasury, 2000), 11.
78. Dept. of Justice, *Gun Violence Reduction: National Integrated Firearms Violence Reduction Strategy* (Washington, DC: Dept. of Justice, 2001).
79. Deposition of Chris Killoy, *Judicial Council Coordination Proceeding No. 4095* (Cal. Super. Ct.), 425–26.
80. Document produced by Smith & Wesson in *Judicial Council Coordination Proceeding No. 4095* (Cal. Super. Ct) (SW17537).
81. Settlement Agreement between Department of the Treasury, Department of Housing and Urban Development and Smith & Wesson (March 17, 2000).
82. Craig Gordon, "Gun Giant Agrees to Regulations; Government Will Drop Lawsuits in Exchange," *Newsday*, March 18, 2000.
83. David Ho, "Officials Praise Smith & Wesson," Associated Press, March 17, 2000.
84. Fox Butterfield and Raymond Hernandez, "Gun Maker's Accord on Curbs Brings Pressure from Industry," *New York Times*, March 30, 2000.
85. Ibid.
86. Documents produced by Sturm, Ruger in *Judicial Council Coordination Proceeding No. 4095* (Cal. Super. Ct.) (SR 20910–69).
87. Philadelphia v. Stephan Chemicals Co., 544 F. Supp. 1135 (E.D.Pa. 1982).
88. Hunnings v. Texaco, Inc., 29 F.3d 1480 (11th Cir. 1994).
89. Suchomajcz v. Hummel Chemical Co., 524 F.2d 19 (3d Cir. 1975).

90. City of Cincinnati v. Beretta U.S.A. Corp., 768 N.E.2d 1136 (Ohio 2002).

91. James v. Arms Technology, Inc., 820 A.2d 27 (N.J. Super. Ct. App. Div. 2003).

92. City of Gary v. Smith & Wesson Corp., 801 N.E.2d 1222 (Ind. 2003).

93. NAACP v. Acusport, Inc., 271 F.Supp.2d 435 (E.D.N.Y. 2003).

94. 151 Cong. Rec. S8910 (July 26, 2005).

95. 151 Cong. Rec. S9088 (July 27, 2005).

96. 151 Cong. Rec. S9226 (July 28, 2005).

97. 151 Cong. Rec. S9017 (July 26, 2005).

98. Webster and Vernick, "Curtailing Dangerous Practices by Licensed Firearm Dealers."

CHAPTER EIGHT: THE SECOND AMENDMENT IS THE FIRST FREEDOM

1. United States v. Miller, 307 U.S. 174, 178 (1939).

2. Ibid.

3. District of Columbia v. Heller, 128 S.Ct. 2783, 2833 (2008) (J. Stevens dissenting).

4. Some of the leading historical texts supporting the "militia purpose" view of the Second Amendment include Saul Cornell, *A Well-Regulated Militia: The Founding Fathers and the Origins of Gun Control in America* (New York: Oxford University Press, 2006); H. Richard Uviller and William G. Merkel, *The Militia and the Right to Arms, or, How the Second Amendment Fell Silent* (Durham, NC: Duke University Press, 2002); and the collection of essays in Carl T. Bogus, ed., *The Second Amendment in Law and History* (New York: New Press, 2000).

5. Warren Burger, interview on *MacNeil/Lehrer NewsHour*, show #4226, December 16, 1991.

6. Paul Finkelman, "The Living Constitution and the Second Amendment: Poor History, False Originalism, and a Very Confused Court," *Cardozo Law Review* 37 (2015): 623.

7. See Adam Liptak, "Ruling on Guns Elicits Rebuke from the Right," *New York Times*, October 21, 2008.

8. Douglas W. Kmiec, "Guns and the Supreme Court: Dead Wrong," *The-Tidings .com*, July 11, 2008, http://www.the-tidings.com/2008/071108/kmiec.htm.

9. Richard A. Posner, "In Defense of Looseness: The Supreme Court and Gun Control," *New Republic*, August 27, 2008, 32.

10. J. Harvie Wilkinson III, "Of Guns, Abortions, and the Unraveling Rule of Law," *Virginia Law Review* 95 (2009): 253.

11. Ibid.

12. Ibid.

13. *Heller*, 128 S.Ct. 2816.

14. Ibid., 2816–17, 2820.

15. Ibid., 2817n26.

16. Ibid., 2820.

17. Ibid., 2815n24.
18. Ibid., 2851 (J. Breyer dissenting) (quoting Abrams v. Johnson, 521 U.S. 74, 82 [1997]).
19. Ibid. (J. Breyer, dissenting).
20. Ibid., 2821.
21. James Oliphant, "Gun-Rights Ruling Could Ricochet across Nation," *Chicago Tribune*, March 16, 2008.
22. Bonidy v. USPS, 790 F.3d 1121, 1126 (10th Cir. 2015).
23. United States v. Masciandaro, 638 F.3d 458, 457–76 (4th Cir. 2011).
24. Allen Rostron, "The Continuing Battle Over the Second Amendment," *Albany Law Review* 78 (2015): 819, 821.
25. See generally, Rostron, "Continuing Battle Over the Second Amendment." See also, New York State Rifle and Pistol Association, Inc. v. Cuomo, 804 F.3d 242 (2nd Cir. 2015); Heller v. District of Columbia, 801 F.2d 264 (D.C. Cir. 2015).
26. Moore v. Madigan, 702 F.3d 933, 949 (J. Williams, dissenting).
27. Heller v. District of Columbia, 554 U.S. at 626.
28. Adam Winkler, *Gun Fight: The Battle over the Right to Bear Arms in America* (New York: Norton, 2011), 165.
29. Kachalsky v. County of Westchester, 701 F.3d 81 (2nd Cir. 2012), *cert. denied,* 133 S.Ct. 1806 (2013); Drake v. Filko, 724 F.3d 426 (3rd Cir. 2013), *cert. denied,* 134 S.Ct. 2134 (2014); Woollard v. Gallagher, 712 F.3d 865 (4th Cir. 2013), *cert. denied,* 134 S.Ct. 422 (2013).
30. Moore v. Madigan, 702 F.3d 933 (7th Cir. 2012).
31. Friedman v. City of Highland Park, 577 U.S. ___ (2015) (J. Thomas dissenting from denial of certionari).
32. Spitzer, *The Politics of Gun Control*, 17.
33. *Washington Post*, "Most Say Amendment Covers Individuals and Militias," poll, March 16, 2008, http://www.washingtonpost.com/wp-dyn-content/graphic/2008/03/16/GR2008031600072.html?sid=ST2008031502430.
34. Johns Hopkins Center for Gun Policy and Research, "Large Majority of Americans—Including Gun Owners—Support Stronger Gun Safety Policies," June 3, 2015.

EPILOGUE: BEYOND MYTHOLOGY TO LIFE-SAVING LAWS

1. The account of the Virginia Tech shooting is taken from *Mass Shootings at Virginia Tech, the Report of the Review Panel* (Richmond, VA: Virginia Tech Review Panel, August 2007), hereafter referred to as Panel Report.
2. Ibid., 71.
3. Ibid., 73.
4. Dept. of Justice, Bureau of Justice Statistics, *Improving Criminal History Records for Background Checks, 2005* (Washington, DC: US Dept. of Justice, Office of Justice Programs, Bureau of Justice Statistics, July 2006), estimates that, as of 2006, 234,628 disqualifying mental-health records were in the

system; General Accounting Office, *Gun Control: Options for Improving the National Instant Criminal Background Check System* (Washington, DC: GAO, March 2000), estimates that at least 2.6 million disqualifying mental-health records should be in the system. See also Jim Kessler, *Missing Records: Holes in Background Check System Allow Illegal Buyers to Get Guns* (Washington, DC: Third Way, May 2007).

5. Owing in large part to the impassioned efforts of some of the Virginia Tech victims and their families, Congress enacted into law the NICS Improvement Amendments Act of 2007, Pub. L. 110–180. The statute provided new financial incentives for states to submit records of prohibited purchasers to the Brady Act's National Instant Criminal Background Check system. This statute is yet another illustration that sometimes it is necessary to enact new laws in order to better enforce existing laws.

6. Everytown for Gun Safety, *Closing the Gaps: Strengthening the Background Check System to Keep Guns Away from the Dangerously Mentally Ill* (May 16, 2014).

7. Panel Report, 82.

8. Ibid.

9. Ibid., 84.

About the Author

DENNIS A. HENIGAN is director of legal and policy analysis at the Campaign for Tobacco-Free Kids and the former vice president of the Brady Center to Prevent Gun Violence. He is the author of *Lethal Logic: Exploding the Myths That Paralyze American Gun Policy*, which he has entirely revised and updated for this book.

For over twenty years, he was a leading advocate for stronger gun laws, appearing dozens of times on national television and radio shows, including *60 Minutes, The Today Show, Nightline, Hardball,* and *Frontline.* He has written and spoken extensively on liability and constitutional issues relating to gun laws and gun violence.

Under his direction, Brady Center lawyers recovered millions of dollars in damages for gun violence victims, as well as winning precedent-setting decisions on the liability of gun sellers. He has been named one of the top ten "Lawyers of the Year" by *Lawyers' Weekly* magazine. His work as a public-interest lawyer has been profiled in the *New Yorker.*

Henigan graduated from Oberlin College and received his law degree from the University of Virginia School of Law.